My work is not my work

Pierre Bernard
Design for the public domain

The child in the industrial society

L'Enfant dans la société industrialisée
Poster made for a conference on this topic
80 × 60 cm / 1976

The starting point for this poster is a photograph of the designer's daughter. The photo, enlarged and framed to the size of the paper, moves from the family album to the poster. A transparent acetate film is placed over this black and white image, and on it, with a few deft strokes, the designer draws the earth as seen from a spaceship. This drawing is then screen printed onto the girl's portrait. Two lines of tiny white lettering across the complete width of the poster divide it into two almost equal halves with the globe at the centre. This gossamer-fine line in the middle draws an imaginary equator, at the same time suggesting the elastic band of a clown's nose. The cropping of the photograph places full emphasis on the child's senses – eyes, nose and mouth – while the superimposed drawing turns the face into outer space.

The image was put together quickly and inexpensively with the tools that lay on every designer's desk in the seventies: felt-tip pens, ruler, transfer letters (Letraset); no computer was used.

In the image of the earth as the centre of the child's face the opposite thought is expressed: the child is the centre of the world, or should be. Child and world, two key themes in Bernard's work, have been cleverly linked here by means of enlargement and reduction. The world, shrunk to a clown's nose, is added to the face of a child.

Meanwhile things are not going too well with the world. It is just after Sputnik, and the surface of the earth is polluted by factories, cars and colossal buildings – a miniature mental map of urban problems that are still with us today. The party nose in the style of a comic book turns out not to be so cheerful after all. The earth, like the moon on the child's forehead, is disfigured by spots. The designer has introduced reflections into the eyes of the child; the open mouth is ambiguous: is this an expression of wonderment, or surprise? The child regards us with an open gaze, but with these and other additions her face, confronted with the world, loses its carefree gaiety. By using his own child as the model for the poster Bernard indicates that the subject of the conference affects him too.

It has been said before that there is a similarity between an aphorism or proverb and a poster: both pregnantly express human characteristics, failings and behaviour, or social iniquities. The nose figures in countless proverbs in every European language, and I shall resist the temptation to give examples here. But it is quite clear that although the little girl who looks out at us from the poster is being led by the nose, she is still looking beyond the end of her nose.

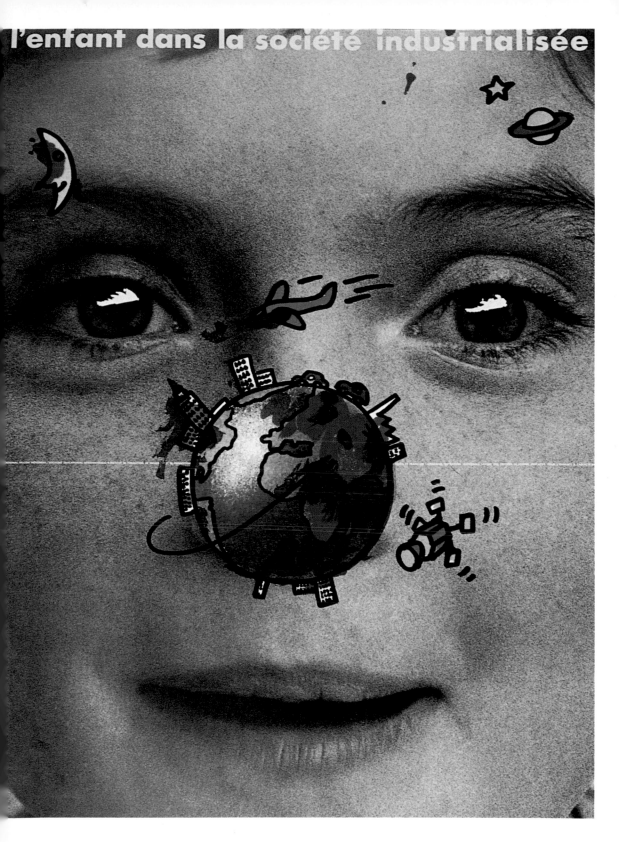

l'enfant dans la société industrialisée

...;&?! «»
THEATRE de SARTROUVILLE
TOUTE UNE SAISON POUR FÊTER ÇA!"
16 ANS
1. 2. 3. 4. 5. 6. 7. 8. 9. 10. 11. 12. 13. 14. 15. 16.

Seize ans
Poster for the sixteenth
anniversary of the Théâtre
de Sartrouville
159 × 117 / 1981

Sixteen years

Like a playing card, this madcap poster can be read in two directions. The theatre celebrates its anniversary and the poster, which reveals the name of the place only in the margin, addresses the local population, inviting them to a festival for a whole season.

The idea expressed by the poster is reversal: the partygoers turn everything upside down, and the master of ceremonies on the poster leads the way. Reversal and disguise reveal a hidden truth: it is like *mardi gras* or carnival where people let themselves go and express through their disguises what they keep silent for the rest of the year. The colours too change places, moving to the borders while the central image has to make do with black, white and a bit of yellow.

The poster is constructed as a puppet theatre with a burlesque figure springing out of the colourful frame like a jack-in-the-box. He uses his body as an abacus: two hands can count to ten, but this actor puts an extra hand on top of his head to make it fifteen, and sticks out his tongue on which we see the number sixteen.

The basis for this figure is the designer's silhouette, reducing the person to a type. However, the figure is not unambiguous. It plays several roles: the jester, ridiculing and heckling, the frightening werewolf, a clown laughing and crying at once. But its quintessence is the wild joy of play. The fingers on the head are the fool's cap, the werewolf has forgotten to take off his watch, his teeth have half-fallen out of his mouth, and even his spiky underarm hair helps make him less frightening. The eyes are those of an animal but the light behind the figure's head makes them less aggressive. All in all, its performance is a source of hilarity.

The farce is also expressed in the punctuation marks in the poster's upper and lower margins. Lines of typographical characters like these are familiar to the designer from type founders' and printers' type specimens, where they show how richly endowed the typecase is. Here they are inverted to emphasize the absurdity of the image.

Bernard first became acquainted with circus and theatre posters in Poland. Back in France he incorporated that tradition in his work. There are at least two other posters in which he portrays the designer as puppeteer (for an exhibition of the work of his Breton colleague Alain Le Quernec, 1981, and for the Grapus exhibition in Lahti, 1988). What theatre and graphic design have in common is that they both play with representation and identity. The two art forms create a separation between spectacle and spectator and then proceed to demolish the distinction in an act of identification and participation. Both invite interaction with the audience. They suspend reality in the play and we, the audience, know that it is fiction – yet we still go along with it. Theatre and design both work with someone else's text, drawing on the tension between the text and its staging. The aim of both is to move, entertain, stimulate and provide food for thought.

Let's go

On y va
Poster commissioned by
L'Avant Garde, magazine
of the French Communist
Party Youth Movement
120 × 80 / 1977

The French expression 'on y va' is both an exhortation and a statement: either 'come on, let's go' or 'we're on our way'. The five letters are the building blocks of the poster, which is in the most literal sense a typographic poster – except that this poster transforms the letters into images. The book typographer arranges black letters on a white ground; the poster designer has them appear as colour on a black ground. This dual status of the letter as both sign and image gives the words ON Y VA the character of a rebus.

The composition of the poster is perfectly symmetrical. The vertical axis runs through the tail of the Y, and the horizontal axis is marked by two yellow blocks to the right and left of the Y. They keep the Y company in its lonely position at the centre. The other four letters are positioned symmetrically in four fields.
The vertical axis dominates not just because of its length: the upward movement is accentuated by the change in the colour of the letters. They offer a view of a world behind the picture plane, a fantastic landscape where it is simultaneously morning and evening. In this surreal atmosphere the sans serif capitals lose their geometric neutrality.

The monumental format of the Futura-like letters turns the everyday expression 'on y va' into a slogan. Handwritten lettering plays through the lapidary formula, as if marked in chalk on a blackboard; these added fragments of text strip the message of its formal character and inject movement into the otherwise static image. In this way three of the five capitals are absorbed into new words: TOUS, IVRY and Vers, creating a second slogan that adds detail to the first: 'Tous à Ivry à la fête', followed by a third: 'Vers le changement!' The everyday expression 'on y va' can be read in three different ways: 1 World, here we come! 2 Everyone come to the celebration in Ivry! and 3 Join the movement and help achieve its goal: change!

That the change of course advocated here is political in nature is clear enough from the poster's tiny headline, with the name of the organizer of the event in a typewriter font, supplemented by emblems placed unobtrusively in the top right corner. Marx, painted by Michel Quarez as a hitch-hiking hippie, is on his way to the same goal: a Red France.

The handwriting in the poster gives the message a personal character and, like the subculture version of Marx, points to the identity of Grapus, whose signature is found at the bottom left. The five capitals themselves have been personalized, too. By scraping off the emulsion of the colour layer by hand, streaks and stripes have been allowed to break through the even colour of the letters.

You cannot tell from the poster that it was a compromise. Grapus's first proposal – a subculture version of Lenin – had been rejected by the organization. Bernard resorts instead to typography, ironically quoting the poster of the hitch-hiking Marx that had been approved by the same client the previous year, and makes the most of the possibilities a typographic poster offers an inventive designer.

TOUS

ON

à

Y

IVRY

4,5 JUIN

à la fête

VA

le changement!

La crieuse
Emblem for International
Women's Year commissioned
by the French trade union
federation CGT
50 x 40 / 1975

The hawker

The United Nations declared 1975 International Women's Year, marking the start of a decade in which women's rights were to be in the spotlight. As a result of political activism on the part of women, in 1979 the UN General Assembly adopted the Convention on the Elimination of all Forms of Discrimination Against Women, widely seen as an international bill of women's rights. The French trade union federation *Confédération Générale du Travail* used International Women's Year to campaign for equal pay for equal work or work of equal value. This emblem for the CGT was used in various ways.

The typewriter face fits the aesthetics of the grainy image. The slogan 'changer notre vie!' (change our life) has been placed at an angle. The woman speaks out and makes this statement herself, as indicated by the quotation marks. Inserted in the figure, the statement moves from the legal and social level (*changer*) to the personal level (*notre vie*); the poster is not just a call to employers, but to women themselves to fight for their rights.

Bernard drew two female heads, one in profile and one full face, and then manipulated the two photographically to blend them into a single image. Silhouette and dot-screen have the same effect. The individual expression disappears and two types of women emerge: the woman who faces the outside world and speaks out, and the woman who turns inward and remains silent. This use of photomontage and dot-screening is inspired by the work of the Polish designer Roman Cieslewicz, who had been working in Paris since 1963. He used this technique for his poster of the theatre version of Kafka's *Trial*: the head of Kafka is reproduced three times in a coarse screen and decreasing size until it disappears down its own throat.

The implicit iconographic references are even richer. The right-facing open mouth of the silhouetted profile is an unmistakable reference to a poster by Cassandre, whom Bernard greatly admires. In 1925 Cassandre designed an open-mouthed street vendor in profile for the evening newspaper *L'Intransigeant*. The newspaper vendor becomes symbolic of the medium itself. She speaks out, loud and clear, telling us what she sees and hears. Cassandre replaces the traditional female portrait with a mechanical stylization in an aesthetic that grafts the technology of the telegraph to the old function of the town crier. But Bernard's work differs from Cassandre in that he adds a psychological dimension – *changer notre vie!* The traditional female image and the mask-like feminine silhouette are as inner and outer aspects of the same person: private sensibility and public action.

Behind both this emblem and Cassandre's *crieuse* lies the French archetype of the combative woman, Marianne, symbol of the French Republic. One of her incarnations was created in 1836 by the sculptor François Rude in a relief on the Arc de Triomphe (Departure of the volunteers in 1792). On another Grapus poster the warlike female figure calling the troops to battle exhorts us to see an exhibition of political posters in Grenoble (p. 90).

Speak out!

Prenez la parole!
Poster commissioned
by the municipality
of Vitry-sur-Seine
120 × 80 / 1977

A young man dressed in jeans and a sweater is partially hidden behind two areas for text, one blank, the other written on. One of them he is holding in his hands: a text balloon with the words 'prenez la parole!' (speak out!) written in slanting capitals with a felt-tip pen. Through the image and across his chest runs the second text field, a crossbar which – edged with the colours of the French Republic – connotes the sash that French officials wear at formal occasions. The young man is in the street; only the lower half of his face is shown, but as a type he is easily recognized by his 'alternative' clothing and hairstyle. This and his slightly swinging pose represent the playful, politically active generation of the late sixties who vociferously mounted the societal stage to question the establishment.

This is a multipurpose poster for a series of public meetings organized by the town council in Vitry-sur-Seine. The theme, place and date of each meeting were added in the text bar – hence the idea of the town crier or a man wearing sandwich boards announcing an event. Here the poster fulfils its most elementary role: 'The circus is in town! Roll Up! Roll Up!' If the text bar is blank, like the one reproduced here, the unwritten space acts as an open invitation to speak out freely, a wall poster to be covered with words and symbols of the citizens' own making.

The theme of the poster is freedom of speech, a right presented here as a duty or command. However, the mandatory character of the imperative 'prenez la parole' is softened by the anti-authoritarian appearance of the messenger carrying the order on a tray – the order thus becomes an invitation – and by the informal writing style of a comic book. Exactly who is giving the order is something we are not told.

The same year Grapus designed a wall poster for the neighbouring municipality of Ivry. (pp. 108-109). This included local news presented in a blue-white-red frame like that of an airmail envelope. It featured snapshots of local people, primary colours, silhouettes and simple drawings alongside the official stamp and photograph of the town hall – in one window a text balloon rises with the telephone number of a help line. This form of public information is both visual and bilingual, speaking as it does both the language of the town hall and that of the man in the street. Mixing the official with the informal, it represents both the sender and the receiver of the message.

The interaction with local residents that the local authority aims to achieve is already present in the manner in which the poster and wall newspaper address the citizenry. The language of public administration and the language of daily life enter into a symbiosis in a style of communication motivated by democratic intentions.

In addition to being a statement about the role of citizens in the political process, this poster tells us something about the social role of design. The young man in the image is Pierre Bernard himself. Here, however, he is not chanting slogans against authority as in May 1968. Rather, he is mediating in the public domain between a left-wing town council and its citizens.

Architectures

Graphus 86

la Villette

→

Cover of an issue of a
magazine dedicated to
Parc de la Villette
31 x 24 / 1986

Architectures. La Villette

The three geometric forms of the logo of La Villette stand out sharply against
the white paper of the magazine's cover – the back cover bears the same image
reversed. The square, triangle and circle have been drawn with a felt-tip pen.
The shadow suggests that together these stacked elements form a tower balancing
on the point of the triangle. At the top of the image the title is written by hand at an
angle; at the bottom there is a hand-drawn arrow.

In the logo, positioned on the edge of the page in accordance with La Villette's
house style, the three elementary forms are neatly lined up as befits a typographic
symbol. In the illustrative variant seen here, however, they are arranged in three-
dimensional space, in addition to which they are clearly not in a state of
equilibrium. Their colouring, while monochromatic, is not flat as in the logo: they
have plainly been drawn and coloured in by hand. The stacking and the shadow turn
this image into a miniature edifice, albeit an unstable one – as if a child were playing
with building blocks. It has the simple structure of a nursery rhyme, a simplicity
that contrasts with the complexity and advanced engineering that arc features of the
Parc. This 'little building' is almost a pictorial version of one of the site's bright red
'follies', designed by the architect Bernard Tschumi. The playfulness with which
the basic forms from the Bauhaus repertoire are used in the logo is thus taken a step
further. The formal grammar of the Bauhaus mutates into a child's game with
elementary building blocks.

When this design was made, the American researchers Ellen Lupton and J. Abbott
Miller had yet to publish their study of the historical origins of the constructivist
visual language of the Bauhaus. [Lupton/Miller 1991] They argue credibly that it
can be traced back to the nineteenth-century experiments in teaching material of
the German *Reformpädagogik*, in particular that of Friedrich Fröbel. Bernard,
who cannot have been aware of this finding, intuitively discovers the toys-and-
nursery-school background of the Bauhaus idiom, as well as its ludic possibilities.

As in the logo, this illustrative use of the Bauhausian ABC – triangle, square and
circle – is ambiguous. The basic forms are maintained but the disciplining and
dogmatic aspect of the idiom is dismissed.

In this design for a professional architectural journal we can feel the pleasure
with which a child can repeatedly court disaster on a miniature scale in a corner of
the playroom by demolishing the towers it has built. Sock it to 'em!
Einstürzende Neubauten.

13

Grapus

Poster for the Grapus
exhibition, in the Musée
de l'affiche, Paris
80 × 60 / 1982

This self-portrait of the group portraying its professional profile and political orientation was designed for the first Grapus retrospective in Paris. Grapus presents itself as a mischievous imp, displaying self-irony with a wink in the direction of the Smiley face.

In the centre of the image is Mickey Mouse, a favourite target in the work of Grapus. He is the symbol of the American political-economic-cultural system and, by extension, of the Disneyfication of European culture. Mickey Mouse, icon of a prudish, conformist, middle class culture, is here transformed into an *enfant terrible*. Mounted on a spring, the mouse's head leaps into the image like a jack-in-the-box. The male yet asexual Mickey Mouse is turned into a woman: two cut-out 'breasts' and taped-on pubic hair for a moustache make the mouse a transvestite.

The poster positions the design collective in the context of the three economic-political systems that dominated the twentieth century: Russian Communism, German fascism and American capitalism. Three propaganda systems, too, which also left their marks on graphic design. Their symbols are mocked, profaned or called into question. French chauvinism is ridiculed by picturing the cocarde as a black eye. This poster is indeed, as Savignac said, a minor public scandal. The faded hammer and sickle, taking the place of an eye, suggest waning loyalty to the French Communist Party. The slicked-down lock of hair, a salient element of any caricature of Hitler, replaces the official Nazi symbol. Passing references to the mass media, television and the press, appear in the tiny antenna on the mouse's skull and the grain in the hammer and sickle.

Pen and brush, calligraphy and photomontage are all put to provocative use. Here we recognize the malicious pleasure of the child preferring to colour outside the preprinted lines of the colouring book. The outline of the ears serves as a palette on which the artist provides less than convincing evidence of his drawing and painting skills.

It would be difficult to imagine a greater contrast than that between the sharply defined lines of the arrow, borrowed from the semiotic universe of modernism, and the visual noise in the mouse's ears. The laminated arrow directing the passer-by to the Grapus exhibition is clamped trophy-like between the teeth, stamping them as anything but followers of the International Style. Set against the sharp, clear-cut arrow are scribbles and splodges, the sans serif type does battle with handwriting, the deformed symbols clash with a pictorial image. The style remains close to graffiti and caricature, far removed from museum art, the sleek images of advertising and hackneyed political symbols. This is a fine example of the anti-aesthetics of Grapus.

The concept of the poster kills two birds with one stone. It criticizes both political propaganda and the commercial visual culture of the Disney factory. The principle of the independence of the reflective designer is emphatically reaffirmed through satire.

du 27 octobre au 7 février AU MUSÉE de l'AFFICHE - PARIS
82 83 Grapus. 18 rue de Paradis 10e

Secours Populaire Français

The hand is a recurrent motif in Bernard's work. The hand juggles – man at play; the hand protects, shelters – the caring man. The hand is held up as a warning or a command. The open, extended hand – man showing solidarity; the hand clenched as a fist – man demanding his rights. In 1981 he drew a hand with wings for the logotype of Secours Populaire Français, a non-denominational, non-religious aid organization. He had come up with the idea of a flying hand a year earlier for an SPF poster: an aeroplane whose fuselage becomes an outstretched hand. In the logo the metal wings are replaced with feathered wings, and the hand takes on its final form as a winged hand – a variation of the winged foot that appeared on a Grapus poster in 1978.

Here the hand is open and outstretched, turned slightly upwards, the fingers slightly spread. The contours are drawn with a rough, porous, line. It is not particularly decorative or elegant, nor does it suggest power or wealth. The hand carries and grasps nothing. It is empty, handing over neither money nor goods. It simply symbolizes willingness to help in any way whatsoever, and betokens the values of solidarity and respect.

The hand reaches out to a non-present Other in a gesture that is both expressive and purposeful: it merely expresses readiness to offer person-to-person help. There is nothing ritual about the gesture: it is not a token of consolation or blessing. This is about action, about real and meaningful aid.

The hand is a universal symbol of strength, will and power: of man's grasp on the world. The clenched fist, the symbol par excellence of militant organized labour, represents desire for power and anger about injustice. As a sign of power the hand has a dynamic aspect: it is poised to act and conquer. Open and extended, it symbolizes the opposite of power; the willingness to lay down arms, the proffered hand a greeting, a sign of peace and reconciliation. The addition of wings strengthens the dynamic aspect of the extended hand as an emblem of reciprocity and peace. Hegel called the hand of man *der beseelte Werkmeister seines Glücks* – the inspired maker of his own happiness. It can make happiness for others as well.

What is the origin of these wings? Do they come from the winged helmet on a packet of Gauloises? Are they a reference to the winged shoes of the Greek god Hermes, messenger of the gods, or of Hermes as the escort of souls on their way to Hades? Or do they stem from the Judaeo-Christian world and are they the wings of an angel? The classic symbol of the winged foot appeared in a work by Grapus in 1978, and in 1981 Grapus painted a banner for a peace march in Paris on which Picasso's dove of peace was given human feet. We see an analogous addition in the SPF logo, though here it is a human hand that is given an animal attribute.

Vincennes Must Stay

Exister Vincennes
Poster for the People's
University of Vincennes
50 × 60 / 1979

The university reform demanded by the student movement in May 1968 failed to materialize, but in January of the following year an experimental college opened its doors in a northern suburb of Paris. The college, which offered subjects such as film, urban planning, psychoanalysis, fine arts and drama, was to become the University of Vincennes. Among those who helped to make it happen were such progressive intellectuals as Deleuze and Lyotard. Abandoning the ivory-tower mentality of the past they turned instead to the topics of the day. The new university was open to those who lacked the required diplomas – i.e. to working class people – so that it soon came to be known as the People's University of Vincennes.

With the turning political tide came attempts to reverse the changes, and in 1979 the 'alternative' university of Vincennes was threatened with closure. Grapus were among those who supported the campaign to keep it open. At the bottom of the poster we read: 'affiche editée et vendue par les communistes de vincennes pour la défense de l'université. travail offert par l'atelier grapus janvier '79' (Poster published and sold by the communists of Vincennes to support the university. Work offered by the Grapus studio January '79).

Political action may have been what prompted this poster, but the way it presents the theme – the pleasure of learning – lifts it above the occasion. The human values on which the visual argument is based have a temporality different from that of the political struggle to realize them. Incidentally, the university still exists, as the Université de Saint-Denis, though it has been largely brought into the mainstream.

At the centre of the image is a tiny book, brightly lit and held by the fingertips of a labourer's hands, dirt still under the nails. This almost ritual gesture emphasizes the precious nature of the text: it is a treasured yet accessible gem. The little book is picked up and shown to us – and to anyone familiar with Catholic liturgy, the analogy of this demonstrative gesture and the central gesture of the Eucharist is obvious. The printed text assumes the place and significance of the Host: take, eat, this is my body.

The image unites two worlds: manual labour and literary culture. The spectator is in the position of the reading protagonist. Because we see not his face but only the book in his hands, we read with him, over his shoulder. We are invited to identify with the studying worker and protest against the closing of his university.

Bernard, a designer who has a sophisticated sense of colour, chooses here to make the poster entirely in black and white. This may have been partly for reasons of cost, but it is as surely a reference to the documentary photography of the interbellum and to book typography. The play of black and white is repeated in the widely spaced capitals of the title. Its two strong horizontal lines create a visual contrast both to the diagonals of the arms and to the minuscule print in the book. The text is a poem written by a worker studying at the University of Vincennes. Take, read, this is my poem.

centre national

des

Arts Plastiques

ministère de la Culture

National Centre for the Fine Arts

This logo was used on a range of products and is part of an interesting house style designed by Grapus in 1983–1987 for the CNAP, an agency of the French Ministry of Culture. The house style included annual reports, press material, invitations, business cards, stickers, and stationery for the management and various departments of the Centre.

The logo is based on a deconstruction of one of the symbols of the French Republic, the *cocarde tricolore* or tricolour rosette. It juggles not only with the rosette's form but also with its colours. The rosette is made up of three concentric circles in the national colours of France: blue, white and red. The emblem of the CNAP is made up of three incomplete circles around a centre. The red circle bursts open into colours, initiating a spiral. The sharply contoured line broadens, first hesitantly, in a different shade of red, and then more boisterously in blue and yellow, and ends in a nebulous splash.

This line of colour is flanked by a second, a circle of ink-filled calligraphed letters. A segment of a third, typographic circle bridges the space between the words 'Centre' and 'des'. Of the three symbolic colours of the rosette, red at first dominates, then turning into the process colours magenta, cyan and yellow. Paradoxically enough, these printing colours are applied with a free painterly gesture. Where cyan and yellow meet there are smudges of green. The political symbol of the rosette is thus transformed. The purple dot in the centre makes it an eye, the play of colour a palette.

The emblem is based on both a formal and a semantic contrast. The periphery of the circle is mobile, not orbiting around its centre but instead becoming the starting point for an expanding movement. The power of colour prevails over geometry, the symbol of political freedom becoming the symbol of the freedom of artistic expression. The CNAP is expressly presented as an institution of the State, but its task as promoter of the fine arts is somewhat at odds with this; the emblem becomes a dynamic yet coherent embodiment of the contradiction between the status of the CNAP and its function. The logo is the synthesis of a conventional symbol and an expressive image.

N.B. In 2005 a new logo was designed by the M/M Paris studio. If the Grapus logo represented the CNAP as a public institution with a specific cultural mission, the M/M logo neglects the political dimension and – in keeping with the spirit of the times – uses ornamental typography to present the CNAP almost as a brand.

National Parks of France

Parcs Nationaux de France
Poster
118.8 × 84 / 1990

In 1989 France's seventh national park was opened, on the island of Guadeloupe. To mark this expansion it was decided that the parks should have a common visual identity, and after a limited competition the commission was given to the Atelier de Création Graphique.

What does the designer take as a starting point to symbolize the unity of the nation's parks? What image does he find for the vastness of biodiversity? What image can there be to represent the individual's experience of the overwhelming beauty and infinite richness of Nature? One of the natural species might be an obvious choice, but what is the French equivalent of the panda? The designer finds himself faced with the task of building an ark on which, like Noah, he will put all of creation. But for the public domain of the parks which make up almost one per cent of French territory, a religious symbol would be inappropriate. Where Bernard did find inspiration at the beginning of the design process was in the famous fifteenth-century tapestry *La Dame à la Licorne* (p. 233) in the Musée de Cluny: 'Its "thousand flowers" motif inspired me when I conceived the emblem for the national parks. The configuration of a poetic island, the diversity and density of carefully observed nature and the presence of mythological animals seemed to be adapted to the metaphoric content.'

So Bernard reinvents the age-old symbol of the spiral, of which Paul Klee said: 'Spirals are the beginning of all blossoms that will develop from this initial movement.' A designer must be aware that symbols cannot be fabricated, but old symbols can be newly interpreted. In a lengthy and laborious process of positioning and repositioning, the spiral is built up on a large sheet of paper from innumerable silhouettes of plants and animals. Note that the silhouettes are not designed: instead, they have been taken ready made from books on flora and fauna. This emblem conflates into a single icon the beginning of the cosmos and the swarming of natural species on the earth, as if an unknown demiurge slings the species into cosmic space.

The surprising element of this emblem stems from a reversal of perspective. The Nature that surrounds us is projected as a nebula in deep space. What was once close by in our experience is suddenly far away. The observer of Nature loses himself in an infinite space, but at the same moment this experience brings what was far away close by. Losing yourself in Nature you feel connected to the cosmos.

A second reversal has to do with the treatment of form. In visual communication it is usually assumed that an emblem or character is primarily recognizable as a result of its closed and well defined outline. The spiral form is at once open and closed, designed to explode and expand at the edges. The Cluny tapestry shows us a static world in which everything is in balance, but this emblem for the national parks is all motion. Nature is in the throes of evolution, an eruption of energy. Each plant or animal silhouette is in itself clearly defined, but when they are all put together the effect – due to the unpredictability of their positions – is of a repeatedly broken, mobile, fractal contour of the spiral: a supernova as a super-sign.

Les Parcs Nationaux de France ont une nouvelle image

Parcs Nationaux de France

1986 MARTIGUES

15/26 JUILLET

ONZIEME FESTIVAL POPULAIRE
MARTIGUES PORT DE BOUC SAINT-MITRE

bureau du festival dans l'île
tél. 42 49 24 54 (55)

1986 Martigues

At the mouth of the channel connecting Etang de Berre to the Mediterranean, the town of Martigues (Bouches-du-Rhône) lies on an island that has been inhabited for 2500 years. Like many French towns, Martigues holds its cultural festival every summer; the 1986 festival was the eleventh. Grapus was commissioned to design a letterhead, postcards and a poster.

Bernard designed this curious image of a cloud in a box three years before his famous logo for the Louvre. We see the cloud from an unusual angle, not from below but from above. It is at once close by and far away – an auratic object. With its indeterminate, vague outline it floats between the cool surfaces of the box. The fleeting object is veiled and protected by the timeless, austere geometry of the box until it is opened. Traces of small, fiery spots on the edges of the carton soften its taut perfection. The sublime character of the tableau is both reinforced and undercut by the fact that the box seems to be anchored in heavy clay. Thus the image represents the four elements.

The surrealist quality of the image is increased by the hyper-realism of the photomontage. Since the handwritten title of the poster is partially hidden from view by the open cardboard flaps, the three-dimensionality of the composition is emphasized and the text en passant integrated into the image.

The poster condenses two ideas into a single image. The first is inspired by the location of the festival, on the Côte Bleue: the deep blue of the inside of the box is a reference to the cloudless, dazzling blue sky of the Mediterranean. And it echoes the name of the festival – Cargo Bleu (blue freighter) – the logo of which we see depicted at the bottom left. The second idea is totally different: the concept of the cultural festival as a gift, a surprise package. Something valuable is kept or sent in the box; when you open it, it turns out to be a cloud, a gift from heaven.

The value of culture is expressed by the contrast with the mundane packaging and the untilled, heavy soil. The box does not contain a product that can be bought, but instead evokes the precious experience of a person who loses himself in the clouds.

The complexity of the image is not immediately obvious. It emerges as a condensation of a rich dialectic of concepts: high and low, light and heavy, heaven and earth, dark and light, nature and culture, culture and market. Its charm also works, however, for those who are unaware of this dialectic.

N.B. This seemingly simple image evokes associations with two works from the history of modern art. In 1919 Marcel Duchamp sealed 50 cc of Parisian air in an ampoule. Upon his return to New York he gave this object, *Air de Paris*, to his friends Louise and Walter Arensberg as a gift. In 1938 the surrealist René Magritte painted a blue sky as a construction of perfect cubes in his work *The Progress of Summer*.

Hugues Boekraad

My work is not my work

Pierre Bernard
Design for the public domain

Lars Müller Publishers

Contents

Preface

This book is not an ordinary monograph about a designer: it is about the contribution made by a particular designer to the quality of the public domain. It was written at the request of the Praemium Erasmianum Foundation to mark the award of the Erasmus Prize 2006 to Pierre Bernard. The Erasmus prize is a European culture prize, and the book accordingly not only looks at the aesthetic qualities of Bernard's oeuvre but also examines its cultural, social and political significance.

I have approached Bernard's work in three ways. To begin with I analysed images that I considered characteristic of a particular facet of it. Then I selected sixteen projects in order to gain a broad overview of his clients and the communication strategies that Bernard has followed over a period of some forty years. Finally I examined certain basic concepts with the aid of which it is possible to investigate and understand the methods, the functions and the effects of communication design in the public domain.

This book is not just a book *about* a designer: it has also been *designed* by a designer. For a period of six months or so Reynoud Homan was my travelling companion – sometimes literally – and we did the picture editing together. The quality of his design work is something the reader will be able to judge for himself, but it is my duty and pleasure to say that this book owes its very existence partly to its designer's tact, meticulous care and powers of endurance.

To paraphrase Pierre Bernard's expression: this book is not my book, it is first and foremost *his* book. Not only because of the work presented in it, but also because of the generosity with which he gave of his time, knowledge and material.

But if these two designers have made my work on this book both possible and less daunting, the same is true of Dorien Pessers and Frederike Huygen, who assisted me in the preliminary research and in the final editing respectively. Finally I would like to thank Marsha Emanuel for her helpful remarks about the draft of the English translation, and Harry Lake for his sterling work in helping to prepare the final version.

With its decision to award the Erasmus Prize 2006 to Pierre Bernard, the Praemium Erasmianum Foundation has – I hope – set a dual process in train. On the one hand the design world has been reminded of the importance of the public domain as an area in which to work. On the other, the award draws the attention of clients and potential clients to the contribution that communication designers make to the quality and vitality of the public domain.

Hugues Boekraad, October 2007

Grapus was founded by Pierre Bernard, Gérard Paris-Clavel and François Miehe who met at the Atelier Populaire de l'Ecole Nationale des Arts Décoratifs in May 1968. Grapus started to function as a graphic creation group in 1970. François Miehe left the group in 1978 and established his own studio. The directors were then, in addition to Pierre Bernard and Gérard Paris-Clavel, Jean-Paul Bachollet, who arrived in 1974, and Alexander Jordan, who joined in 1975. Grapus closed its doors in 1990.

Participants in the Grapus studio between 1970 and 1990: Maria Arnold, Christine Baillet, Rik Bas Bakker, Joseph Balette, Jean-Marc Ballée, Lindsay Bartolini, Dirk Behage, Geneviève Bentolila, Claude Benzrihem, Leslie Blum, Paul-André Bungelmi, Simone Christ, Gérard Delafosse, Evelyne Deltombe, Eszter Domé, Marc Dumas, Anne Castebert, Mathieu Csech, Anne Dasriaux, AnnieDemongeot, Ibrahim Denker, Pierre Di Sciullo, Fokke Draaijer, Sylvain Enguehard, François Fabrizi, Richard Ferrand, Eugénie de Freitas, Gérard Gaillard, Anne Gallet, Vanina Gallo, Valérie Gandon, Jean-Louis Gigue, Sylvia Goetze, Michèle Guieu, Claire Herlic, Katie Herzig, Thomas Hirschhorn, Denis Imbert, Anne-Marie Latrémolière, Alain Lebris, Martin Le Chevalier, Patricia Lemorvan, Thierry Lemunier, Annette Lenz, Martine Loyau, Malte Martin, Ronit Meirovitz, Pierre Milville, Annick Orliange, Pancho, Muriel Paris, Vincent Perrottet, Claire Prébois, Marjolaine Preiss, Michel Quarez, Michel Robledo, Alain Roth, Thierry Sarfis, Théa Sautter, Ivan Sigg, Cornélia Staffelbach, Elian Stephan, Jean-Luc Soulier, Chantal Sueur, Pierre-Laurent Thève, Michel van der Sanden and François Vannière.

The Atelier de Création Graphique was established in 1991 by Pierre Bernard, Fokke Draaijer and Dirk Behage, two young Dutch graphic artists who had joined the Grapus studio the previous year. Fokke Draaijer left the studio in 1995 and Dirk Behage in 1997, both to set up their own studios.

Participants in the Atelier de Création Graphique between 1991 and today:
Fabienne Benoit, Johannes Bergerhausen, James Bolton, Stéphanie Brunel, Lucille Clerc, Cyril Cohen, Antoine Corbineau, Chantale Danjon, Julie de la Celle, Guillaume Chavanne, Béatrice Delas, Virginie Démonio, Anne Drucy, Sylvain Enguehard, Richard Ferrand, Justine Gaxotte, Isabelle Guillaume, Luc Guinguet, Nicolas Haeberli, Boris Igelman, Milène Journe, Ofer Kahana, Agnes Korink, Jacqueline Kübler, Ohyun Kwon, Thomas Lélu, Livio Loïal, Sébastien Marchal, Fanette Mellier, Sophia Païva-Raposo, Pierre Péronnet, Grégoire Romanet, Kathleen Rousset, Johannes Ruesch, Julien Samani, Milena Schärer, Bianca Sistermans, Dominique Soubranne, Laurent Stosskopf, Frédéric Teschner, Karin Trägenap, Wijntje van Rooijen and Jeanne Verdoux.

Today, the Atelier de Création Graphique, under the direction of Pierre Bernard, includes: Béatrice Delas, Guillaume Grall, Anaïs Lancrenon, Julien Lelièvre and Uli Meisenheimer. Claudine Durand is in charge of management.

My work is not my work

I hope my comrades will not see the title of this book as betraying some kind of malicious intent: in fact, it is intended as a mark of acknowledgement and indebtedness.

The entire Grapus period (1970–1990) and the first years of the Atelier de Création Graphique (starting in 1990) were characterized by the strive to arrive at a form of collective working. All those who were involved endorsed this goal, which they proudly professed as a political – not to say revolutionary – stand.

This ambition led automatically to a kind of polyphonic dialogue between the designers in the collective. Each member was forced to listen to each of the others and each was challenged to express his own constructive criticism. This *modus operandi* boosted our energy tenfold and considerably enlarged our room for experiment. At the same time we were each being given the ideal preparation for doing battle with the ideological certitudes of clients of every possible complexion.

Whatever the subject, the effect of all this was that each new job saw a new mix of assertive creativity and graphic experimentation. We were united together, and our common goals showed us the way. Like our verbal exchanges, our image productions were founded in a dialectical process in which form was set against form. And the pleasure that we took in the image that ultimately emerged from this process was the seal upon our friendship.

This dynamic gave us all the sincerely held feeling that our collective oeuvre at the same time became the personal property of each. Speaking for myself, this special alchemy has continued to work its magic to this day.

Together with the author of this book, however, I decided only to present those jobs in which I played what might be described as the lead role, either as the executant or as the creator of the concept, though it was not uncommon for the concept to emerge from the interaction between us. But whether I was the supervisor, the inventor or the executant, I was always an enthusiastic advocate for the end result.

All in all I believe my personal world was built up in those long years that were dominated by youth and a utopian world view, by interchange and collaboration. Today I have sole artistic responsibility for the way the Atelier works, but it remains true that my work would still not be my work without the clarity of vision, the talent and the effort put in by the young graphic designers who have joined me in it.

Pierre Bernard, August 2006

Hugues Boekraad

Visual rhetoric and ethics

Pierre Bernard, designer for the public domain

People regularly change their opinions and may happily revise their political preferences once or twice in their lives, but what is not so easily changed is the fundamental values that guide them through the vicissitudes of life. Although this study
of the work of Pierre Bernard only occasionally draws on biographical data, it is
important to point out the permanence of his ethical orientation. His personal values
are indissolubly linked to the positions he chooses as a designer: his professional
work is never without a subjective dimension.

   Bernard's first and most important decision as a designer was the choice of the
public domain as his field of activity. It is the setting for all sixteen projects presented in this book. The following chapter will sketch in broad lines the nature of
the public domain, its internal structure, its development, its functions and its
importance for the various design disciplines. Bernard has explored every nook and
cranny of the public domain. On the one hand he has moved in the circles of the
oppositional forces in civil society, and on the other he has entered into long-term
professional relationships with public institutions. This shifting of ground has never
involved a shift in the orientation of his values, though there is a growing awareness
of the fundamental values of the public domain. Bernard's principled choice of the
public domain has naturally had its effect on how he defined his profession and put
it into practice. His work can be seen as a particular rhetorical activity. Indeed, the
rhetoric is still there in the work that his studio, Atelier de Création Graphique, has
been doing for one of its institutional clients, the Pompidou Centre, since 2001. It is
these two concepts – ethics and visual rhetoric – that will be considered in this
introductory chapter.

   Bernard's moral, political and rhetorical positions took shape in the context of the
nineteen-sixties, and against the background of French culture and politics. I shall
therefore begin with a few words on that context.

The context of the sixties and the generation of '68
Bernard is of the generation which, in the nineteen-sixties, discovered the contradictions in modern capitalism and in the whole idea of modernization. The revolt of
the new politically active generation reached the universities in May 1968, revealing a crisis in higher education which had been brought about by the influx of vast
numbers of students from social backgrounds hitherto denied access to it. The
resulting 'massification' of higher education led to falling standards and the de
facto abandonment of the notion of education as the general development of human
qualities, in particular the capacity to make autonomous and critical judgements.
True, new social groups may have gained access to the higher regions of culture and

knowledge, but they were being groomed to meet demand in the labour market for people to fill positions in management and production. Similar changes were taking place as a result of increased affluence: young people now had more purchasing power, but this seemed only to offer them entry to the empty happiness of the consumer paradise. The values with which this generation had grown up (thrift, usefulness, solidarity: survival strategies in times of scarcity) clashed with the new promise of affluence and instant satisfaction. The generation of '68 rejected the definition of wealth and happiness in terms of consumption and career and even found the pursuit of this type of wealth reprehensible, given the poverty in other parts of the world, images of which were brought home by television.

In reaction to this, a youth culture developed which claimed the alternative utopian values of solidarity, peace and love. Out of this critical morality arose resistance to the war in Vietnam and the hegemony of the military-industrial complex. The generation of '68 was the first to grow up after the Second World War, and it still had a connection, albeit an indirect one, to that war. A consciousness of the horrors of fascism was still alive, perhaps even strengthened – and slightly distorted – by the authoritarian tendencies of the Fifth Republic under the presidency of Charles de Gaulle (1958–1969). In general, the sixties were about resistance to the unstoppable changes brought about by modernization and a plea to shape life as a personal project based on value consciousness and solidarity with the working class, minorities, outsiders and liberation movements in the Third World. The work of authors like Marcuse, Kerouac, Pfirsig and Foucault had a great influence on ideas of a counterculture.

The Situationists were the avant-garde, particularly in France, of an intellectual opposition that for the first time had an eye for the misery in which students collectively found themselves. They broadened the spectrum of critical theory to the parameters of modern life, such as urban planning, the consumer society, mass culture in general and the entertainment culture in particular (exposed by Guy Debord as the Society of the Spectacle), the control of the masses and their manipulation and domestication in the areas of work, leisure, tourism, etc. The Situationists prepared the ideological concepts of May '68 with their analyses of the concrete reality of urban life as experienced in daily life. Debord applied the early Marxian theory of alienation to the role of the media. Small groups of students were inspired by the Situationists and succeeded in becoming the core of the student movement. The Situationists also developed new forms of action, initiated by the Provo movement in the Netherlands in the mid sixties, and employed such means of communication as films, posters and comic strips.

Politically, Bernard chose the French communist party, which had recruited rebellious young intellectuals since its inception in 1920. After the Second World War, moreover, the PCF had become a symbol of anti-fascist resistance. In his professional practice, however, Bernard was also influenced by new forms of action and communication, the rediscovery of the old medium of the poster, the self-image and style of youth culture, and political satire. He was also exploring the possibilities of the image as the catalyst of emotions and the vehicle of values.

The context of French culture and history
In left-wing iconography, references to the glory of the national past – whether critical or not – are unusual. Not in the case of Bernard, however: he clearly places his work in the context of French culture and history. Although he is receptive to graphic design from such countries as Poland, Switzerland, the US and Holland,

these international influences are synthesized in an oeuvre that is unmistakably French. Love for his culture and his country is not alien to his work, as the poster *J'aime mon pays* clearly testifies (p. 107), and references to the French republic and nation can be found in many of his posters; they act as the self-evident subtext to the text being presented. Symbols referring to the history of France appear in abundance: the tricolore, the cocarde, Marianne, the map of France, and so on.

At the end of the eighties Bernard started taking on large jobs for public institutions such as the Louvre and the national parks. His designs demonstrate the power of these institutions to pass on cultural patterns and values across generations, to enter into dialogue with the past by reinterpreting it and integrating it into the present. The long-term memory of a culture is not the least of the prerequisites for its capacity to innovate.

Through the close connection of his work with contemporary history after 1968, through his identification with the basic values of the French republic, and through his brilliant corporate identity programmes for national institutions, in the international design world Bernard's work has become an icon of French visual culture.

The image

In Poland, where Bernard studied with Henryk Tomaszewski in 1964–1965, he became acquainted with a form of graphic design that harked back to the golden age of the French poster (Toulouse-Lautrec, Cassandre), and its reverberations in the fine arts (Bonnard, Matisse, Picasso, Léger). He discovered the image as the vehicle of social criticism and utopian desire.

The image can present anything, make the impossible happen and expose the contradiction between reality and ideology. It shows what language cannot or must not say. It sharpens the eye for revealing details. The metaphoric image makes it possible, via the detour of a poetic procedure, to comment indirectly on the reality in which the viewer finds himself. A slight distortion – for instance by the displacement or condensation of details – allows the image to express powerfully what is appreciated or criticized. Images can stimulate because they are a more direct mode of address than text. An image can assume the status of a symbol when it mediates values, experiences or meanings that are shared collectively. Creating images is enjoyable, and gives quite a different pleasure from that afforded by the creation of codes, systems or descriptions.

Tomaszewski linked the pictorial tradition of the French poster with an essayistic and aphoristic approach. In his work, typography sometimes made way for a singular calligraphy, and handwriting took on the value of a visual means of expression. On both points Bernard followed his Polish teacher.

Between typographic code and symbol, the image occupies an intermediate space of freedom. As long as it is not fixed in any given interpretation, its meaning is indeterminate. If this is true, I can only offer the reader my apologies for my commentary accompanying the images at the beginning and end of this book, although I do hope my analyses will elicit new associations and interpretations.

One final comment about Bernard's images. They do not stem from a desire for originality: on the contrary, they are the fruit of a striving for comprehensibility. Frequently they are variations on archetypes, proverbial expressions and commonplaces. The power of his images is that they take fossilized metaphors and make them dance, and that is precisely the definition that a French poet gave to poetry: music in the letters.

14 h.30
PARIS
22
octobr
198

HE POUR LE **DESARMEMENT**

e Jean-Jaurès à la rue de la Paix

MOUVEMENT DE LA PAIX

"Si cette terre ne périt pas, elle fleurira."

In the booklet *Hangzhou/Paris* [2005], the report of an exchange project involving French and Chinese students, Bernard writes in his foreword: 'One of the values that are most important to me in this profession is the personal involvement in the topic. It is that which gives emotional authenticity to the graphic approach, and which profoundly colours the communication solution that is proposed.'

Rhetoric

Grapus rediscovered the rhetorical dimension of visual communication. In contrast to science, which attempts to formulate true propositions, rhetoric is a means of formulating plausible statements about matters regarding which scientific certainty is impossible. All the more important, then, is moral certainty, the power of conviction as a prerequisite for convincing others. Rhetoric is the art of public speaking on all questions that are not susceptible of scientific proof: in short, rhetoric is a vehicle of practical reason. In the words of the eighteenth-century Neapolitan cultural theorist Giambattista Vico: 'What is eloquence if not wisdom expressed in an elegant manner, richly flowered and in accordance with healthy reasoning?' For centuries rhetoric was taught to the elites of the nations of Europe so that they could speak in public, be it from the pulpit, from the academic lectern, in the courts, from the tribune of a political meeting, on the battlefield or at the graveside. Rhetoric provided them with the toolbox for the shaping of public opinion.

Here we see a connection with graphic design which is indissolubly linked with the public sphere as it has developed since the Renaissance. Even today rhetoric is a tool of the exercise of power for the political, managerial, legal, scholarly and religious elites. The invention of visual rhetoric as a mode of mass communication in the second half of the nineteenth century was the continuance of the old rhetoric by new, visual means. It brought about an explosion in the printing of posters which, starting with Jules Chéret, furnished the changing urban wallpaper of European cities. Here visual rhetoric is deployed as both a simulation and the return of the repressed: the rhetoric of the spoken text returns in the medium of image reproduction. Graphic design and classical rhetoric have this in common: they are both intended to reduce, if not eliminate, the distance between the sender of the message and its receiver. Communication design is a rhetorical practice of the second degree, both a competence and a theory of that competence, just like classical rhetoric. But the theory of visual rhetoric is still in its infancy.

A closer analysis of Bernard's work by reference to the categories of classical rhetoric reveals its rhetorical character:

Inventio is the formulation of an idea or a proposition to be defended. Relevant material is selected to illustrate the subject and standpoint.

Dispositio is the constellation of arguments that are ordered into a carefully considered and articulated whole.

Elocutio is the verbalization and/or visualization of the thought, the careful – concise or flowery – presentation of the arguments in question in an appropiate stylistic form.

Standpoint, argument and style must be coordinated according to the public's expectations and level of understanding. But at the same time the audience or spectator must be seduced and surprised, invited to reflect and revise or confirm their opinion or attitude. It is of great importance that a style be chosen that is appropriate to the audience and to the occasion.

Some design theoreticians and designers make use of an antiquated notion of rhetoric when they reduce the rhetoric of a design to its aesthetic dimension, suggesting that the stylistic skill of the designer is crucial. In my opinion, the thesis that visual communication is the more or less creative modification of commonplaces is closer to the truth. If effective communication is placed first, the *topica* – the theory of the commonplace – is just as important to a communication designer as the style. Inventive reuse, rediscovery, elaboration or transformation of archetypes and visual clichés are all instruments in Bernard's arsenal.

It is striking how often the work of Grapus and Bernard is tailored to particular gatherings or occasions (conferences, demonstrations, celebrations, performances etc.). Sometimes mottos or slogans are typographically mutated, modified and cast in an unexpected shape. Sometimes a piece of work's effectiveness will stem from a combination of a known text and an unexpected symbolization. The posters, a medium of the street, speak the language of the street, or at any rate the language of a particular section of the population. Bernard injects powerful doses from popular sub-cultures into the moribund corpus of political representation, and in so doing bends the verticality of professional communication to the horizontality of a form of address in which the intended public recognizes itself.

Rhetoric has the disreputable connotation of manipulation: it is thought to hide the real intention of the speaker and stretch the truth. Rhetorical language, it is suggested, resides in the neighbourhood of falsehood and trickery, or even blatant lies and deceit. But no matter how it is used, it has to do with interests and with power. Even in Bernard's case it is a matter of power and interests, but the interests for which he enters the ring are generally those of the powerless: workers, children, prisoners, the jobless, the poor, people who are victims rather than wielders of power. What is brilliant in his idiom is that it avoids any form of miserabilism. The powerless are not portrayed as victims, but as a source of strength, as bearers of human dignity and as persons who have not only the right to speak, but also the right to act; they are not passive. They embody the highest values and are valorized. In fact, the directness of the form of address and the choice of everyday – visual – language create a situation of dialogue: the monologue of the sender reveals itself as an amalgam of various idioms leading to dialogue with the receiver. The presence of the maker's gestures or traces in the image adds to this. The visual orator does not hide himself in an impersonal style but reveals himself in scratches and smudges, in the direct notation, in the handwriting. In this way, in a medium that excludes the personal presence of the speaker, the *actio*, the presentation of the text by a flesh-and-blood person, is replaced by a series of indexical signs that connote his proximity. Here, however, a new paradox appears on the scene: precisely these stylistic characteristics and personal formal language have shown that they can be imitated and copied, like any formal language, in completely different strategies of communication.

The objects of Bernard's graphic design are close to those of classical rhetoric: entertainment through humour and unexpected changes of course, through a playful use of colour, the crossing of boundaries, visual witticisms and typographical gags; informing by means of announcements, instructions, pointing out inequities and particular states of affairs; making people sensitive to issues by appealing to such feelings as pride, endearment, outrage, readiness to act, compassion or anger; mobilizing and activating people by breaking through indifference, by inviting them to participate, to show solidarity, *citoyenneté* and responsibility, to identify or to criticize and resist; and confirmation of or appealing to values which the designer believes, in principle, exist in us all.

43

es
aris.
Pour envoyer les gosses
au soleil...
SECOURS
POPULAIRE
FRANÇAIS
...ersez au CCP 23 33 S Paris.

Graphic design has evolved to become the visual rhetoric of our times. This does not mean, however, that it receives the scholarly attention it deserves. As the vehicle of ideas and values it is effectively buried from view beneath its cargo: its role and effect in the public domain receive even less attention than its role in commercial communication. Researching the methods and functions of graphic design would make it possible to understand its social, symbolic and political effects and if necessary subject them to criticism.

Hugues Boekraad

Design for the public domain

Remarks on the occasion of the awarding of the Erasmus Prize 2006
to Pierre Bernard

The awarding of a prestigious prize to someone working in a design discipline
implies a certain view of the way in which design functions and is perceived in
European society today. What function of design is being honoured? What
definition of design has been used? What image of the world of design does the
award confirm? Can the award offer a way of correcting current perceptions of
design? What criteria for quality were applied in the award process?

1 The image of design today

There is no single notion of or approach to what design is or should be: on the
contrary, there is a whole panorama of notions and approaches. In the media the
prevailing view is that design is a market-related phenomenon, if not actually a
marketing tool. Design seems to be a way of meeting the needs and desires of
consumers, and is strongly focused on the consumer's private life. In television
programmes and magazines aimed at the general public, design is associated
with lifestyle, related to segments of the consumer market that is divided up
into target groups which vary according to age, gender, income, education and
lifestyle. According to this view, design is a way of creating, stimulating and
presenting individuality and distinction. From the point of view of the purveyors
of lifestyle accessories, design is a means of identification and presentation
(or representation) of the consumer's identity, magically incorporated into the
brand.

One of the consequences of this use of design to do what the market dictates is
that it tends to be mainly focused on outward visual aspects of identity. In short,
design becomes subservient to form, and tied to the individual object. The time-
frame or lifetime of a design is brief, following as it does the rhythm of fashion and
trends. Design responds to events, topical matters and the 'talk of the day'. In this
way design acts as an instrument for maintaining or accelerating the existing
patterns of production, promotion and consumption of goods and services. Its
primary function is economic. And as a consequence of that, what defines quality is
success in the marketplace.

This market conformism makes design heteronomous and reactive. It is put into
use in strategies on which it has no influence. Market orientation also determines
the field in which design operates, while markets and brands free themselves from
local or national cultural frameworks and become international.

In the wake of privatization and stronger market forces in some countries,
market-oriented designing has penetrated into the public domain as a policy

instrument borrowed from the private sector. In some countries, indeed, it has reached the very apparatuses of the State itself, carrying out its classic core tasks: defence, policing and justice, and taxation. In countries such as Switzerland and the Netherlands – pioneers in the use of professional communication techniques and styles in the public domain – a chaotic jumble of house styles has arisen for public and semi-public institutions to the extent that the identity of the state is barely recognizable behind them. [Jaquet 2004] The same phenomenon is seen in the institutions of the welfare state: the social services, education, healthcare, social housing and culture.

This development can be appreciated as an expression of a desirable modernization and professionalization in the interaction between government and citizens. It also has its dark side, however, because the distinction between the public and private domain has become less clear, as has the division between different types of commission: State, market and culture. [Boekraad 1994] What is lost when public institutions not only present themselves but also organize themselves as if they belonged to the private sector? The declining prestige of politics is often explained as being a result of the deepening cleavage between citizens and politicians, but distrust and indifference towards politics and politicians are unquestionably also a result of the blurring of the lines between the public and private domain. [Marquand 2004]

In cultural production too, the convergence of the public and private sectors has had an adverse impact. When cultural production is perceived and organized as a form of consumption, it runs the risk of losing its contours and becoming a component of the popular and flexible culture of media and events. Ultimately it becomes a building block and purveyor of a new branch of commerce, the creative industry. However much the porosity of the barriers between high and low culture may be applauded as a form of democratization, it cannot be denied that it jeopardizes some of the functions of art and science. The room for experimentation, for independent thinking and research, for diversity of intellectual styles and dissidence is increasingly limited. In this way the public domain is seeing the same paradoxical situation as the market sector: despite all the emphasis on distinction and identity, a clear tendency can be discerned – in the most diverse social areas – towards greater uniformity and standardization of the procedures and styles of designers. The diversity of visual culture is decreasing rather than increasing.

When we look at the smaller, more specialized publications that inform designers about current trends and developments in the design world, design exhibitions, etc., we see quite a different way of designing, based on different concepts. The literature of design, both national and international, focuses on a specific type of designer: not the large or medium-sized agencies, but the smaller studios and independent designers. They set themselves apart from the crowd by their originality, their own style, their own thoughts, their own oeuvre. This oeuvre has its origins not in any social demand or need, but in the personality of the designer. These designers are seen as authors with their own themes and style, recognizable in the tumult of mass culture: faces in the crowd. Their designs distance themselves from mass culture through irony, parody or humour, by an emphasis on the conceptual quality of the design, by a personal signature or idiom, by distance from current events and by references to the designer's own biography, to distant cultures or forgotten traditions. Their designs, which refer as little as possible to a concrete social context, are characterized by a certain striving after timelessness. Design critics and curators often discuss their work in terms of a mentality which then may or may not be seen as the personal variant of a collective mentality, as embodied in a national culture. [Lootsma 1995] There are still, or again, those who talk of Swiss design, Italian design or Dutch design. In reality these denominations cover a narrow band of design practice in the countries referred to which serves a small niche on the periphery of the art world. In essence, they apply to designers aspiring to the status of fine artists, looking to escape from the banality and uniformity of the mainstream design culture, and seeking sanctuary in all sorts of refuges: specialized design shops or galleries, websites, artists' initiatives, museums. They not uncommonly play a prominent role when Ministries of Culture put on exhibitions in foreign countries of what they call a representative selection of their national design culture.

Yet another picture comes up when we look at those sectors of industry in which scientists, engineers and technologists work on innovation-driven research and development programmes and at a certain moment call upon the capabilities of the designer. In such a case design sometimes makes good its old claim: it brings together knowledge and form in products and processes that are truly new and open up prospects of improving living and working conditions, i.e. the quality of life, for some or all of humanity. Examples include the innovative role of such companies as Olivetti and IBM, the telecommunications industry, or the medical instruments division at Philips. In these capital- and knowledge-intensive industries, design is subject to the dictates of technology and rational, exact thinking, yet it sometimes also contributes to the usability and integration of new functions and devices in users' familiar spheres of work and life. This type of product and communication design is aimed first and foremost at professional markets. Its common feature is an essential function in highly developed societies: it brings about the connection between specialized systems and between those systems and the world in which all of us lead our lives. Technical innovation and the adaptation of new technology to existing cultural patterns are a core function of this type of design. The design teams who carry out this task are relatively anonymous, in contrast with the clamorous signatures of the brand names and images in the windows of glamorous shops.

Looking at this small panoramic view of design we find ourselves asking one or two questions. The first is: do the nature and function of design disciplines allow us to deduce possibilities and objectives that they can realize autonomously? What is the actual value of their promise of unobstructed invention and initiative? Is design not by its very nature a heteronomous activity, bound hand and foot by practices, institutions and systems which have other functions and objectives? Do we not see, in actual practice, that design is only an instrument for more powerful players in the social arena? Are the design disciplines not absorbed by the dominant systems of money and power, and do they not as a consequence lose their own profile?
   This book focuses on a designer who has succeeded in avoiding the dilemma of autonomy and dependence. Evidently it is possible to be a practising designer in a way that credibly combines relative autonomy, originality and social relevance. The prerequisite for this turns out to be a not easily achieved position of equality with clients with whom one shares certain values. This designer moves between the state and the market in a socio-cultural field whose dynamic allows the repeated creation of new alliances. The question of whether this position leads to

. 50-1
e last attempt
ster
Beyerd Museum, Breda
0 × 160 / 1985

worthwhile and meaningful designs is answered, in this book, in the affirmative. The second question has to do with the specificity of design competence. The Bauhaus (1919–1928, under Gropius) and the Hochschule für Gestaltung in Ulm (1957–1968, under Maldonado, Aicher et al.) defined design in terms of its ingredients – art, science and technology – of which it appears to be an ever-changing mixture. But what, then, constitutes the specific competence of design, with its associated evaluation criteria and professional responsibility in a defined area? Is it possible, after all, to define designing as an autonomous practice, as an *ars liberalis*? Is it truly emancipated from the old system of the fine arts on the one hand and from the modern engineering disciplines on the other, to which, since the fifties of the last century, the new subservience, the hegemony of marketing, has been added?

This book will try to formulate tentative answers to some of these questions, not by assuming an *a priori* theory of design but by means of the thematic discussion of a design practice. Before I begin, however, I should point out that given the short time between the announcement of the winner of the Erasmus Prize 2006 and the presentation ceremony, the research into the material covered here could never be exhaustive – quite apart from the size of the Grapus archives in Aubervilliers and those of the Atelier de Création Graphique in Paris. What I do hope to do is to contribute to a better understanding of the complexity of designing as a political, social and intellectual activity, of the use to which graphic design is put in professional communication, and of the crucial importance of the public domain. What role do professional designers play in the public domain, that complex of institutions and activities the proper functioning of which determines, to a large extent, the substance of the democratic state governed by the rule of law?

2 The reflective designer

Let us suggest a new profile of the designer in contrast to the standard notion of the specialist of form and fashion, market and style, namely that of the reflective designer – a figure not unknown in the literature of design, but one who has been so much pushed into the background by the trendy version of the profession that a reappraisal would be appropriate. The sidetracking of this profile stems from the fact that all attention has concentrated on the commercially successful designer, the winner of the competitive struggle that produces a legion of losers. But that is not the only reason: the fact that design is not seen first and foremost as an intellectual activity, a form of reflection, has to do with the equation, characteristic of our culture, of thinking and logic, of thinking and theoretical reason. Although this type of thinking is not absent from the design process, it is not the only type. In my conception of design as a reflective activity, I distinguish a number of different cognitive capacities.

Design is a form of practical reason
Design takes place in the social interaction between the client, the designer and the user. The designer is in the middle of social reality. He plans and effects real inter-ventions in the real world. [Papanek 1972] His designs are produced and repro-duced in series of varying sizes. Tangible material interests assume concrete shape both during the design process and in the result of that process. The client-designer relationship is a business arrangement and is usually regulated on a contract basis.

Both winning commissions and dealing with clients demand practical skills. Nor is it possible to run a design studio and guide the design process without practical insight. The questions, needs and desires for which the design formulates an answer stem from a very practical, human world.

Design is a form of communicative reason
The starting point of the design process is almost always a text, in which someone other than the designer, generally the client or the user, defines the underlying principles, problems and objects of the design process. The interpretation of this text by the designer is the first step of the design process. This interpretation must then be discussed with the client and approved by him. In the case of a more complicated commission, this bilateral adjustment takes place more than once. The reciprocal structure of the dialogue permeates the design process from the outset. In turn, the designed spaces, objects, texts, systems, symbols and images anticipate the interpretative capacity of the users, readers and viewers, whose communicative capacity is thus presumed. Indeed, any form of design presumes a public domain of shared codes. However, they are not mechanically repeated ad infinitum: instead, they mutate and evolve under the influence of, among other things, the unending stream of new designs. In this way, design guarantees the flexibility of social communication.

Design is the exercise of moral categories
Valorization is the affirmation or enhancement of the value of a thing, a person or a state of affairs. It is intrinsic to design in so far as design implies attention to and care for the designed object. Indirectly, valorization extends to client and user. When design is critical in tenor, when it deprecates or polemicizes – i.e. when the value of something or someone is denied – a different, underlying, value is affirmed.

The moral dimension of design also exists in the relationship between client, user and designer. The designer must immerse himself in the culture of the client and keep in mind the values that guide him. The same applies to the user. Finally the designer cannot avoid the question of whether the commission is compatible with his own personal values, and whether its fulfilment offers an opportunity to realize those values. Having a clear understanding of the compatibility of values allows the designer to select his clients with care. Of course, the process of selection is reciprocal: designers choose their clients as much as clients choose their designers. Coherence in the designer's choice of clients based on the values they adhere to is a prerequisite for coherence in a designer's oeuvre.

Artefacts always carry the mark of a specific conception of humanity and culture. Given the nature of the decision-making process in complex organizations, today's designer is often forced to make these usually implicit values explicit.

Design is a function of the power of imagination
The designer looks at the world not just as a field of facts but first and foremost as a field of possibilities. Design is built on an existing state of affairs but tries to change it. The design process is a path from a given fact to a desired situation. As such, design is an expression of the power of imagination, to which, since the Romantic period, almost demiurgical potency has been ascribed. However, human imagination is not a matter of creation *ex nihilo*. Design is almost always a variation on existing models and forms, and in only a few cases is it true innovation. New forms

commonly arise through the selection, transformation and combination of existing techniques and materials, forms, symbols, signs and images. Thus it is not the incidental design but a constellation of designs that determines the character of a culture or an environment. The extent to which a culture or environment leaves room for the innovative imagination to express itself is one of the factors that determine its dynamic.

Design is an exercise of theoretical reason
Design is inconceivable without analysis and abstraction, without research and reflection, without hypothesis, argumentation and conclusion. This theoretical aspect of a project starts with the awarding of the commission, which will naturally be accompanied by information of different sorts and levels of abstraction.
In addition to interpretative processing of this information, an objective analysis is required. This is augmented with information from other disciplines with which the designer is going to have to collaborate: a design, after all, often calls for more than one kind of expertise.

Naturally the designer will also have his own expert knowledge: that is to say, he must not only be au fait with the state of the art in his own field, but also with its history. Now that modernism – which abolished history as a source of innovation – has itself been dispensed with, history has once again, albeit in a new way, become a source of inspiration for forward-looking designers.

In design, unlike fundamental research, theoretical reason remains tied to practical reason because certain requirements imposed on the product of the design process are established at the beginning of the process. The desire to achieve that outcome is the engine driving the hypothesizing in the designer's sketchbook.

Design combines various research methods
Also part of the reflective character of design is that the designer will employ a number of different research methods. In the first place this is a matter of investigating what procedures the designer can best follow during the design process itself, in the discussions with the client and with those carrying out the design. This is because the internal organization of the design process is not the same for every job. The next step is to determine the materials and techniques that will be needed to implement the design. It is not uncommon for this kind of research itself to lead to form-invention. Research into forms is of course the crux of design as an aesthetic practice. This investigation of forms is not separate from the research into theme and content or into the specific functional requirements that the design must meet. Where they are not known to the designer from experience, he will also investigate the design's future users, in so far as it is necessary to anticipate their response. And finally the designer will research the context in which the design is to be realized: the context of the commission and the field of application. For it is in that context that the design will have to fulfil its dual function: to adapt itself and at the same time be distinctive.

All these forms of research lead ultimately to a synthesis of the design proposal or model that is the result of the whole procedure. The design proposal is thus in no sense based solely on intuition, although pure chance and serendipity do play their part. Almost equally important is a type of reasoning that ever since Peirce has been known as 'abduction'. To designers, abduction is the ongoing process of eliminating options that do not appear to lead to the stated goal.

The fact that with so many varied forms of cognitive, analytical and argumentative work no designer can manage without periodical reflection on his own activities during the design process, will come as no surprise. The designer's activity – aimed at achieving a goal – is indeed strategic and teleological, a form of thinking that is dismissed by the experimental sciences but which is indispensable in modern production and communication processes that are based on the same sciences.

3 The public domain

Design disciplines can be classified in many ways. As objects of design Buchanan [1992] distinguishesn between symbolic and visual communication, material objects, activities and services, complex systems, and environments. More usual is an arrangement according to the nature of the design discipline or the designer's speciality (fashion, architecture, landscape, print media, industrial products etc.). Another arrangement is according to types of client: politics, culture, business, non-profit organizations. Less common is distinguishing design activities according to the private or public character of the domain to which they relate. This division allows of a dual perspective of design, from the individual point of view and that of the community. It corrects the methodological individualism practised not only by many designers, but also, in their wake, by design theoreticians and critics. In the introduction to this chapter I pointed out the implications of this market related methodological individualism. The effect is that designing is seen first and foremost as an instrument for the private sector. Producers see design as a means of seduction, marketing, branding, gaining attention, positioning, whereas consumers view it as a means of self-expression, a way of setting themselves apart from other consumers. In the private domain the chief functions of design are differentiation and individualization. The public domain, by contrast, is the territory of generality, of what binds people and transcends them, of their common interests and identity. These interests are defined and sustained in an unceasing and dialectical process of power and counterpower, of images and counterimages, of proposals and counter-proposals.

The heart of the public domain is the state, its organs and apparatuses, for it is the state, above all, that is charged with looking after the public weal. Second, the public domain encompasses the public sphere, in which state and civil society interact. This interaction takes the form of communication amongst government agencies and public authorities, between government agencies and public author-ities on the one hand and the public on the other, and vice versa, and between citizens. Also part of the public domain is public space in the physical sense. And finally the public domain includes the institutions within which culture and knowledge are produced, distributed and preserved.

The dichotomy of the private and public domain is the starting point of this book. All social interaction outside the personal sphere and outside the marketplace is accounted part of the public domain. This pragmatic definition parallels the distinction, customary in the design world, between social, political and cultural clients on the one hand and commercial clients on the other. The public domain is the catch-all term for the first three of these areas. The sixteen projects presented in this book are grouped according to the various sectors of the public domain.

Almost all of Pierre Bernard's work has been done in the public domain, and indeed his work cannot be seen in isolation from the social, cultural and political

p. 56-7
Carrier bag
Louvre Museum, Paris
46 × 34.5 / 1990

context in which it came into being. At every stage of his career as a designer he has made his preference for public commissioners abundantly clear, even defining design as a social activity. This is why the unity of his oeuvre cannot be established simply by looking at its themes, style, methods and values: it also requires an exposition of the specific nature and connection of those areas of the public sector in which and for which Bernard still works. It is the public domain that is the unifying link in Bernard's projects.

As a theoretical concept the public domain actually leads an uncertain existence. The concept takes different roles in different scholarly and scientific disciplines, and it is therefore impossible to homogenize the various definitions into a single coherent theory – at least, to the best of my knowledge such a theory doesn't exist. Besides, the realities to which the term 'public domain' refers are not static but ever-changing. The boundaries between the private and the public domain are not, after all, fixed: their demarcation is at stake in a permanent political and social battle which is fed by political ideologies. These ideologies, in turn, resonate in academic theorizing. That is why I shall confine myself in this introduction to a brief exposition of a few concepts borrowed from cultural anthropology and the theory of law that are relevant for understanding the role of communication design in the public domain.

The public domain and the symbolic order
Broadly speaking, the public domain is what individuals necessarily have in common to be able to exist as individuals. The public domain is thus not a cultural supplement, but a basic prerequisite for community living and survival. In this sense we can speak of a public domain as soon as people succeed in developing shared institutions such as language, family, religion, etc. These institutions are predicated on the human capacity to symbolize: to render the physical and social environment manageable, comprehensible and meaningful, for without order and meaning the world would appear to us as an unfathomable chaos experienced only through impulses or drives. Society and survival are impossible without regulation of drives.

The pre-eminent means of signification, of course, is language. Language makes it possible for an individual to take a position as a subject, language is the vehicle of intersubjective communication, and language is the medium by which we interpret and construe the situations and surroundings in which we interact with others. Language is thus not primarily the expression of personal or shared preferences or intentions, but it does constitute the community in which, under certain conditions, individual use of language becomes possible. (Of course, every society also has other symbolic forms of expression that fulfil the same function, such as images, music, song, dance and rituals.)

Personal experiences, too, bear the stamp of the symbolic order that is characteristic of a culture in its totality. All cultures are familiar with the stages of human life between birth and death, with the alternation of peace and war, of past, present and future, of the shelter of one's own clan and the potentially hostile outside world. But the form in which these experiences are symbolized varies from culture to culture.

The constant changes in the social order create an inherent instability that must repeatedly be restored to unity, even if it is only a fictive unity. Gurvitch [1950] is of the opinion that symbols 'act as a sort of liquid and omnipresent cement that forces its way in everywhere to restore the constant breaks and imbalances between levels.' Gurvitch probably overestimates the elasticity of cement. Some cultural changes cannot be dealt with by rearranging the patterns of the symbolic order. If social patterns are put under pressure from changes in the economy or technology, or through migration and war, cracks will appear in the symbolic order that cannot so easily be sealed but take the form of a lasting deficiency or hiatus. New symbols or even new kinds of symbolic construction are then needed. The necessity of such compensating symbolic constructions is one of the reasons for the rise of modern communication design, and of all design disciplines in so far as they fulfil communicative functions. To give the history of communication design in relation to social, cultural, economic and political changes promises greater insight into its real functions than a history couched in terms of the autogenesis of forms, or a history presented as the result of external technological determinations.

The sixties and seventies of the last centrury – notoriously a period in which established institutions and symbols came under attack – were also the birthplace of a large-scale resymbolization, at the level of the institutions, of social groups and of private lives. I shall look at this period of radical change in more detail later on.

Symbolic order, public morality and design
The symbolic order as a signification system is not value-free. Indeed, it is a way of clearly identifying value and the absence of value and attributing them to human behaviour, characteristics and objects. Thus the symbolic order also produces a topography of good and evil, friend and foe, virtue and vice, commandment and taboo, rights and duties, honour and disgrace. It acts as a moral navigation system which individuals are expected to follow. In language it is the thesaurus of proverbial sayings that points the way to the moral values of earlier generations. Within the symbolic order, social institutions fulfil an analogous function by attempting to keep socially accepted value configurations intact in the undulating swell of generations.

Even on this fundamental, anthropological level we can distinguish five functions of graphic design in the context of public communication: *orientation* in an environment which without signification would be a frightening chaos to us; *identification* which, by allowing us to recognize ourselves in others, allows us both to establish our own identity and to identify with others; *representation* of symbolic meanings which renders the invisible visible and the absent present for all; *integration* of the various symbols and signs in a code that is valid for the whole community; and finally *valorization* as a dual, circular process: the attribution or denial of values to people, objects and characteristics (e.g. courage or cowardice, wisdom or stupidity), and the affirmation of the value system on the basis of which this attribution takes place.

Symbolization constantly conquers strangeness by means of artefacts, which themselves adapt to the existing artefacts of the world we live in. For the professional designer this symbolization and adaptation are core tasks. In our technologically highly developed culture social changes are often introduced by developments in the sciences. Scientific or symbolic systems construct their own reality: their object of knowledge. True, in time they do have a real effect on daily life and social relations, but only after selective absorption by systems such as the economy or political power. Here again design disciplines are necessary to mediate between those systems and the world in which we live.

The public domain and the rule of law
The distinction between public domain and private domain and the separation of powers in a system of countervailing powers, human rights, fundamental rights and

principles of law are the normative organizational principles of a constitutional state governed by the rule of law.

Modern law is a symbolic system with a special character. 'Law is not revealed by God or discovered by science, but is through and through the work of men. ... It is true that notions of justice change over the course of time and also from country to country. But what does not change is the need for a shared idea of what is just in a given country or age. Law is the institution that embodies this idea.' [Supiot 2005, pp. 24-25] Law, according to Supiot, is a symbolic system in which the moral values of a society are crystallized.

The central legal figure of the public domain is statute law: a set of regulations to which all are subject, established by parliament. The central legal figure of the market is the contract, which is a *consensus ad idem* between two individuals, based on calculation and negotiation and intended to promote private interests. The contract can only exist by the grace of an underlying system of law that guarantees the freedom of contract and makes it possible for individuals to enforce its observance. From the point of view of the contracting parties this public infrastructure is generally out of sight. Important market players, of course, know how to find their way to the legislators if they want to see a given stipulation removed or a new one added. And the party to a contract who is confronted with non-observance will know how to find his way to the courts. But in chasing after their personal interests private parties fail to see their dependence on the public domain. Just as the law cannot be reduced to a contract, so society cannot be reduced to the sum of individual interests. Methodological individualism forgets that personal rights can only be exercised in the context of a community of law that is endorsed by all.

The law and its ethical consequences for design
What does design have to do with law, jurisprudence and contracts? Copyright, contract law, delivery conditions, etc. are all matters of private law with which the designer as an entrepreneur is confronted. But public and administrative law, e.g. regulations concerning quality, the environment, procedures and the like also limit his actions. However, as a creative individual the designer believes that he is outside the sphere of the law. In his introduction to *Das Gesetz und seine visuellen Folgen* [2005] Baur observes that 'the vast majority of designers and artists surround themselves with an aura of anarchy and deviation, giving the appearance of living more freely by taking no interest in anything touching on the question of law and order and by cultivating their favourite, almost legitimate status as outlaws.' [p. 13] He then goes on to ask the question of what, beyond design, determines the prevailing aesthetic of our urban environment. According to Baur, it is largely determined by laws, norms, rules, rites and other regulated processes. The law appears here as an external constraint on creativity.

This book on Bernard takes a different view. Here the law is not seen as an administrative rule system regulating the actions of individual citizens but as the heart of the public domain in which it embodies the central values of our culture in the catalogue of fundamental human rights. It is not the relationship of law to aesthetics that is the central issue, but the constituting role that moral values play both in the public domain itself and in design for the public domain: in other words, the relationship between ethics, law and graphic design. What are the ideas of social justice that nourish the oeuvre of a designer? Does he work for the Establishment or for counterforces? What are the values that determine his selection of clients?

What power does he legitimize by means of representation? Of what power does he contest the legitimacy?

The past two centuries have demonstrated that the freedom of the autonomous arts is only assured within a constitutional state, even if the idea of the rule of law plays no part whatever in the artist's consciousness. At the present time such freedoms are again under pressure, on the one hand through the withdrawal of state support and the privatization of the cultural sector, and on the other through the obsession with security to which, for the benefit of the 'war on terror', more and more civil freedoms are being sacrificed. The rule of law, or parts of it, is in danger of being suspended, moving step by step towards a state of emergency. Freedom of speech, and particularly freedom of expression for artists and designers, will be the first victim. This is one of the reasons why designers and artists have every interest in adopting the core values of the democratic rule of law as their own and not in comforting themselves with the illusion that they are outside or above the law.

The rule of law and civil society
The normative structure of the state governed by the rule of law was laid out in the eighteenth century by Montesquieu and the Social Contract philosophers as an Enlightenment project. It was put into effect by the French Revolution and has been further refined since then. From the outset, however, there was a dialectical tension between the substantial rationality of the liberal state under the rule of law and the instrumental rationality of the private, free market garanteed by the same liberal state. In the second half of the nineteenth century these internal contradictions in the new political and social order culminated in the clash between labour and capital. The state was called upon to arbitrate in the conflict, and from that moment on would develop from a nightwatch state into an intervention state, and finally into an all-embracing welfare state. The state was no longer an independent supervisor of the Social Contract, more a party within it, and as such found itself at the centre of political conflicts. The state gained the function of a platform on which conflicting interests were fought out. It was not the sovereignty of the state but its officiality that legitimized the outcomes of the social and political battle. It was in this force field of an industrial society that the functions of the state were extended in the nineteenth and twentieth centuries.

The interaction between state, market and citizens resulted in a public domain that can no longer be clearly distinguished from the private domain of the market. Civil society has also lost its autonomy relative to the state, now that important sections of civil society have become matters of government policy. The state has been socialized as society became 'statified' [Habermas]. The public domain became the space in which the public interest was defined and promoted in a continuous dialectical process of power and counterpower. Since the eighties the centre of power has shifted to the market. 1989 saw the emergence of a market triumphalism which – partly under the influence of the European Union – legitimized and reinforced a neo-liberal climate that urges the retreat of the state. In several European countries, privatization and deregulation are bringing about the delegation of institutions and functions of the public domain to the market. Even state apparatuses are reorganizing themselves according to business models. Consequently, the practical relevance of the distinction between the private and public domains has decreased. However, as a normative and critical category the public domain has lost none of its significance. On the contrary, there is now a

p.62-3
Graphic Design, World Views. A Celebration of Icograda's 25th Anniversary
Book jacket
Icograda (International Council of Graphic Design Associations)
.5 × 26.5 / 1990

GRAPHIC design, WORLD views
A Celebration of ICOGRADA's 25th Anniversary
Edited by Jorge Frascara

between labour and capital about the form, speed, direction and social consequences of the progressive modernization of the state and economic production was finally pacified by means of social legislation and fundamental social rights. The state was thus at once platform for, participant in and object of the struggle. The political battle over social reform and legislation went hand in hand with new disciplining strategies to qualify the masses for the labour market through education, healthcare, housing and social security. The result was the welfare state in which the state and the market were tightly interwoven in a constant process of modernization, one result of which was a scaling up in the economy and education. In secondary and vocational education, teaching factories sprang up. Huge numbers of students flooded into the universities. Partly because of pressure from this 'massification' of education, the ideal of the education as an end in itself was abandoned and replaced with job-oriented courses. The universities underwent a process of deculturalization.

The sixties and seventies

Against this background, a new fierce struggle arose in the sixties for access to the spheres of power and political decision-making. There was a change in the way people saw politics, and social change was sought in new areas. The established order was attacked by a broad movement of democratization that left almost no social institution unaffected. Social criticism, expressed primarily by the student movement and inspired by the neo-marxist Frankfurt School, focused on the close-knit relationship of state, academia and business, and the instrumental rationality to which society and science were subjected. According to Habermas, all kinds of systems were colonizing the world in which people live their lives and suppressing views of reality not determined by the media and those in power. He called for reactivation of the constitutional values of the public domain by means of democratic forms of organization and new communication models that would allow domination-free debate.

The key words of the second half of the sixties were public sphere and democratization. Public institutions – universities, museums, theatre companies, healthcare, social services, legal aid, even the armed forces and the prison system – now became the targets of action groups demanding direct, participation-oriented democracy. Newspapers, radio and television began to play an active political role. In the Christian churches, both ordinary believers and clergymen were demanding changes in the liturgy; the Word of God was to be interpreted in the light of political positions and social engagement. Patriarchal and authoritarian relationships such as those between the sexes and between parents and children were now open to debate. Battles for equal recognition under the law were fought for homosexual relationships and alternative forms of cohabitation. Works councils and trade unions demanded, and were given, new powers. Even the quality of the physical and social environment in the street, neighbourhood and city was placed on the political agenda by agitators and squatters resisting the transformation of the city into a transport and consumerist system. The countryside was rediscovered by the environmental movement, which claimed nature as something that needed protection because it was finite. The peace movement succeeded in expanding the geography of the political agenda: there were demonstrations against the war in Vietnam, on behalf of dissidents in the communist bloc, against nuclear weapons and cruise missiles. The Third World movement opened up a global perspective. American imperialism was pilloried, as was the poverty gap between North and

South. Solidarity was expressed with freedom movements in colonial or formerly colonial areas and in Cuba and South Africa, and finally there were campaigns aimed at bringing down military dictatorships, notably those in Greece, Spain, Chile and Argentina.

A countervailing public sphere
The result of this explosion of political consciousness and activism was a multiform public domain that produced new forms of visual agitation, new means of communication and new communicative styles. Printing shops, stencil machines, posters and flyposting, wall newspapers and megaphones all helped make the fast distribution of mass information possible. These oppositional messages were also different from commercial and official sources of information in their spontaneous, unpolished form. But there was more than just a change in the content and forms of communication. There was also the discovery of the political power of the image, and, particularly, the power of the image reproduced in the media. Walter Benjamin's brilliant essay on *The Work of Art in the Age of its Technological Reproducibility* [2006] was rediscovered by the student movement and opened the eyes of many to the limitations of a notion of democracy which placed the text at its centre: the spoken text of parliamentary debate, the written text as the basis of bureaucracy, the legislative text as the basis of legal pleadings and the verdicts of the courts. Power and manipulation, persuasion and seduction all make use of a double register: the language and the image. Alongside the old-established rhetoric of the word there is the visual rhetoric of the image. In short, what was discovered – following in the footsteps of the Situationists – was the phenomenon of the society of the spectacle and the relationship between power and the media. Marshall McLuhan was celebrated as the pioneer of media theory. In linguistics great things were expected from semiotics; meanwhile classical rhetoric was dusted off – by Barthes, among others – and research into persuasive public speaking was taken down some new paths.

The political activism of the sixties launched an offensive of dissent and created an alternative communication circuit based on the democratic principle of argument and counterargument. Minorities unrepresented by political parties acquired a voice and a face in the public domain. Abuses caused by governments or companies were exposed by means of black books and the publication of confidential minutes.

In short, the whole political discourse changed: the speakers, the topics, the public, the style and the language. Who seized the floor? Young people who saw themselves as an extra-parliamentary opposition. They gained an eye for the structural relationship between the economy and political power and addressed issues that were outside the scope of the political economy. Reality as it was lived, subjective experience, personal stories – often expressed in accusatory or confessional literature – all were put to political use. Those who had the floor evaded the dogmatism and wooden language of the traditional left wing parties and unions. Their audience consisted primarily of people of their own age, and their discourse was coloured by a subcultural idiom.

The eighties and nineties
At the back of the stage, meanwhile, an economic, neo-liberal restructuring was going on which in the eighties – presided over by Reagan and Thatcher – proceeded apace. The state – certainly the welfare state – was seen as an obstacle to economic

RCK

26 février — 12 mai 2003

PARIS
PREMIERE
PARIS-PREMIERE.FR

MCTROBUS

growth and social dynamics. Far-reaching privatization and deregulation operations were started to give the market new impulses. The public utilities that were
so characteristic of the public domain in telecommunications, transport, energy,
housing, etc. were hived off or privatized. British and American business models
based on shareholder interests swept the European continent by storm. The growing
influence of the European Union on the economic policy of the member states also
fostered the neo-liberal climate. The so-called Rhineland model that had dominated
relationships between employers and employees after the war came under pressure
from the Anglo-American model, which was more confrontational. The new
business models were no longer based on the industrial economy but on the service
economy which took off in the seventies, partially as a result of new information
and communication technologies. Knowledge, information and access to
information became the most important capital goods. Technological innovations
not only brought massive increases in productivity, but also changed the labour
process and industrial relations. Employees were now expected to be flexible
and willing to undergo lifelong training. The chief characteristic of the new, post-
industrial worker was no longer manual labour but brainwork coupled with
communication skills. The communication society had arrived, though not in
Habermas's sense of social and non-hierarchic communication but rather in the
sense of the new society steered by the market and new information and communication technology. Human engineering, corporate communication and public
relations were put to use as strategic management instruments. Becoming an
important part of these management strategies was an image policy in which
private companies adorned themselves with the feathers of a public morality.
Benetton set the tone in controversial advertising campaigns in which a direct link
was suggested between the brand and a better world without racism, where Aids
would be combated with vigour and its victims treated with compassion, and in
which seabirds would no longer suffocate in filthy fuel oil. Business and industry
entered the public and even the political domain vaunting a veneer of social
responsibility.

Business leaders regained their status as heroes in the front line of modernization.
They were sought as advisers to and supervisors of public institutions like universities, hospitals, and museums. With their managerial approach to organization
models they also introduced commercial communication models into institutions
of the public domain. One effect of this was that in the design world too the
distinction between commercial and public communication began to blur. It looked
as if all communication was turning into marketing communication.

Meanwhile as the eighties progressed, the original activists withdrew from the
stage, exhausted, in a noiseless *Rückzug ins Private* (retreat into the private sphere).
They too finally embraced the ideal of individual self-realization. The eighties were
proclaimed to be the 'me, me, me' decade, characterized by a fixation on lifestyle,
physical appearance and health, and by a preoccupation with personal relationships
and personal feelings. The fixation on the personal life extended to the political
sphere, where the persona and looks of a politician became more important than his
political agenda. The ultimate mass medium, television became the vehicle for the
far-reaching personalization of politics. Political activism declined and – if it
existed at all – failed even to reach the television screen. Now, political opposition
came from NGOs to which responsible citizens demonstrated their solidarity with
their chequebooks.

In the constitutional state under the rule of law the interminable tensions of democracy are pacified and channelled by means of legislation, jurisdiction and administration carried out by bureaucratic apparatuses. These are expected to have a particular organization, professionalism and morality attuned to the optimal realization of the public interest. As an ideal type (in the sense in which Weber used the concept), bureaucracy is in sharp contrast to the organization, professionalism and ethic of the market. The chief characteristics of a bureaucracy are the absence of competition, impartiality on the part of public bodies, equal treatment for all citizens, objectivity and predictability in the actions of government, and reliability of information.

Bureaucratic institutions present themselves in countless forms of visual communication: house styles and logos of the government bodies themselves, statistics, infographics, passports and identity documents, tax forms, public information campaigns and so on. I take the Netherlands as my example not just because I am familiar with the Dutch situation but because, after the dissolution of Grapus in 1990, Pierre Bernard asked two Dutch designers to establish with him the new studio Atelier de Création Graphique in 1991.

In the eighties the public domain in the Netherlands gained the reputation in the international design world of being a 'designer's paradise'. [Huygen 1985] The new 50, 100 and 250 guilder banknotes designed by R.D.E. Oxenaar between 1981 and 1986 elicited a particular mix of amazement and admiration. Oxenaar's banknotes were adorned with warmly coloured motifs from nature: a snipe, a sunflower with a bee, a lighthouse by the sea. The lettering was matter-of-fact, clear and taut, the general layout uniform. [Bolten 1987] Remarkable about this iconography was that it had not been prescribed by the Dutch central bank: it had been the designer's own idea to break with the conventional allegorical representations and historicizing portraits. The new themes reflected emerging ecological awareness and were at most a reference – via the sunflower – to the history of art. At the heart of a state monopoly – the minting of coins and emission of banknotes – the designer acquired a high degree of independence relative to his client and the printer. He even incorporated his thumbprint into a lock of Spinoza's hair on the thousand-guilder note. In what other country would a designer have the freedom to depict his girlfriend's pet rabbit, as Oxenaar did in the watermark of the 250 guilder note?

Even before this operation by the Dutch central bank, modernization had already started in another area of security printing: postage stamps. In 1965, for the first time, drawings by children were reproduced on five benefit stamps. Equally ground-breaking were the five children's benefit stamps designed by Slothouber and Graatsma in 1970: each stamp bore a cube in three colours, playing with elementary forms and colours. Individual expression and a geometric system do not point to shared values or a common history but to an aesthetic (counter)position. [Boekraad 1993]

The drive towards modernization of the communication systems in the public domain in Holland began in the early sixties at KLM, now merged with Air France but then still the national flag-carrying airline of the Netherlands, with the Dutch state as its principal shareholder. It is telling that KLM had to call upon a British designer, F.H.K. Henrion, for its new house style. [Wells 1990] He simplified the crown in KLM's logo to a graphic construction. The house style manual in which the construction of KLM's new logo was specified, was officially presented in

1964. In hindsight, this was the starting signal for a wide-reaching clean-up operation in public communication, in which old heraldic symbols were subjected to de-historicizing revamping if they were not done away with altogether. The other large state company in the transport sector, the Dutch Railways, followed the example of KLM not long after (1966–1970). The two designers given the task of creating the new corporate identity, Wijsenbeek and Dumbar, had both studied at the Royal College of Art in London. [Teunissen 1987]

The success of this modernization operation in two public companies led to the rise of the house style in other sectors of the public domain. The logo that Wim Crouwel of the Amsterdam agency Total Design created for the city of Rotterdam in 1972 had a great impact in the design world. The emblem shows a honeycomb structure projected onto a plan of the city. Today that logo has long since disappeared: thirty years after it was welcomed as modern and innovative, it was rejected by a designer of a new generation as 'closed and authoritarian'. Crouwel's logo was perceived as representing a centralized vision of the city, not the heterogeneous diversity of its population. In fact, Crouwel's concatenation of hexagonal modules represented the infinite expandability of the modern city and its association with the industriousness of the honeybee. [Boekraad 1999]

Rotterdam's adoption of a modernist visual language stirred similar desires in other city councils. To understand this one has to know Rotterdam's position in the psychogeography of the Netherlands. Rotterdam, at that time the largest seaport of the world, was considered to be both cosmopolitan and a major focus for industry. The city centre, bombed flat in the war, had been rebuilt and was a showcase of modern architecture. Economy and design were thus closely engaged and the city was crying out for the modernist communication model offered by Crouwel. Hundreds of towns and cities found the temptation to adopt a similar house style in the Swiss mode irresistible. The Provinces and finally the ministries in The Hague followed suit. (House style for the Ministry of the Interior in 1976, by the agency BRS.) The professionalization of Dutch graphic design was greatly advanced by this wave of public commissions, as well as the implicit recognition of the public benefit provided by the previously obscure profession of graphic designer.

What were the motives for this tide of modernization in the public domain? For what problems was this new visual communication the remedy? Often the process was set in train by the increasingly large size of organizations, since increased scale makes it difficult to see an organization as a single entity. Visual communication combats the proliferation of historical forms and styles. What is required is a consistent image. The costly investment in a house style is often legitimized by pointing out the economic benefits: cost and time savings as a result of the standardization, particularly of forms. Other motives less commonly mentioned by clients are of a completely different nature: often an institution wants repackaging to repair damage done to its image. Nor should the role of fashion and trends be underestimated – 'this institution moves with the times' is the message required.

The rapid modernization of the visual communication put out by the Dutch government cannot be seen in isolation from the government's own loss of image as a result of declining public confidence in that same government. In the sixties, protest movements like the Provos and the student movement had successfully attacked the patrician culture of government. The government's discreet yet authoritarian style, widely perceived as arrogant, had now become an irritation. In reaction to that weakened image, the government's style of communication changed and the search began for openness, transparency and public consultation.

As the last decade of the century got under way, new management styles came into fashion for public institutions. Administrative law made way for the science of public administration, which preached the separation of politics and policy-making. [Osborne/Gaebler 1992] The implementation of government policy would be more efficient and less expensive, it was thought, if the rationality of business models were adopted in the public domain. Privatization and deregulation were the magic formulas with which the administrative machinery could be drastically reorganized. This brought with it another change in the style of government communication. In the new representation and communication, the public character of public bodies was pushed farther and farther into the background. Whereas in the sixties the democratization of the public domain was at the heart of a fierce political struggle, we are now seeing a process of de-democratization and privatization of the public domain. Organs of the state present themselves as market players and address citizens as if they were customers and consumers. In the cities, public officials are turning into city marketeers trying to interest private investors in urban development and economic opportunities. Exaggeration and mild forms of deceit which are accepted as inevitable side-effects of the functioning of the market are finding their way into public communications. Youthfulness, dynamism and innovation are ascribed to administrative bodies that have been in existence for centuries. With the introduction of models borrowed from commercial communication, the principle that criticism, protest and dissent are desirable in a democracy, and indeed essential for the political process, is fading away.

We are at risk of forgetting that bureaucracy still fulfils many functions that do not lend themselves to being left to market forces. The government maintains public space, looks after security, acts as a general regulator and supervisor, provides information and issues licences, permits and consents, organizes cultural events, subsidizes institutions. It supports the elderly, the infirm and the disabled, it provides social support, it maintains law and order, and it steps in whenever some disaster or crisis befalls the nation. The skills required of the new-style public servant for all these and similar tasks include specific forms and styles of communication.

There is no common good that leads automatically to a single form of public communication. Neither the rigid systematism of modernism nor the extravagance of postmodernism naturally lends itself to the enormous diversity of public communication. What is required is an equally differentiated rhetoric that can establish rules for speaking in different situations, for different audiences and for the multifarious objectives of governments. The structure of the public domain implies a few common basic rules for this differentiated rhetoric: communication should be based on truth and reliability, centred on the dignity of the citizen, on what ties citizens together and maintains the community as a prerequisite for individual life. For the communication designer in the public domain that means an understanding of the democratic and constitutional values that are to be symbolized.

. 74-5
e citizen
ster
ernard's entry for the
cond International Poster
ennale, Warsaw, January
68
gital reconstruction, 2006

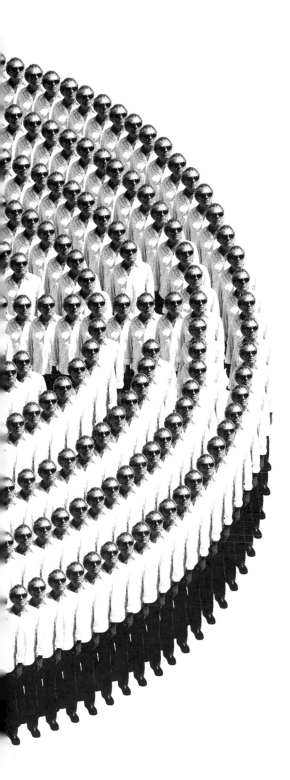

Solitary adjective and noun
[Latin *solitarius*, from *solus*, lone]
Someone who is alone or lives and acts alone.
Synonyms: distant, secluded, alone, lone, lonely,
introverted, unsociable, hermit, recluse, empty, deserted.

Solidary adjective [Latin *in solidum*, for the whole]
**Feeling or having a sense of solidarity, i.e. being allied with
or sympathetic to a group through having shared responsibilities
or interests.**
Synonyms: allied, united, engaged, involved, sympathetic,
ready to give help or support, sharing responsibility, participating,
of one mind.

the citizen

Sixteen projects
for the public domain

Politics

Social

Cultural

National heritage

Science

Public space

Politics

Activism and engagement

Within ten years of its establishment in 1970 Grapus had also been recognized outside France as a unique phenomenon in European graphic design. Its originality stemmed from the combination of an explicit visual style and a clearly delineated political profile. Grapus was committed to the aims of two large left-wing organizations: the French Communist Party (PCF) and the radical labour union Confédération Générale du Travail (CGT). Grapus's work for these two organizations is the subject of the following two chapters. In my opinion, the images in this chapter, which cover a period of almost forty years, demonstrate the continuity of Bernard's political and professional engagement.

Despite its political activism, Grapus never succumbed to the temptation to create a blueprint for a new world to set against the established order. Instead, the group steered a somewhat erratic middle course between the Scylla and Charybdis of the left-wing intellectual: on the one hand a strategy of demystification and on the other the utopian strategy.

The unmasking strategy is based on the idea that we live in a myth. The essays that Roland Barthes collected in *Mythologies* [1971] are a textbook example of such a strategy. Using advertising texts and images, he exposes the truisms and commonplaces of everyday life. His lucid analyses show how images falsify the material, historical and social conditions in which we live. The myth, says Barthes, posits the historical condition of man as natural and eternal. The unmasking of this mystification is the task of the critical intellectual, and consequently of the reflective designer as well.

The opposite of the demystification strategy is the utopian strategy. Utopia glorifies an alternative order that has likewise distanced itself from reality. Paradise, impossible to realize in the here and now, is either projected into the future or set in exotic faraway antipodes. An early form of such a utopia is the myth of the noble savage living at one with nature in an extra-historical, harmonious world. Fictions like these were being projected onto liberation movements in the Third World by action groups in the sixties and seventies who identified with their political struggle. And children still want the Indians to win! The utopian strategy may have had a powerful mobilizing function in the twentieth century, but it became entangled with political ideologies and practices that have cost the lives of millions. Man's capacity for projection has also proved its destructive potential.

The two mechanisms of demystification/rejection and utopian projection/glorification operate at the poles of the imaginary order. The image is the perfect medium for depreciation and appreciation, because it makes the transition from reality to unreality (and vice versa) quite naturally. The boundary between representation and misrepresentation is fluid. The image is situated between the order of reality and the order of symbolic systems.

In his early work Bernard made use of both strategies. In May 1968 he made the poster *la police vous parle tous les soirs à 20 h.* (The police speak to you every evening at 8 p.m.) in which he accuses French state radio and television of false reporting about the revolt of students and workers. The poster attacks the authority that had taken control over the media; and the caricature is justified because what it denounces is itself a caricature of the journalistic imperative of truth.

In 1975, for an exhibition at the Pompidou Centre on advertising campaigns, Grapus created a masterpiece of the unmasking genre. The poster features a poster. A hand pointing at the spectator stabs straight through the head of a man who is standing with his back to us. Shreds of the punctured paper curl up like pieces of skin in the neatly trimmed hair. The idea behind this poster is related to the original meaning of 'campaign': a series of military operations. What battle does advertising fight? The territory that advertising seeks to conquer and occupy is the human brain.

The origin of the image with the compelling index pointing at the observer is well known. The famous poster featuring Field Marshal Lord Kitchener appeared in the streets of Britain early in the First World War, and in 1917 James Montgomery Flagg designed the poster *I want YOU for the US Army* to do the same job in the United States. The German army used a similar image in its recruiting campaign. In quoting this pictorial motif, Grapus links advertising to the task of the mass media in time of war.

The back of the man's head is also a quotation. A man viewed from behind is a recurrent theme in the work of Magritte, one of the ways in which he elaborated his motif of the masked man. The man in Grapus's poster instantly recalls the figure in Magritte's painting *La réproduction interdite* of 1937. Collar, shoulder line and haircut are virtually identical.

On the Grapus poster, not only is the head of this faceless individual punctured, but also the poster on which it is depicted. The person represented is located somewhere in the imaginary world. Penetrated by the compelling finger and fist, the anonymous citizen becomes a sign of an empty identity to be filled in from the outside. The passivity of the featureless man is deceptive: in and around his head a battle is going on for the interior wallpaper of his mind. This struggle of brand and mask is denounced as a form of violence.

Both strategies – that of accusation/unmasking and that of glorification/utopia – are combined in an ingenious manner in the series of nine posters that Grapus submitted in 1972 to the Warsaw poster biennial. Three of them are reproduced here (pp. 84-85), each featuring a straw hat at its centre. They tell the story of a long and bloody war. In the first image, an Asian country is subjected to carpet-bombing in broad daylight. The horrors of war are not shown on the second poster, only their sinister reflection, colouring the sky red. In the third image, the straw hat shines against a peaceful sky, which is once again blue; the clouds have not moved a millimetre and the straw hat is in the same place in the sky as before. Have years gone by, or only seconds? The hat has not moved, but precisely because of that, its meaning has changed: its motionlessness makes it a symbol of indomitability.

Before the Vietnam War, the straw hat was a symbol of Asian rice-growing and, more generally, of the Asian continent (e.g. in the pictogram system drawn by Gerd Arntz for Otto Neurath's picture statistics). From a Western perspective, the straw hat was associated with underdevelopment and poverty. In this series, the scope of meaning of this symbol was enriched by redrawing the triangular sign into the image of an object with a finely articulated structure of rushes, made by human hands. The texture and structure of this image contrast with the harsh geometry of the bombs. Against the background of bombs, the hat becomes a shield against them. The flexible straw defeats the hard metal and the vulnerable helmet becomes a shelter and roof for a whole nation. The handmade wickerwork resists the industrially produced violence. The straw hat, originally a symbol of a vulnerable nation, now symbolizes the resilience of that nation.

The readability of these posters rests on the play on familiar symbols: both hat and shield are objects we associate with physical safety. The posters also allude to a collective representation widely used during the Cold War, namely the nuclear bomb umbrella, the security concept developed by NATO. Straw hat or umbrella: in either case it is a matter of repelling an external threat. The syntagmatic series is the same: a nation protects itself from bombs with a shield, but the paradigmatic substitution of the umbrella by an Asian hat makes a totally different (visual) statement. The third poster, the dénouement of the war story, is purely utopian and imagines a world without violence. The war story ends with a return to a fictitious origin of paradisiacal peace.

At the end of the sixties anti-imperialist, at the end of the nineties an 'altermondialist': Bernard's political engagement with the Third World continues. Four of the works reproduced in this chapter comment on the triumph of neo-liberalism in the nineties. What they show us is a negative utopia. Two dollar signs placed on either side of the globe – their vertical bars displaced to strike through the earth – create a cry for help: *S.O.S.* (1991). On the poster *The debt ...or the earth* (1992) two joined hands swing between the letters N and S like the needle of a compass. The thumb gestures refer to an arena in which there is a fight for life or death. The double-page spread with stock market data (*people/money*, 1998) visualizes the contrast between the profits of multinational companies and the poverty and malnutrition of the Third World. These images are held up to us as an accusation. The percentage sign on the cover of *Domus* (1998) also connotes the world dominance of capital: shareholders of the world, unite!

In these designs Bernard makes abundant use of typographic symbols: columns of figures, dollar signs, percentage mark and the North-South indicator on the compass. They are taken from the rich world of accounting and navigation and transplanted to the barren world of starvation to formulate a critique of political economy. Bernard offers no vision of a better world, but a state of affairs which he rejects. Distributed in the wealthy part of the world, these posters are a visual plea to convict a symbolically represented defendant.

'What is an advertising campaign?'
poster for an exhibition presented
by the Centre of Industrial Design
Pompidou Centre, Paris
120 × 80 / 1977

«qu'est-ce qu'une campagne publicitaire?»

exposition présentée par le Centre de Création Industrielle
Centre national d'art et de culture Georges Pompidou

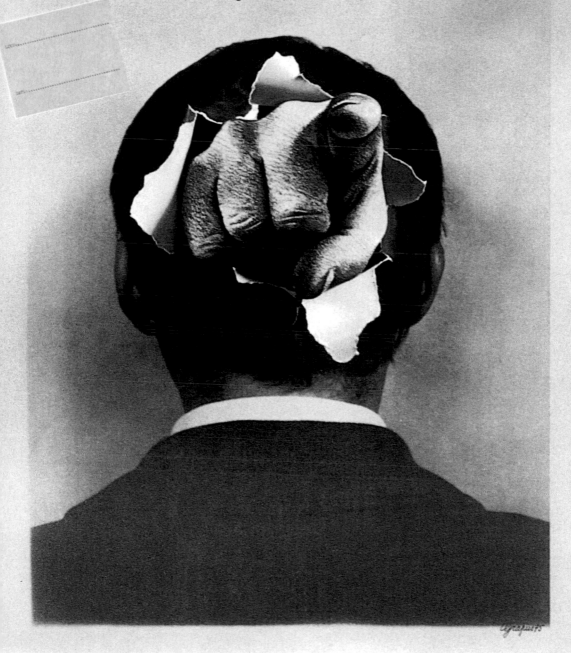

Series of nine posters
Grapus's entry for the
Fourth International Poster
Biennale, Warsaw
120 × 80 / 1972

pp. 86-7
March to Paris of miners and
steelworkers from Lorraine
poster
Trade Unions of Longwy
60 × 80 / 1979

23 mars 1979 MARCHE SUR PARIS pour

notre région, sauver la sidérurgie, les mines.

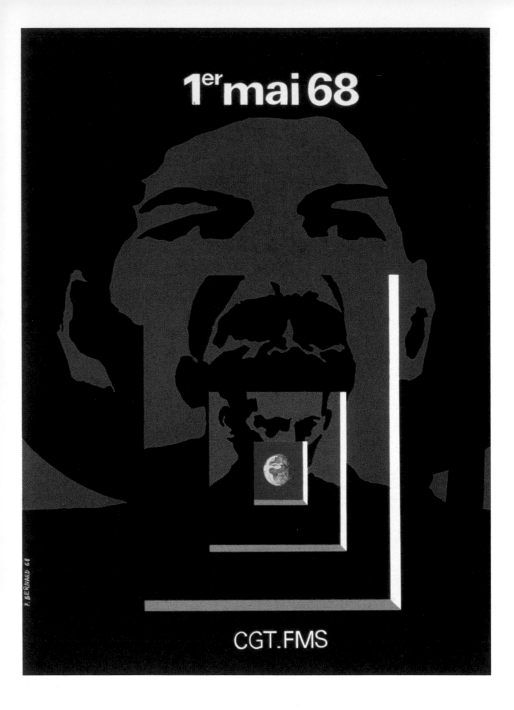

First of May '68
poster
Confédération Générale du Travail/Fédération Mondiale des Syndicats
(General Workers Confederation/World Federation of Trade Unions)
80 × 60 / 1968

Three-day Marxist literature fair
poster
The Paris Federation of the French Communist Party
80 × 60 / 1972

3 JOURS DU LIVRE MARXISTE
ancienne gare de la bastille 3, 4 et 5 mars 1972

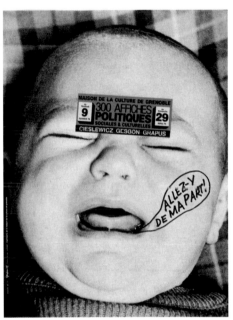
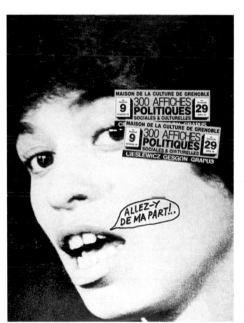

Tell them I sent you!
five posters for a poster exhibition
Cultural Centre of Grenoble
60 × 40 / 1979

For a better life, reduce
the pace of work and cut
working hours
banner
General Workers
Confederation Paris (CGT
Paris)
150 × 600 / 1972

Long live 14 July 1789
poster
City of Le Havre
300 × 400 / 1978

Apartheid Racism
poster
National anti-apartheid rallies
60 × 40 and 160 × 120 / 1986

Long live the youth centres
and cultural centres
poster
Association of Youth
Centres and Centres for
Everyone
80 × 60 / 1983

The debt... or the earth
poster
The United Nations Rio
Conference '92
60 × 40 / 1992

Rich shits on poor
poster for an exhibition on
human rights
Artis 89
80×60 / 1989

%
cover for *Domus* no. 793,
May 1997
32.5×24.5 / 1997

pp. 98-9
S.O.S
painted canvas for a travelling
exhibition Plea for the Earth
Culture in the City Association,
Allonnes
300×400 / 1993

Conquered states ... can be held by the conqueror in three
different ways. The first is to ruin them, the second for the
conqueror to go and reside there in person and the third is to
allow them to continue to live under their own laws, subject
to a regular tribute, and to create in them a government of the
few who will keep the country friendly to the conqueror.
Niccolò Machiavelli, *The Prince*, 1513

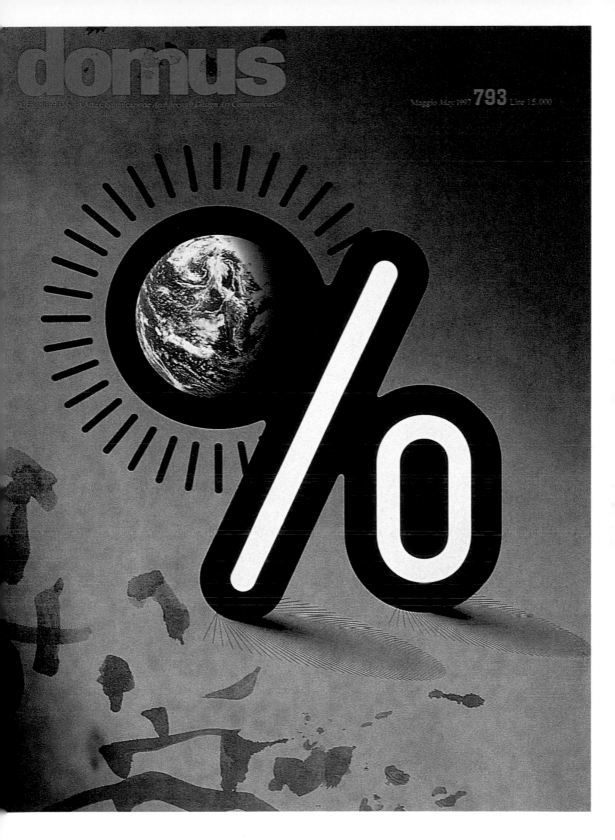

domus

Maggio May 1997 **793** Lire 15.000

SALUT, J'EN PROFITE
POUR VOUS RAPPELER
QUE LE PAPIER VIENT
DES ARBRES.

A + M

On peut tenir les Etats conquis...de trois manieres
differentes.La premiere consiste à les ruiner.la
deuxième,pour le conquerant,à aller y résider en
personne, et la troisième, à leur permettre de
continuer à vivre selon leurs propres lois, soumis
à un tribut régulier et de créer chez eux un
gouvernement avec quelques-uns d'entre eux qui
maintiendront une relation amicale entre le pays
conquis et le conquérant

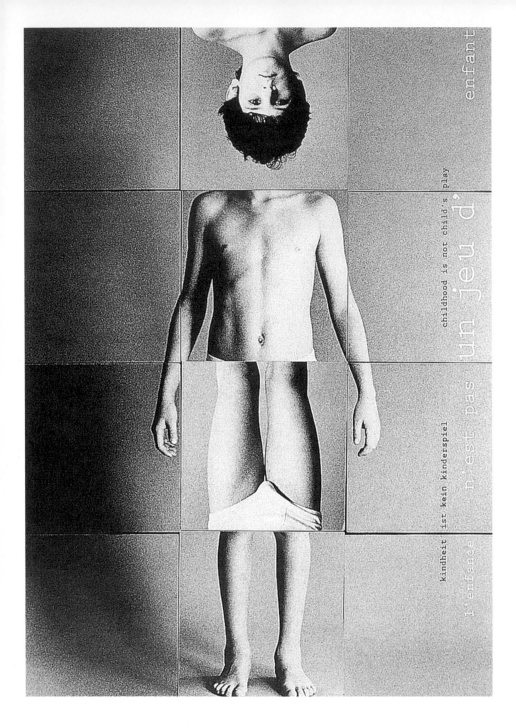

Childhood is not child's play
poster
Competition organized by the
Poster Museum, Essen,
Germany
84 × 59.4 / 1998

International Observatory of
Prisons
poster
84 × 59.4 / 1993

pp. 102-3
Wishful thinking: People and Money
one of five spreads on 'wishful
thinking' in a magazine
Mill Paper
30.5 × 25.5 / 1998

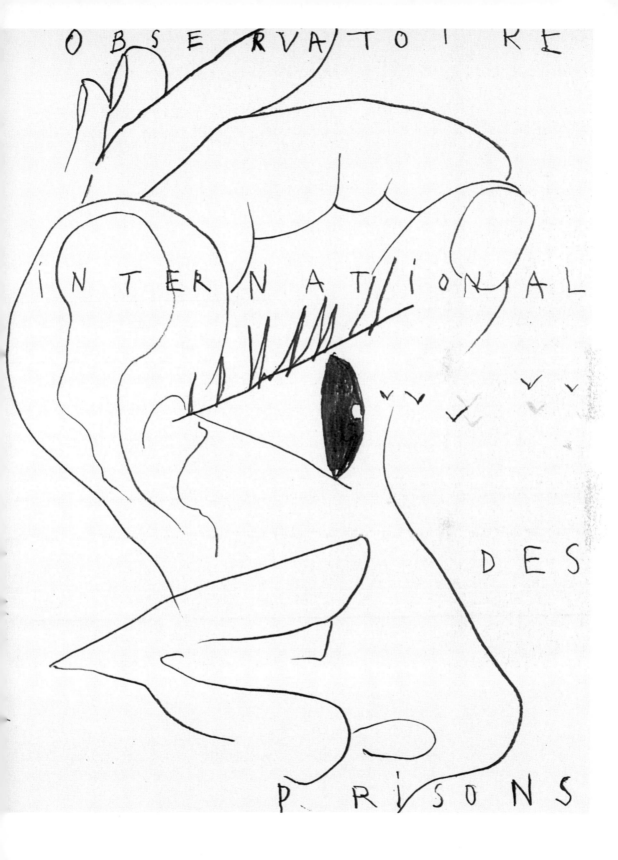

money

foundations for world understanding

French Communist Party

Work for the
Parti Communiste Français
(PCF), 1973–1984
Posters, buttons, logo,
emblems, magazine,
campaigns, New Year
cards, etc.

Bernard's work for the French Communist Party is a salient component of his oeuvre. After all, Communist parties are not as a rule associated with artistic renewal and aesthetic quality: more with dogma, centralism and propaganda. In France the party stands for the radical wing of the labour movement, which for a long time has been stronger than the reformist wing. It was precisely its radicalism that made it attractive to many writers, intellectuals and artists who were looking for a political expression of their discomfort about, and rejection of, the existing social order. In the thirties the PCF had been in the vanguard of the anti-fascist forces, and during the Second World War it had played a leading role in the Resistance. During the Cold War it became a magnet to those opposing French colonialism and the role of the United States on the global political stage.

As Bernard explains: 'In May 1968 I was very impressed by François Miehe, a dedicated communist who played a leading role in the graphic workshop of the École des Arts Décoratifs, where a constant stream of posters was produced that were put up all over the city. This was Communism in practice. Most of the students of the school were ultra-left-wing, yet they were typical representatives of bourgeois culture and outspokenly anti-Communist. I found their attitude objectionable. In my opinion May '68 was not just about the interests of students, but the interests of the working class. Those interests, I believed, would be in better hands with the PCF. When in August the party distanced itself from the Soviet invasion of Czechoslovakia I decided to become a member. My image of the party was also influenced by the role it had played in the Resistance, but there was another, professional interest at work. I knew of course that great painters like Picasso and Léger had been party members. As a designer I wanted to work for the forces of revolution. My artistic ambition and my vocabulary as a designer, I expected, could come into their own in the service of the party.' [Boekraad 2006]

In 1970 Bernard, along with Miehe and Paris-Clavel, founded Grapus. The name is derived from *crapules staliniennes*, Stalinist scum. By turning this term of abuse into a title of honour, Grapus instantly made their position clear. They saw themselves not as individual artists – they did not sign with their individual names – but as a democratically organized action group of designers who wanted to offer their talents for social change. They rejected individual engagement as a form of bourgeois individualism.

Bernard may have been a member of the PCF for about fifteen years, but he never realized his ambition of influencing the communication policy of the party and the closely allied trade union, the Confédération Générale du Travail. Grapus's work for the party never evolved into an organic and long-term cooperation. This was probably because their professional, independent stance towards their clients did not fit in with the hierarchical structure of the party and the confederation. The ideas of Grapus about communication, their autonomous analysis of the commission, their choice of a visual aesthetic that was clearly influenced by the spontaneity and radicalism of their generation, all stood in the way of an institutional cooperation. Grapus retained the character of a militant action group, partly because of the work they produced independently. As they expected, this did not stop them finding like-minded clients in the lower echelons of the PCF and its world – workers' councils, local chapters and unions of the CGT, left-wing city councils, *Maisons de la Culture*, non-profit organizations and action groups of various types, the peace movement, and so on.

Why did Grapus want to change the image of the party? In their opinion, the PCF's existing image coincided neither with the culture and reality experienced by its members, nor with its objectives. To quote Bernard: 'Nowadays, every political party is aware of how important communication is, but in 1970 there was no such awareness and there was little room for us. The party had a hierarchical structure with strict leadership from the top; style and content of communication were decided by the leadership. On the other hand, there were strong local sections. The party's communications were focused primarily on social actions, strikes, campaigns and party meetings. All there was for Grapus was an occasional commission. It was only with the communist youth organization that we achieved a more permanent arrangement, for their weekly magazine *Avant-garde*. But even that experience only lasted a couple of months. We constantly had to negotiate with the editors, which meant that we were unable to create a consistent image. But we did do a number of successful posters for them.' (He refers to work like the irreverent poster on which Michel Quarez portrayed Marx as a hitchhiking hippie with biker's goggles on his forehead.) Jean-Paul Bachollet, Grapus's manager from 1974 onwards, says: 'They were reluctant to trust us with all their communications *en bloc*. Indeed, they didn't even see communications as a coherent whole.' [Cat. Grapus 1985]

The poster *On y va* was designed in 1977 for the *Jeunesse Communiste* – the youth section of the party. This image has become very well known, but it led to a false perception that Grapus had renewed the party's image. In the words of Bachollet: 'The Parti Communiste Français does not want us, Grapus, to renew its image because the party is itself incapable of deciding what image it wants to project, and that has been the case for some time.' [Ibidem] By the time Bachollet made this statement, Bernard had left the party, and Grapus's work for it was a thing of the past.

The misconception just referred to was also fuelled by another commission, for a party campaign in 1973 entitled 'Union du peuple de France'. Bernard designed an emblem with a childishly drawn sun and the handwritten text *Union du peuple de France pour le changement démocratique* (Union of the people of France for democratic change). Here he reinvented the sun emblem that had been used during the French Revolution [Starobinski 2006], endowing it with an aesthetic that evokes Miró. The intention was to create a simple and recognizable symbol in primary colours that would be easy for anyone to imitate. It was friendly, optimistic and timeless, a panegyric to *joie de vivre* and a symbol of pre-political humanitarian engagement that would bring people together. 'We had a theory that handwriting would be better than typography at making it easy for the observer to make the message its own', says Bernard. 'After all, typography is associated with the world of products and institutions. We thought we were taking a step towards a general image for the party. But six months later the PCF abandoned the slogan and the symbol disappeared from the streets.'

The 1979 poster *J'aime mon pays* (I love my country) for a PCF membership campaign in Seine-Saint-Denis is indicative of Grapus's attitude towards the party. The party provided the text, which consisted of three parts: 1 (*premise*) I love my country; 2 (*diagnosis*) France is in decline, its independence is in danger, the democratic and peace loving part of Europe is under threat; 3 (*conclusion/remedy*) I will join the Communist Party.

The depiction of France is a geographical relief map from a school atlas, i.e. a map without borders, roads or cities. The capital letters of the premise are deliberately sloppy, with the 'j' and the 'i' in lower case. They are carefully placed across the image surface but some of them fall outside the national boundaries. The map takes no account of France's independence nor of its decline, mentioned in text 2. Laid out as a newspaper clipping, it is relegated, along with the handwritten conclusion, to a subordinate position at the bottom of the page, overshadowed by the main text. The poster associates patriotism with the enduring nature of the physical world, as opposed to the ephemerality of politics. By chopping up the text and giving it such an idiosyncratic treatment the design distances itself from the message.

A subtle shift in the meaning of a political symbol can be seen in the poster for the sixty-year-old PCF. The parallelogram of the flag is slightly distorted: its outline is ragged like a sheet of blotting paper and the monochrome red is attached to a multicoloured flagpole. Related to the spectrum, the colour red loses its monopoly.

At the end of the seventies and the beginning of the eighties the PCF was internally divided about the undemocratic structure of the party and its relationship with the Soviet Union. 'We abandoned the idea that it might be possible to reform the party's communications. It was a period of mourning: *c'était fini*. The party had lost its credibility, the nadir had been reached. At a cell meeting one evening in 1984, a representative from a higher echelon made it clear to me that my party membership would not be renewed the following year. My opinions were too deviant, my criticism was "not constructive". I left the party.' [Boekraad 2006]

We generally associate political posters with protest or propaganda. Both are found in Grapus's work for the PCF, but only sporadically. Even where the party and its symbols are represented, Grapus goes against expectations: a rhetorical technique calculated to avoid cliché and convention.

Grapus's work for the PCF is characterized by a range of ways of addressing the audience and various rhetorical strategies. The predominant feature is an encouraging and stimulating style that combines political action with the pleasure of living life to the full.

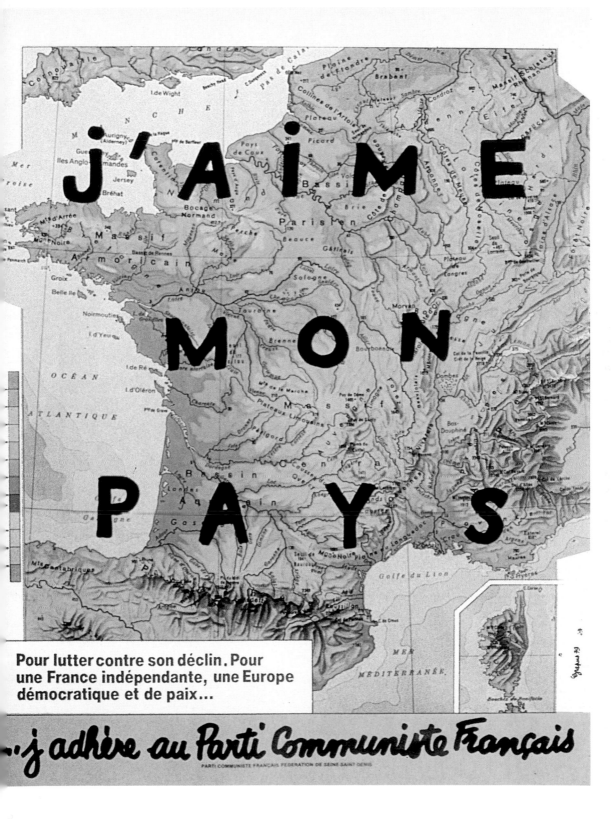

J'AIME MON PAYS

Pour lutter contre son déclin. Pour
une France indépendante, une Europe
démocratique et de paix…

…j adhère au Parti Communiste Français

PARTI COMMUNISTE FRANÇAIS FÉDÉRATION DE SEINE-SAINT-DENIS

ALLO ! ALLO !

IVRY

Journal mural d'informations municipales · Renseigneme

VIVE LE 14 JU

L e 14 juillet 1789, le peuple de Paris prenant la Bastille ouvrait la voie à la liberté contre l'oppression.

Le 14 juillet 1977, le peuple de France réclame le droit au travail pour tous, un salaire décent, la garantie d'une vie plus heureuse, plus humaine.

Il se prononce pour un bon programme commun réactualisé, la sécurité, la paix, l'indépendance nationale.

Il exige le respect des libertés démocratiques, le respect du suffrage universel, les moyens financiers pour les communes de développer une politique sociale.

Ivryennes, Ivryens, participez nombreux aux festivités :
le 13 juillet au soir, dans les quartiers
le 14 juillet à 21h. esplanade Georges Marrane

Le conseil municipal

FÊTE
jeudi 14 juillet
esplanade Georges Mar
à 21h
ALLOCUTION
de Monsieur
le MAIRE

spectacle
de variétés
avec
Les Troubadou
LENY
ESCUDERO

fête
des
libertés

vers 23h
feu d'artifice
sur le
terrain Glanda

AVIS
de concours

MAIRIE D'IVRY-SUR-SEINE
(Val-de-Marne)

EMPLOIS	DATE DES CONCOURS	DATE LIMITE DES INSCRIPTIONS
ADJOINT TECHNIQUE concours sur épreuves externe et interne	21-22 et 23 septembre 1977	20 août 1977
concours sur titre	vers le 25 octobre 1977	
REDACTEUR concours épreuves externe et interne	5 octobre 1977	1er septembre 1977
COMMIS concours sur épreuves externe et interne	19 octobre 1977	1er septembre 1977

...l'agen
culture

MOCKINPO
dans les quar

Une tournée Iv
d'un spectacle thé
qualité, a permis a
bitants de six quar
la ville de d
comment MACKI
fut libéré de se
ments.

Mise en scène pa
France Duverger.
Une de nos concl

70 15 71 · Juillet 1977 N°2

ILLET!

BOURSES scolaires

Les familles ayant des enfants entrant en classe de 4ème à la rentrée scolaire 1977/1978 sont informées. que les dossiers de demande de **bourses** départementales sont à leur disposition au bureau municipal de l'enfance - 4, rue Raspail.

Date limite pour déposer les demandes en préfecture :

Enseignement secondaire : 31 octobre 1977,

Enseignement technique : 31 octobre 1977,

Enseignement supérieur : 1er décembre 1977.

POUR APPELER
Le centre médico-social 672 38.38
La bourse du travail 672 49.38

MUTUELLE PLEMENTAIRE
s personnels
départements,
s communes
établissements
s et hospitaliers

à l'assemblée générale du
ont décidé, à l'unanimité,
e montant de la cotisation
u 1er JUILLET 1977 de la
te

IE 1 (bénéficiaire du régime
.00 F au lieu de 35,00 F
IE 2 (tous affiliés au régime

général) : 38,10 F au lieu de 35,10 F
Ces modifications ont été approuvées
par arrêté préfectoral du 7 juin 1977.

OUF !
des idées pour vos loisirs

2 A 6 ANS

Les enfants de 2 à 6 ans seront reçus dans les écoles maternelles aux heures suivantes :
juillet : 7h à 19h, Péri et Thorez-7h.30 à 19h. Langevin, Barbusse. Solomon, Rousseau et Robespierre.
août : 7h à 19h. Makarenko et Thorez ; 7h.30 à 19h. Robespierre et Joliot-Curie.

Les enfants de 6 à 12 ans seront reçus de 8h à 18h. Ils iront tous les jours, au centre aéré du Bréau, situé vers Dammaries-les-Lys (60 kms d'Ivry) ou en pique-nique.
Prix pour la journée, repas compris : de 2 à 10.50 F. suivant les ressources de la familles.
Pour les inscriptions où tous renseignements complémentaires. adressez-vous au service des affaires scolaires et de l'enfance, 4 rue Raspail - tél 672 24.00 - poste 308.

12 A 16 ANS
SEJOURS ET SORTIES

Les loisirs information jeunesse organisent en juillet et en août :
DES SEJOURS :
. lac des Settons : 18 au 22 juillet ; vélo, baignades, équitation, randonnées.
. Méridon : 25 au 28 juillet vélo, promenades, randonnées.
. Mesnil St Père : 1er au 5 août et 8 au 12 août ; voile, vélo, baignades, découverte de la forêt, hébergement en bungalows.
Dives sur Mer : 22 au 26 août ; baignades, vélo, randonnées, camping sous tente.

DES SORTIES :
. à la mer : 19 juillet et 18 août - Honfleur ; 26 juillet et 30 août - Dives,
Départ à 7h retour vers 21h.
. en forêt : 15 juillet et 28 août - Compiègne ; 28

juillet et 3 août - Fontaine-bleau ; 23 août - Orléans.
Départ à 9h retour vers 18h.
. en vélo : 12 juillet ; 11 août ; 25 août.
Les itinéraires des randonnées seront choisis par les participants.
Pour toutes les sorties d'une journée, il faut apporter son repas.
Des activités de plein air, des jeux, des rencontres, chaque jour à Ivry.
Pour s'inscrire : adressez-vous au 17, rue Raspail - Tél : 672 24.00.

POUR LES RETRAITES
JUILLET AOUT

visite du parc animalier des Yvelines :
Départ entre 13h et 13h.30, des foyers.
Mercredi 13 juillet

croisière de Veneux les Sablons à Samois :
Départ entre 9h et 9h.15 des foyers

Mardi 19 juillet
Jeudi 4 août
Apporter votre pique-nique, pour déjeuner au BREAU.

visite du chateau de Pierrefonds :
Départ entre 8h et 8h.30 des foyers.
Jeudi 28 juillet
Déjeûner au restaurant Promenade dans la forêt avec visite de la clairière de l'armistice et des vestiges gallo-romains.

une journée à la Collinette :
Départ entre 7h.30 et 8h, des foyers.
Mardi 26 juillet
Mardi 16 août
Mardi 6 septembre
Déjeûner à la Collinette.

inscriptions : à l'annexe de la mairie bureau n° 4.

RETOUR des CENTRES DE VACANCES de juillet
HERY/UGINE (Savoie), le dimanche 31 juillet vers 7 heures, esplanade Georges Marrane
LES MATHES (Charente Maritime), le dimanche 31 juillet vers 7 heures, esplanade Georges Marrane
LAVARE (Sarthe), le samedi 30 juillet vers 18 heures, esplanade Georges Marrane
CHEVILLON (Yonne), le samedi 30 juillet vers 17h.30, esplanade Georges Marrane

---

pharmaciens de garde

10 juillet
ANDRE - 185, avenue de Verdun
14 juillet
ZAZOUN - 15, rue Jean le Galleu
17 juillet
VETEAU - 7, place Gambetta
24 juillet
JANNOT - 55, rue Jean le Galleu
31 juillet
BICHARD - 10, rue Lénine
7 août
BRUNET - 5, rue Marat
14 août
PINAUT - 1, rue Amédée Huon
15 août
RIBOT - 40, rue Marat

21 août
CHABANE-SCHILTON
52, avenue Maurice Thorez
28 août
GUEDJ - 70, rue Lénine

médecin de garde

Médecin de garde : la nuit de 20h à 8h, le samedi à partir de 16h, les dimanches et jours fériés. Tél :

660 55 20

60th anniversary of the
French Communist Party
poster
The Urban Committee of
the French Communist
Party in Blanc-Mesnil
60 × 80 / 1980

'No neutron bombs, Mr Reagan'
poster
Youth Movement of the French
Communist Party
60 × 80 / 1981

Culture has no Party,
just partisans
poster
French Communist Party
60 × 80 / 1984

union du peuple de France pour le changement démocratique

*

union
populaire!

POUR LA VICTOIRE
DU PROGRAMME COMMUN
DE LA GAUCHE UNIE

Parti communiste français 14e

Union of the French people
for democratic change
campaign poster
Central Committee of the
French Communist Party
83 × 60 / 1974

Union of the French people
embroidered emblem
30 × 35 / 1974

People's Union!
sticker
For the 14th arrondisse-
ment chapter of the
French Communist Party
ø 20 / 1973

pp. 114-15
All right! How do we start?
poster
Federation Seine-Saint-Denis of
the French Communist Party
120 × 160 / 1980

.........LE CHÔMAGE.................L'EMPLOI................LA RETRAI

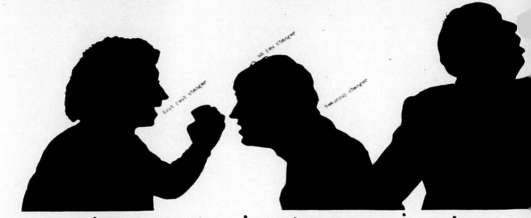

..LES SALAIRES...........LA VIE CHÈRE......LA VIE TRISTE........

........LES LIBERTÉS.................L'AUTOGESTION.................

.... LA FORMATION DES JEUNES........ DES AUTRES............

JSPORTS............. LA CULTURE ....LES LOGEMENTS.............

ALORS!

ESTE .... COMMENT, COMMENCER ? **PCF** 93.......

262-12-25

Social

General Workers' Confederation

Work for the Confédératio
Générale du Travail (CGT
since 1972
House style for the Paris
chapter, logos, action and
campaign buttons and
posters

The Confédération Générale du Travail (CGT), founded in 1895, is France's most radical trade union federation. It was not until 1919 that a competitor based on religious beliefs, the Confédération Française des Travailleurs Chrétiens, arrived on the scene. In 1947 the Force Ouvrière was established as a social democratic alternative to the CGT, which had been dominated by the communists since the Second World War. In 1964 the Confédération Française Démocratique du Travail (CFDT) came into being when the Christian union federation was secularized. In about 1970 membership of the CGT was about three times that of the CFDT, with which it had allied itself in 1966-1970 in a joint programme of social demands. Since the eighties, membership of the CGT has declined, and by 2005 the two federations were roughly the same size with 700,000 and 800,000 members respectively.

Grapus designed a great deal for the CGT, albeit not on a regular basis. They never created a system of graphic communication as such for it. Apart from the house style for the Paris chapter, there was no long-term working relationship, but rather incidental assignments, about thirty of which can be found in the Grapus archives in Aubervilliers: buttons for the metalworkers' union, postcards, posters, books of stickers with slogans, and so on. They also designed logos and posters for the CGT's membership campaigns and conferences.

The logo for the Paris chapter of the CGT (1972) is the schematic representation of a group of demonstrators in an urban setting. They personify the labour unions working together in the CGT, and lean upon the letters which function as a pedestal. The letters read as a banner carried across the full width of a street demonstration, but are, at the same time, a massive spatial object. Motion is suggested by the arms and by the addition of a blue and a red cloud between the group in the foreground and the Eiffel Tower in the distance.

In the Grapus archives there are dozens of sketches which allow us to follow the development of this logo step by step. At the initial stage of the design process, ideas were put forward by several members of the collective. The first rough sketches are based on traditional symbols of proletarian solidarity: hands. The confederation's militant character is underlined by placing this symbol on a protest sign. These preliminary ideas were apparently discarded.

A second approach explored the typography of the logo: a three-dimensional, almost sculptural typeface was developed for the letters CGT. This is the starting point for the final version in which the two-dimensional typography is transformed into a three-dimensional typographical object. After this, a drawing of a group of five people was produced from a photograph. At first the group was situated in front of the lettering, but it was later replaced by a group of four drawn in the style of Léger and placed in or behind the type sculpture.

In the colour studies in felt-tip pen and pencil we see the figures become more and more abstract and no longer distinguishable as individuals. They become silhouettes, melting together and fusing with the logo as if anchored in it. Their massiveness increases and the gesture of the brotherly arm on the shoulder becomes more

Sketches for a logo
General Workers Confederation,
Paris (CGT Paris)
[Grapus Archives, Aubervilliers]
1972

CGT at the heart of the struggle
for a new life 1895–1975
sketches and photomontages
for a poster
CGT Paris
[Grapus Archives, Aubervilliers]
1975

prominent. The coherence of lettering and image is increased by the fact that the left arm of one of the figures reaches over the bar of the T. One way or another, then, there is still a place for a hand – not the fist for fighting, nor the handshake of solidarity.

Finally, the addition of the Eiffel Tower places the group in an urban space. The proximity of the blue cloud makes the group larger and more monumental: indeed, one of the figures walks with his head in the clouds.

The unity of the whole – logo, group and background – is reinforced by being printing in two colours, blue and red, on a white ground.

The image exudes strength and solidarity, determination and readiness to act, but also self-confidence, cohesion and optimism. The reference to Léger has a slightly historicizing effect, but the emblem does not hark back to the mummified symbols of the labour movement. The Eiffel Tower, icon of Paris, regains something of its original association with technology and progress.

The contrasts in the representation between near and far, figure and group, typography and image are gradually resolved during the design process by varying the shading of the colour and the texture of the planes. Abstraction and simplification bring about a fusion of all the elements of the emblem in a single, irregular, pregnant contour.

In 1975 Grapus designed the emblem for a national conference of the CGT. Again the design process can be reconstructed on the basis of drawings, photographs and photomontages stored in the archives. The slogan of the conference, 'Le CGT au coeur de l'action pour une vie nouvelle' (The CGT at the heart of the struggle for a new life), is represented literally.

First a drawing of activists in a circle was made. This image was realized as a photomontage based on a photograph of a row of people in front of a blank wall. The circle of people forms a halo around the name of the organization, which leaps out from the centre to the foreground.

The concept of this emblem is indebted to the tradition of representing a crowd around a central figure or symbol, as in the work of the Russian constructivist Gustav Klucis in the early thirties. Just like the logo for the Paris CGT, this logo was both miniaturized into a button and enlarged into a poster.

Finally, a few remarks about two other CGT posters, one campaigning for an increased minimum wage and another addressing unemployed young people. Both show not a mass, class or group, but an individual. In each case the individual is only partially visible: the face of the woman is half concealed behind the pay slip she holds up to us, whereas the figure representing the unemployed man is reduced to an anonymous shadow. Here Bernard uses a device that was employed again a year later in the *Martin Eden* poster for the theatre group La Salamandre (p. 182). The rhetoric here is not so much that of struggle and action as that of vulnerability.

union des syndicats c.g.t. de paris

85 RUE CHARLOT - 75140 PARIS CEDEX 03

TEL. 887.44.63 C.C.P. 2746-74 PARIS

l'union des syndicats
c.g.t. de Paris vous présente
ses meilleurs vœux pour
l'année 1973.

New Year greeting on letterhead
CGT Paris
29.7 × 21 / 1972

Sticker
CGT Paris
ø 20 / 1972

Join the CGT
two posters (text and logo)
The 6th Congress of the CGT Paris
50×50 and 50×50 / 1976

Join the CGT
poster
CGT Paris
60×40 / 1972

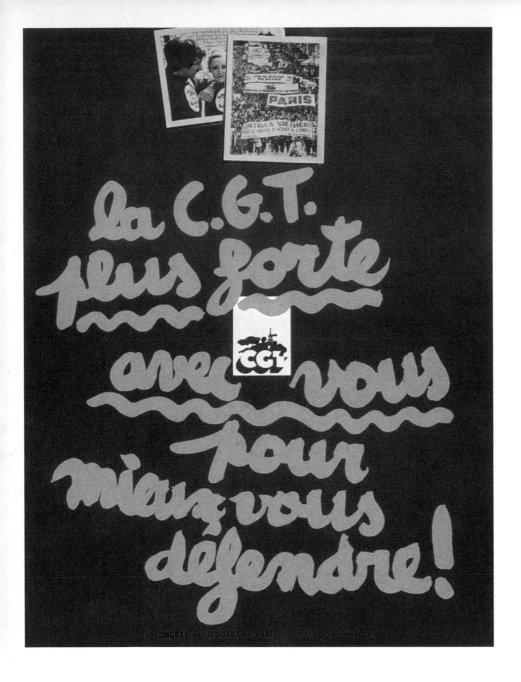

The CGT – stronger with you,
the better to defend you
poster
CGT Paris
71 × 52 / 1975

Buttons
CGT Paris, PCF
ø 5 / 1975

126

union du peuple de France pour le changement démocratique

PARTI COMMUNISTE FRANÇAIS

AU CŒUR DE L'ACTION 1895 1975 POUR UNE VIE NOUVELLE

CGT

CGT

«..changer notre vie..!»

CGT

PARIS

JEUNES CHOMEURS AGISSEZ
POUR LE DROIT AU TRAVAIL
POUR VOS REVENDICATIONS
DANS LE COMITE CGT DES
JEUNES SANS EMPLOI DE
VOTRE QUARTIER

CGT
PARIS

Grapus 76

UD CGT PARIS 85 rue Charlot Paris 3°

2500 francs minimum wage
campaign poster
CGT Office Workers
66 × 48 / 1978

Young and unemployed? Act now!
Call for new members of the local
young unemployed committee
poster
CGT Paris
80 × 60 / 1976

Born to be born

Né(e) pour naître
Travelling exhibition of
twenty panels with an
accompanying publicatio
for the Groupe de
Recherche et d'Action po
l'Enfance (GRAPE)
Panels 90 x 60 and
publication 34 × 22 /1983

The exhibition and its companion publication were produced on commission from GRAPE, an interdisciplinary research group set up in 1975 consisting of dedicated professionals: doctors, psychologists, educationalists and sociologists. The group is still active today. Initially they concentrated on preventive care and aid for young children (later extended to adolescents) growing up in precarious situations. The group undertook several initiatives, such as establishing a free children's help line and a counselling service offering expertise to local organizations in the area of youth care. It also published the monthly magazine *l'Enfant d'abord!* (Children first!), edited by Nadia Monteggia, who also wrote the texts for the exhibition panels. The exhibition made a tour of children's clinics and teacher training institutions and was even welcomed at the Pompidou Centre.

On the cover of the brochure we see a man and a woman from the back. They are looking at the panels of the exhibition *Né(e) pour naître*, which are all reproduced in the brochure itself. On the back cover of the brochure the couple have turned towards us: the woman is holding a baby in her arms. As in many Grapus projects, the models are members of the collective, in this case Alex Jordan and his wife Noreen O'Shea. On some panels children of friends are used as models.

In the centre of each panel is an image (a photo, collage, photomontage or drawing) illustrating a particular theme: the development of the foetus, birth, breaking away from one's parents and individuation, acquisition of language, sexuality, aggressive behaviour, growth and socialization. These images are framed on four sides with blocks of texts and series of small images. They provide medical, psychological, sociological and legal information relevant to the theme. Intended for social workers and parents, the texts are informative, based on scientific insights, intelligently and sensitively phrased. The reference to Jacques Lacan's neo-Freudian writings on developmental psychology is striking.

The title *Born to be born* refers to the duality of a child's birth: as a biological and subsequently as a linguistic and social being. The child must put aside its mother's milk to be able to taste the flavour of words (*quitter le lait, pour le goût des mots*), i.e. enter the symbolic world. The child arrives in the world, according to the authors, as a stranger with no luggage: only its DNA backpack has been filled. But its future is determined neither genetically nor socially (through its parents' position in the economic system). The dependent creature is recognized, acknowledged and cherished by its parents. Parents and child will have to fill the empty suitcases so that the child, once independent, will be properly equipped to begin its own adventurous journey, which will not be without detours and setbacks. This preparation for life during the first three years of human existence is the subject of the exhibition, which follows the baby through this crucial first period of its life.

The images propose a timeline in which there is a triple movement: from the dual unity with the mother's body to independent freedom of movement; the expansion of the child's small world to the world of others; and finally – less common in a developmental psychology model – the broadening of perspective from the human environment to the space of the universe. The final image shows, enlarged to fill the sky, the fingerprint of an individual in the firmament.

« Les parents ne font pas de miracle.

Ils font mieux. Ils font l'avenir. »

Né (e) pour Naître...

« Je suis né pour naître, pour retenir le pas de tout ce qui s'approche, de tout ce qui cogne à ma poitrine comme un nouveau cœur tout tremblant ».

Pablo Neruda.

Une Petite Enfance dans la Vie. Avant la conception quelque chose de lui existait déjà dans l'imaginaire de ses parents. Puis être réel, unique, distinct, éclos de leur rencontre, l'enfant a germé au secret du ventre. Naître. Venir au monde... Le monde aussi vient à lui pour qu'il devienne un être humain.

Cette exposition retrace la saga du bébé, du petit enfant, les temps forts des premières années de la vie. Tout ne s'y décide pas mais c'est là que se compose l'identité d'une femme ou d'un homme. C'est là aussi la source profonde où puise le futur de chacun, son activité et sa création.

Le Groupe de Recherche et d'Action pour l'Enfance vous convie à l'étonnement devant l'enfant présent au souvenir de l'enfant passé. Dans la rencontre du quotidien et de la mémoire se tisse une espérance : que l'humain s'émerveille assez de lui-même pour aimer vraiment la vie qu'il engendre.

LE GROUPE DE RECHERCHE ET D'ACTION POUR L'ENFANCE
EST UNE ASSOCIATION LOI 1901.
IL ASSURE LA FORMATION DES PROFESSIONNELS DE L'ENFANCE.
REÇOIT GRATUITEMENT VOS APPELS TÉLÉPHONIQUES
SUR « ALLO PETITE ENFANCE » (1) 296.22.85.
APPORTE SON CONSEIL AUX MUNICIPALITÉS.
ÉDITE LE JOURNAL MENSUEL « L'ENFANT D'ABORD »
GRAPE, 70 GALERIE VIVIENNE 75002 PARIS
(1) 296.22.32

La conception de cette exposition a pu être réalisée avec le concours de la Fondation de France

Central to the exhibition is the idea that interaction between parents and child can be a source of unworried pleasure and is a prerequisite for individuation. From conception the child is carried in its mother's womb, but in its earliest years it is also enveloped and carried along by a familiar environment of smells, colours, sounds, words, touches and responses. Growing up, according to the authors, means renouncing the desire to be carried: experiencing loss in order thereby to gain. It is only then that the child can become the subject of its own desire, gradually learning to live its own life and build its own identity.

At first sight, the individual development of the human child hardly seems an obvious topic for a Marxist design collective. But appearances can be deceptive. Members of the collective, too, are parents! The theme of the child returns more than once in Bernard's work. This communication project demonstrates that knowledge-based information is not incompatible with the personal signature and subjectivity of a sensitive designer.

The quality of the design stems primarily from the images. They often have considerable wit and there is a surrealistic slant to them. The phrase *la sexualité n'est pas ce que vous croyez* (sexuality isn't what you think it is) in relation to a one-year old boy who gazes out at us with the confident earnestness of a small-town burgomaster deserves to become a catch phrase. The collage *au Fil du Temps, Grandir* (as time goes on, growing up) seems to be an illustration to a fairy tale that has yet to be written. The stacking of a stool on a chair on a table against the background of a night sky expresses the impossible compromise between awakening perception of the cosmos and metaphysical longing on the one hand and the limited motor capacity of a child on the other.

The typography of the brochure is worth a critical comment. The possibilities of using varied typography for articulating a complex subject like this on different levels of information have certainly not been fully exploited. In this respect, Bernard and his comrades still had a long way to go. The words that close the first life phase of the child, on the last panel, *à suivre* (to be continued) also applied to the designers.

133

Il n'y a pas de modèle familial unique. Familles limitées aux parents et aux enfants, familles élargies, d'autres éléments de la parenté, unions libres... familles mono-parentales ou de la famille, selon s'ajoutent ou s'crient de la famille, et leur évolution les différents modèles familiaux et leur évolution. Regardons chez vous, et autour de vous !

Environ 800 000 femmes élèvent seules leurs enfants. Connaissent-ils leur père ? Le savent-ils ? Combien d'hommes élèvent-ils seuls leurs enfants ? Qu'en est-il des mères ?

L'activité salariée des femmes représente un apport économique vital. Et aussi l'effet de vos débats y compris au sein des couples. La place des femmes dans la chaîne économique et leur propre prise de conscience jouent la recherche d'un nouvel équilibre de la famille.

Il importe que chaque parent réfléchisse en fonction de sa propre réalité familiale, à la présence réelle en temps et en attention qu'il offre à son enfant.

... Au Creux...

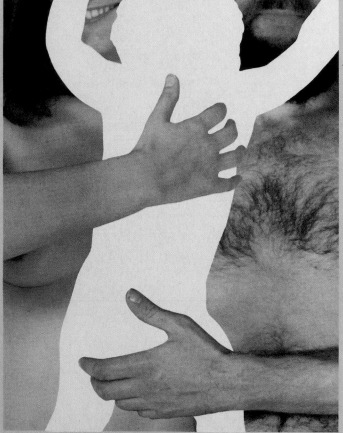

Son premier monde etait rond
tissé d'ombres
et de contacts,
de paroles et de désirs.
Dans le nouveau monde
tout cela se retrouve
diffracté, modifié
par l'étrangeté du cadre.

D'abord bercé dans le ventre,
il l'est maintenant
dans les bras,
il peut sentir la peau,
les odeurs, la voix plus claire
et plus précise.

Le familier fait retour
dans le dépaysement.

« Une mère » ?
Pour porter. Pour prendre
le relais du foyer utérin...
Ce n'est pas forcément
la même personne :
l'une peut donner le jour,
d'autres la vie...

La sécurité du cadre,
l'intérêt sincère des personnes
qui s'en occupent,
portent l'enfant à vivre.
Surtout quand se transmet
au cours des soins
le plaisir qu'il soit là et le désir
qu'il s'épanouisse.
Le « j'aime que tu vives »
est la main invisible qui porte
l'enfant vers le monde
après que le corps l'y a mis.

« Un père » ?
Pour porter aussi
dans son désir et dans ses bras.
Pour garantir à l'enfant
son origine et la moitié
de ses racines.

... de Vous...

un père peut-il faire la mère ?

L'un des deux parents peut remplacer l'autre dans les soins et le partage. Mais les termes père et mère désignent aussi des places qui ne sont pas identiques pour l'enfant. Et lui ne les confond pas.
Même si les adultes s'efforcent de ne pas marquer la différence « sociale ». le petit perçoit nettement cette qui s'exprime à travers le corps, la voix et de multiples et subtiles façons.

Père et mère désignent des fonctions différentes — à ne pas confondre avec égales — auprès de l'enfant pour que celui-ci se construise dans la différence. C'est plus difficile mais non impossible pour un parent seul.

... Je suis l'Enfant Réel,

Accueillir un nouveau-né,
c'est comme un premier
rendez-vous d'amour
avec un être
encore jamais vu.

Le bébé, lui, est prêt
pour la rencontre.
Par ses manifestations propres
et sa résistance à loger
dans un moule préparé à l'avance,
il se fait connaître
et découvrir dans l'étonnement,
l'agacement, la déception,
l'attendrissement.
Il fait de son père et sa mère
des parents !

Au fil des mois
la rencontre s'approfondit
au rythme des nouveautés
de l'enfant qui grandit.

L'enfant aussi porte son parent
à se retourner sur son enfance.
Être avec un enfant, c'est retrouver
l'enfant que l'on fut.
Poursuivi, cerné, débusqué par le présent,
le bébé d'hier revient.
Il faut le rejoindre pour s'accorder
à la nouveauté
de l'enfant qui est là.

Par son père et sa mère l'enfant
est inscrit dans les lignées familiales
dont les réseaux tissent
l'histoire humaine
dans l'espace et le temps.

Avant de germer
au secret du ventre,
il existait déjà dans la tête
de ses parents :
« Il sera... », « Elle aura... ».

Pourtant, cet enfant-là
qui arrive était inimaginable
car l'enfant réel n'est jamais
l'enfant rêvé.
Attendu, il apporte la surprise.

Mais c'est un étranger
particulier, car il est
aussitôt « reconnu ».
On cherche la ressemblance,
et on la trouve.
C'est sans doute cette illusion
qui permet aux parents
d'accepter l'inconnu.

Faisons Connaissance.

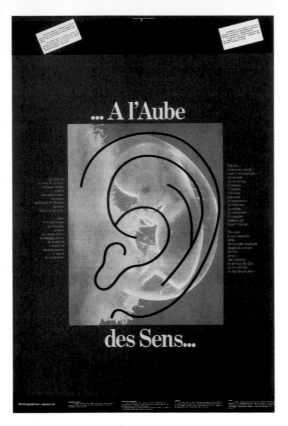

... A l'Aube

des Sens...

... Mon
Développement,

... Je suis
Incomparable.

La Sexualité
n'est pas

ce que
Vous Croyez!

quitter le Lait,

pour le Goût
des Mots.

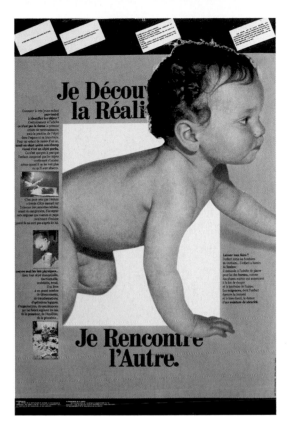

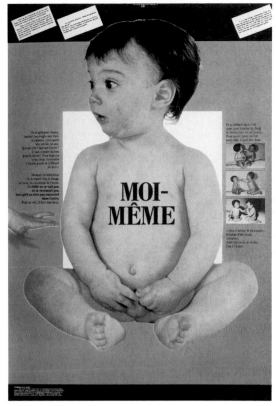

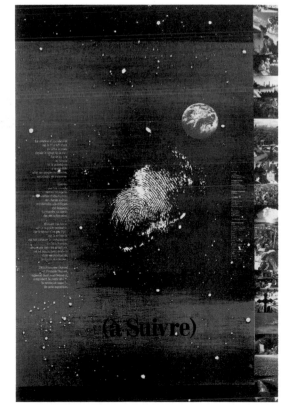

The ZUP family album!

L'Album de famille ZUP!
Book published on the
occasion of the festival of
La Rochelle,
commissioned by the
Maison de la Culture,
104 pp.
34.1 × 24 / 1982

Design
Grapus in collaboration
with Martine Barraud,
Noak Carrau, Lucette
Delibes, Marsha Emanuel,
Anne Gallet, Lucia Villar
Guanaes, François Miehe,
Sophie Mougenot, Marc
Pataut, Vincent Perrottet,
Noreen O'Shea, Pierre-
Laurent Thève
Publisher
Festival de la
Rochelle/Grapus/éditions
Marval
Printed by
Marchand, Paris

Early in the sixties the French Ministry of Culture launched the Maisons de la
Culture. The purpose of these cultural centres, financed jointly by central government and local councils, was both to decentralize culture and to broaden its accessibility: it would be possible for people living outside the big cities to come into
contact with culture. Each Maison de la Culture determined its own programme
and was headed by an artistic director. Places with a left-wing majority on their
councils tended to invest a great deal of energy in cultural activities and never
failed to make a progressive mark on the cultural programme. For Grapus, the
Maisons de la Culture were welcome clients who regularly filled the collective's
order book.

In La Rochelle, a medium-sized town on the south-west coast of France, the
Maison de la Culture held an annual festival. In 1982 it decided to involve residents
of the suburb of Villeneuve-des-Salines, a newly built priority urbanization zone
or *zone à urbaniser en priorité* (ZUP) providing social housing for some 6,000
people. The Maison de la Culture, located in the centre of the town, asked Grapus
to develop an activity for and in the district itself. Could Grapus organize a poster
exhibition such as they had set up on earlier occasions for other Maisons de la
Culture? At this time Grapus consisted of five members: the four designers Pierre
Bernard, Marc Dumas, Alex Jordan and Gérard Paris-Clavel, plus manager
Jean-Paul Bachollet. The commission from La Rochelle was accepted, but it was
decided that it should be thoroughly analysed. The client took the view that communication between the cultural centre and the inhabitants of the district was not
what it should be. But could that communication deficit be solved by a short-lived
exhibition of posters? What did the inhabitants themselves want?

Grapus sought contact with neighbourhood associations, local clubs, societies
and care organizations, and with the concierges of apartment blocks. What emerged
from these meetings was a different perspective: communication between the
inhabitants of the neighbourhood itself was poor. Armed with this intelligence,
Grapus decided to redefine the client's brief: the objective of the project should be
to let the inhabitants express themselves and put them in touch with one another.
Grapus came up with the idea of conducting interviews with a relatively broad
selection of local people and using the material gathered as the starting point for a
book which would be given to all residents. And the question that the interviewees
would be asked was: 'What does happiness mean to you?'

In the words of Bernard: 'Four or five members of Grapus worked with friends and
family on this project, and at least as many interns. I contributed to the book as a
designer but was primarily responsible for the organization of the project as a
whole. The book was to include stories from the oldest to the youngest inhabitant.
One of us was to respond to each of those stories with an image. The book was to be
given to all of the inhabitants in order to increase contact between them. We took a
picture of everyone interviewed. I've lost count of the number of times we drove
back and forth between Aubervilliers, where we had our studio at the time, and La
Rochelle; there were always two of us together. Back in the studio we would work
on how best to respond to the stories we had heard. We wanted to show the diversity

of the neighbourhood, so the images had to be as varied as possible. On the basis of an excerpt of our conversation and our memory of the person we had talked to we made one image per person. Each page of the book combines text and image.

It was an expensive project, in addition to which we overspent our budget – something that happened from time to time. At one of the meetings with the client and the people from the neighbourhood, the residents were enthusiastic but the Maison de la Culture thought it was becoming too expensive. We defended the project by arguing that the production of the book would cost less per inhabitant than the subsidy for an opera ticket and would reach more people. Not only would the residents of the neighbourhood talk about it but the rest of the city would become interested, through the local radio station, for example, which had taken an interest in the project. As a result of ZUP! the inhabitants of La Rochelle would start to talk to one another and about one another.' [Boekraad 2006]

L'album de famille ZUP! is constructed on the principle of seniority, opening with the oldest inhabitant and ending with the youngest, a newborn baby. Alice Bouron, aged 98, answered the question about happiness like this: 'It's difficult to explain ... happiness does not exist ... it's a myth.' The youngest, Elza Bozier, just burped. Instead, her photo is the only one printed, bigger than life size, in full colour. Missing ages, between 97 and 86, are represented by black pages.

The inhabitants' words are given exactly as they were spoken. Their stories of happiness and unhappiness, and the Grapus members' memories of these people, did indeed lead to an extremely varied range of images. For financial reasons the book was produced entirely in black and white, yet it ends in colour with a portrait gallery of Polaroid photographs of those interviewed.

The interaction between residents, designers and photographers resulted in a book full of images which are not conventional or idealized representations, nor literal illustrations of the text. They are visual reactions just as people react to one another in a conversation – differing sharply in tone and style. There is empathy, respect and tenderness, but also humour, mockery and sarcasm. This polyphonic book allows differences to be heard and seen, but it is also the orchestration of many different design styles, brought together in a common project.

This project is a model of horizontal communication. Grapus was able to bend the original brief – vertical communication between an institution and its public – because the institution also wanted the target group to be an active participant. Here Grapus valorized participation so radically that the institution itself almost disappears. The book becomes a form of communication in which it is not the institution that determines the discourse. This is not a transmitter sending out a message packaged by a designer: instead, the designers have made the message come from the receivers, coaxing out their words and replying with their images to initiate a reciprocal communication process. The book, the residue of many conversations, is a stone thrown into a pond, drawing wider and wider circles in the community. This gift from the community to its inhabitants and from the interviewed inhabitants to the community has a structure of reciprocity, which the designers hoped and expected would be continued in everyday face to face communication.

The project replaces monologue with dialogue and ends in a polylogue, an exchange between many. It envisions the democratization and decentralization of the communication process itself. Beneath the monotony of the new suburb there is a colourful array of life stories to be told and visualized. The residents lose their anonymity. Their names are written into a family album of a new kind.

141

Well, I played football for a while with my friends, but with football you're always in the same position, it's always more or less the same: you pass, you kick the ball about a bit, you move forward a bit – whereas with rugby there are several sides to it: you have touchdowns and you have conversions – taking conversions is great because you do it all yourself. Whereas kicking for goal, that's no fun. And there have to be eleven of you to be able to play. Rugby's something else, it's got its own spirit, that sort of thing...

Happiness... is being on my own when I want to be, and then when I want to be with my friends being with them right away.

15 Eric Beuzet

The band is called 'Drive in'; we play rock, psychedelic rock actually: rock's too simple, we find ... psychedelic rock, it's music that's, umm, based on sounds that are very... made with lots of effects.

14 Frédéric Lopez

●●● Ah !... j'ai joué un moment au foot avec des copains / mais alors → je trouvais que... le football, on reste axé / c'est toujours la même chose : on fait une passe → on joue à la baballe → on avance un petit peu / tandis que le rugby, il y a plusieurs faces : aussi bien la touche, que les transformations, → surtout les transformations on peut faire ça tout seul tandis que les tirs au but, c'est pas marrant → il faut être onze pour pouvoir jouer... et puis le rugby c'est autre chose, il y a un esprit... tout ça...

Le bonheur... c'est être tranquille quand j'en ai envie et puis quand j'ai envie de rencontrer des copains → être tout de suite avec eux.

●●● Le groupe s'appelle « Drive in », on fait du rock... du psychédélique justement, parce que le rock, c'est trop simple → on trouve... psychédélique / c'est de la musique... recherchée à base de sons très / faits avec beaucoup d'effets.

15 ERIC BEUZET

FRÉDÉRIC LOPEZ 14

●●● On n'a pas tellement de contacts avec   au plafond pour dire : « baissez un peu la
ses voisins... quand on en a → c'est frapper   chaîne » → il y a ces contacts-là, mais il y en
a d'autres aussi...

PATRICK BOUYER

●●● J'ai travaillé comme femme de service à   Le bonheur ? beaucoup de choses...
ROTO DIESEL / je préfère garder mon
bébé

LEONIDA MARCHESSEAU 26

We don't have much contact with the neighbours. When we do, it's because they're knocking on the ceiling to say 'Turn the radio down' – there are contacts like that, but there are others too...

27 Patrick Bouyer

p. 144

We come from the Auvergne, from Puy de Dôme, we lived in Saint Eloy-les-Mines. My husband was a miner. Yes, you were always afraid that an accident might happen. In the beginning it was really difficult to get used to it! But then, after the start, the routine – he spent thirty years down the mine, that's not so bad.

When he would come home late, I worried of course, but then later on, routines are like that, it's like everything else.

You know, it's the same thing with cars these days – there are just as many accidents as there used to be in the mines back then. I'm afraid in a car, that's because there is too much traffic. People drive like madmen. I'm afraid in a car; I don't close my eyes, but I brake before my husband does.

55 Marianne Fujarski

I worked as a cleaning lady at Roto Diesel, but I prefer taking care of my baby.

Happiness? Lots of things…

26 Leonida Marchesseau

p. 145

I sing, yes – Edith Piaf songs, because I have more or less the same voice, ah well, I am the same size as she was, 1.46 m.

I like rock; I like modern dances – oh the 'duck' dance, oh, oh, oh, we were doubled over with laughter!

I used to like Elvis Presley, but I also like Eddy Mitchell – maybe because he's such a hunk.

54 Simone Diévart

●●● Nous on vient de l'Auvergne → du Puy-de-Dôme... on habitait à Saint-Éloy-les-Mines / mon mari était mineur, oui... on avait toujours la crainte qu'il y ait un accident qui arrive / au début, c'était dur pour s'habituer hein !... puis après la première fois, la routine → il a fait trente ans de fond, c'était déjà pas mal...

Quand il rentrait tard, je portais peine bien sûr... mais après, c'est une routine tout ça → c'est comme tout le reste.

Vous savez, avec les voitures c'est pareil maintenant → il y a autant d'accidents qu'y avait dans les mines dans le temps. En voiture, moi j'ai peur, ça par contre... parce qu'il y a trop de circulation → ils roulent comme des fous les gens, / la voiture me peur... je ne ferme pas les yeux, mais je freine avant mon mari.

C'est la vie, plus de poissons que de tristesse

mon dieu pauvre pêcheur,

Ils vont faire disette, mais faute en est au preneur.

Mais voici le printemps,

comme nous ont besoin de batifoler

Ils reviendront avec le temps, à vos hameçons se suicider

1,46

●●● Je chante oui → des chansons d'Édith Piaf parce que j'ai une voix à peu près pareille / ah ben, j'ai la même taille qu'elle, 1,46 m...

J'aime bien le rock / les danses modernes j'aime bien → la danse du canard... ah ! la la qu'est-ce-qu'on a pu rire avec ça !

J'aimais bien Elvis Presley, mais j'aime bien Eddy Mitchell → c'est peut-être parce que c'est une grande carcasse...

I have seven children! Why? I didn't really want seven children; I had them because there weren't any contraceptives like today. If there had been contraceptives in my day, believe me, I wouldn't have had seven – and certainly not in eight years! I might have had seven, but much more spaced out, whereas I had seven in eight years! Well, you know, life hasn't always been a bed of roses; thank goodness I have a husband who always helped, otherwise...

We're not unhappy, we are alive.

Happiness to me is living together, the two of you, understanding one another, having children – that's my idea of happiness.

I rent out rooms to students during the summer; in June I'm having an eighteen-year-old boy, a Swede; in July a Swedish girl, and if all goes well an American girl.

41 Jeanne Renoux

The morning starts with the alarm clock, looking after the kids, getting them ready for school. After that there are errands, housework, making lunch. Then it's midday. After lunch the children have to be got off to school again. Still, the afternoons are a bit quieter, you can relax a bit. Then it's evening and back to the kitchen again.

Happiness is cosiness, being together at home with husband and children.

40 Denise Cabioch

I can't just do nothing all day long, after all... I can't just sit around like... there are people who sit in their chair from morning to night and from night to morning... At the Third Age club, I come here on Tuesdays and Thursdays to play cards; it keeps your mind occupied. Here we play cards, belote or hearts.

I've been here for eighteen months; I think the people are nice enough, we get along; always here... well, what goes on outside, umm, that doesn't concern me.

Happiness is when there are two of you together, monsieur.

67 Paulette Berdèche

Yes, I would like to have some happiness, I've had a lot of unhappiness. I lost my husband four years ago, and two years later I lost a son, he was forty.

The happiest moment of my life, monsieur? I haven't had many. I had my husband, and was very unhappy. I had four children. I stayed with my husband because of my children, otherwise I would have done what everyone else does: I would have left him, wouldn't I?

I watch the telly to pass the time; I like westerns best because there's more action in them. I go to the market because it's something to do. It helps pass the time.

66 Jeanne Martineau

147

The Book of Children's Rights

It was only in the twentieth century that growing awareness that children too have human rights led to an extensive system for their legal protection. After the adoption of the Universal Declaration of Human Rights in 1948, eleven years passed before the United Nations approved a Declaration of the Rights of the Child. Thirty years later, in 1989, the Declaration was followed by the United Nations Convention on the Rights of the Child. In 1990 the Convention was ratified by France.

Each UN convention requires member states ratifying it to publicize its text. Exceptional about this book are the commission itself and its design. Government institutions in the field of child and youth care are usually satisfied with folders and brochures. In this case, however, the general council and the departments of communications and *l'Enfance et Famille* of Seine-Saint-Denis, just north of Paris, took the initiative – in cooperation with institutions for child care – to offer future parents a book on children's rights.

The rich and complex structure of the book, according to the preface, makes this presentation of the Convention 'a house in which there is a place for hope. Parents are invited to walk around in it, to make new discoveries and enhance their self-confidence'.

The book is intended for the child itself, and its name should be written on a printed bookplate on the first page. Thus the government addresses the child via its parents. The bookplate is reminiscent of the custom, common at wedding ceremonies in some Protestant churches, for the couple to be given, as a gift from the congregation, a family Bible in which their names are inscribed and in which they can later add the names of their children. This analogy suggests that the fundamental constitutional texts of the democratic state have a comparable status to the holy scripture of a community of believers. In France, certainly, this is a plausible comparison given the almost sacred status of such founding texts as the 1789 *Déclaration des droits de l'homme et du citoyen* (Declaration of the Rights of Man and of the Citizen).

The book opens with a quotation from Victor Hugo: 'Today's utopia is tomorrow's reality'. *Le livre des droits de l'enfant* is a book inspired by hope, not by the dark reality in which children all over the world so often grow up, a reality which, I should add, is also shown in this book. The articles of the Convention are the scarlet thread running through the book. They are not presented in the order in which they appear in the Convention, but are grouped into themes which refer to the various aspects of children's lives. The articles of the Convention are printed, commented upon and explained, as well as being accompanied by historical, educational, literary, academic and political texts on the theme in question. This approach makes it possible to form a bridge between the formal, abstract language of law and the actual experiences of parents and children. This creates a rich and layered panorama of the world of children in an intelligent and carefully considered montage of texts and images.

The form of address is neither moralizing nor paternalistic. The government does not put on the strict face of authority, but rather that of mediator. No single model is presented as the right way to bring up children: parents are acknowledged as those

Le Livre des droits de l'enfant en Seine-Saint-Denis et partout sur la planète
(The Book of Children's Rights in Seine-Saint-Denis and everywhere on the planet)
156 pp., 50,000 copies
23 × 19 / 2001

Concept and editing
Nadia Monteggia
Direction
Pierre Bernard
Design team
Thomas Lélu,
Fréderic Teschner,
Cyril Cohen,
Uli Meisenheimer
Picture research
Dalloula Haiouani

who are responsible for raising their offspring. The book supports them in this task, informing them, encouraging them and repeatedly pointing out the developmental potential of children and identifying the concrete conditions which are necessary for its realization. This is the government showing itself as close to its citizens. The book ends with a practical list of addresses of aid agencies that parents can turn to. All in all, the book exudes vitality, joy and responsibility. The two worlds, that of the law and that of the child, come together in a unique synthesis.

Nadia Monteggia, the book's editor, explains the aim of the publication like this: 'The question was how parents needed to be approached. We had to think about the diversity in their concrete reality in order to be able to allow each one of them – whatever their age, cultural origin, level of education or standard of living – to find a point of recognition helping them to enter the book and find their way. The fertile interaction between texts and images which arose during the writing and design process of the book will create the possibility for every parent to take from it what they need and to revisit the emotions of their own childhood, for that is what nourishes their relationship with their child.' [Press file of *Le livre des droits de l'enfant* 2001]

In the words of Pierre Bernard: 'The idea we had was that of a family book, something like a family photo album – a book that establishes the links between a child and its family, but also describes it as a unique human being. The family in this case is humanity: mankind today in all its diversity, constantly in the making, perpetuating itself for aeons and evolving towards ever greater humanity. That is the desire that inspired us and it is that message of hope that motivated us to make this book. Thus, rather than choosing symbolic images to illustrate a given view, we have preferred to create a continuum of images that weave the book together, showing and explaining the multiplicity and richness of different cultures, both those of yesterday and those of today, both here and elsewhere. The African woman nursing her baby reminds us of other icons bridging the centuries. Today's child in his pedal car appears alongside his eighteenth-century counterpart sitting majestically in his little chariot, the old master alongside the press photo. There is a universal and timeless message in this juxtaposition: the right of – and the absolute necessity for – each child to develop its own form and to cooperate with the form of tomorrow's humanity. Texts and images relate as dialogue and echo, never as mere illustration.' [Ibidem]

The book is divided into twelve chapters, each with its own theme. Each chapter opens with a spread on which its theme is presented in texts and images. The articles of the Convention are integrated into the image. Chapter openings are marked by conspicuous changes in type size and colour. Only the legal texts, printed in black on white, escape this flood of colour. The book combines various text genres and levels of information that are indicated by means of two typefaces in different sizes. They create a hierarchy in the text and suggest different ways and speeds of reading it.

Most of the images are in colour. They vary in nature and origin, ranging from reproductions of old masters depicting children to drawings by children themselves and photographs from family albums, representations of children in non-European cultures, and documentary and press photographs. The presentation of the images is adapted to their content: the informal bric-a-brac of a bulletin board, the objective presentation of a documentary photograph, the respectful presentation of art historical icons. The images permit direct access, concretizing the abstract words of the law and bringing the theme closer to home. All kinds of readers can recognize themselves in the book, so they can identify with the message.

The book's picture editing and presentation contribute significantly to achieving its goal, i.e. to raise children in such a way that they are guaranteed the best possible chance of realizing their potential.

The *Livre des droits de l'enfant*, a collective production of the Atelier de Création Graphique, was produced under Bernard's direction. It was only right that the commissioning authority should be recognized for its part: in 2001 the General Council of Seine-Saint-Denis was awarded the *Grand Prix de la communication publique*.

L'enfant a droit à l'éducation.

L'enfant a droit à l'éducation
sur la base de l'égalité des chances.
L'État a l'obligation de garantir un
enseignement primaire et secondaire
gratuit et obligatoire, accessible à tous,
et l'accès à l'enseignement supérieur
en fonction des capacités de chacun.
L'État doit favoriser l'assiduité
des élèves, mettre à leur disposition
les services d'une orientation scolaire
et professionnelle. Il doit aussi veiller
à ce que les règles de la vie scolaire
respectent la dignité de l'enfant.

Les États doivent coopérer
pour éliminer l'ignorance et
l'analphabétisme, faciliter l'accès
aux connaissances scientifiques
et techniques notamment dans
les pays en développement.

article 28

L'éducation a pour but de favoriser
l'épanouissement de la personnalité
de l'enfant, le développement de ses
dons et aptitudes. Elle doit lui inculquer
aussi le respect des droits de l'homme
et des libertés fondamentales.
Ainsi que le respect des parents,
de la culture d'origine et d'adoption,
et des autres civilisations.
Elle vise à préparer l'enfant à assumer
plus tard ses responsabilités dans
une société libre, débarrassée
du sexisme et du racisme, dans un
esprit de tolérance, d'amitié et de paix.
Elle doit aussi former l'enfant
au respect du milieu naturel.

article 29

Le livre des droits de L'enfant

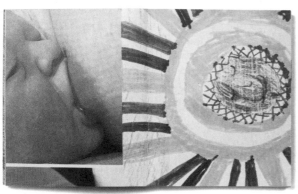

« Qu'est-ce qui rend la société possible ?
Les droits de l'individu ».

La convention internationale des droits de l'enfant est une étape importante du progrès humain.

La longue marche des droits de l'Homme*

« C'est un être humain habillé en enfant, il possède les émotions et les sentiments de son espèce, mais n'a aucun des droits ».

Howard Buten, psychologue, clown et écrivain d'origine américaine.
À cinq ans, je m'ai tué, éditions du Seuil.

Le paterfamilias romain avait le droit de refuser le nouveau-né, les pères gaulois décidaient de la vie ou de la mort de leurs enfants.

Pendant des siècles, l'instruction fut surtout le privilège de ceux dont la famille détenait le pouvoir et l'argent.

En 1212, la Croisade des enfants en a rassemblé 30 000. De la figure du martyr à celle du héros, les enfants ont toujours été utilisés.

L'enfant a longtemps été considéré comme un adulte en miniature et un être dont il fallait réprimer les mauvais instincts par les brimades et les coups.

Jean-Jacques Rousseau a dénoncé les libertés du système éducatif et inspiré une lente évolution des mentalités et des mœurs à l'égard des enfants.

De nombreux enfants abandonnés ont été recueillis par l'œuvre charitable créée par Saint-Vincent de Paul.

Employés parfois dès l'âge de quatre ans dans les manufactures, les ateliers et les mines, les enfants-ouvriers ont payé un lourd tribut à l'industrialisation. 1881-1882, l'enseignement primaire devient obligatoire, laïc et gratuit pour les 6-13 ans (jusqu'à 16 ans en 1959).

L'abolition du travail des enfants et l'instauration de l'enseignement obligatoire ont été des facteurs déterminants pour le développement des pays industrialisés.

Textes fondateurs des droits humains

1215
La Grande Charte, Angleterre.

1679
L'Habeas Corpus votée en Angleterre protège l'individu contre les arrêts arbitraires.

1689
Bill of Rights, Angleterre.

1776
La Déclaration d'Indépendance des États-Unis comporte une ébauche des droits de l'Homme.

1789
La Déclaration des Droits de l'Homme et du Citoyen, proclamée par la révolution française établit que tous les hommes naissent et demeurent libres et égaux en droit.

1793
La nouvelle Déclaration des Droits de l'Homme et du Citoyen, élargit la notion de droit, notamment à l'instruction et à l'assistance.

1794
L'esclavage est aboli une première fois sous Robespierre. Il a été rétabli dans les colonies françaises par Napoléon en 1802. Ce n'est qu'en 1848, et cela grâce aux pressions du mouvement abolitionniste et à la ténacité de Victor Schoelcher, qu'il sera définitivement interdit.

1918
Déclaration des droits du peuple travailleur et exploité, République soviétique de Russie.

1936
Complément à la Déclaration des Droits de l'Homme, France.

1948
Déclaration américaine des droits et devoirs du citoyen, Bogotá–Amériques.

1948
Convention pour la prévention et la répression du crime de génocide, New York–Nations Unies.

1948
Déclaration Universelle des Droits de l'Homme, Paris–Nations Unies.

1950
Convention européenne de sauvegarde des droits de l'Homme et des libertés fondamentales, Rome–Europe.

1965
Convention internationale sur l'élimination de toutes les formes de discrimination raciale, New York–Nations Unies.

1966
Pacte relatif aux droits économiques, sociaux et culturels, New York–Nations Unies.

1966
Pacte relatif aux droits civils et politiques, New York–Nations Unies.

1975
Acte final de la conférence sur la sécurité et la coopération en Europe, Helsinki–Europe.

1976
Déclaration universelle du droit des peuples, Alger–Univers.

1980
Convention pour l'élimination de toutes les formes de discrimination à l'égard des femmes, New York–Nations Unies.

1981
Charte africaine des droits de l'homme et des peuples, Nairobi–Afrique.

1984
Convention contre la torture et autres peines ou traitements cruels et inhumains ou dégradants, New York–Nations Unies.

1990
Convention relative aux droits de l'enfant, New York–Nations Unies.

1998
Traité créant une Cour pénale internationale, Rome–Nations Unies.

À suivre...

1819

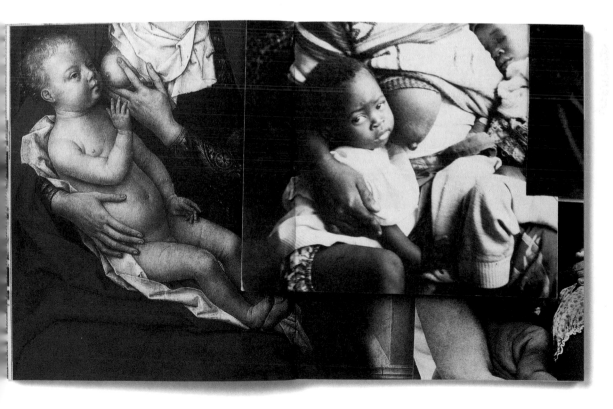

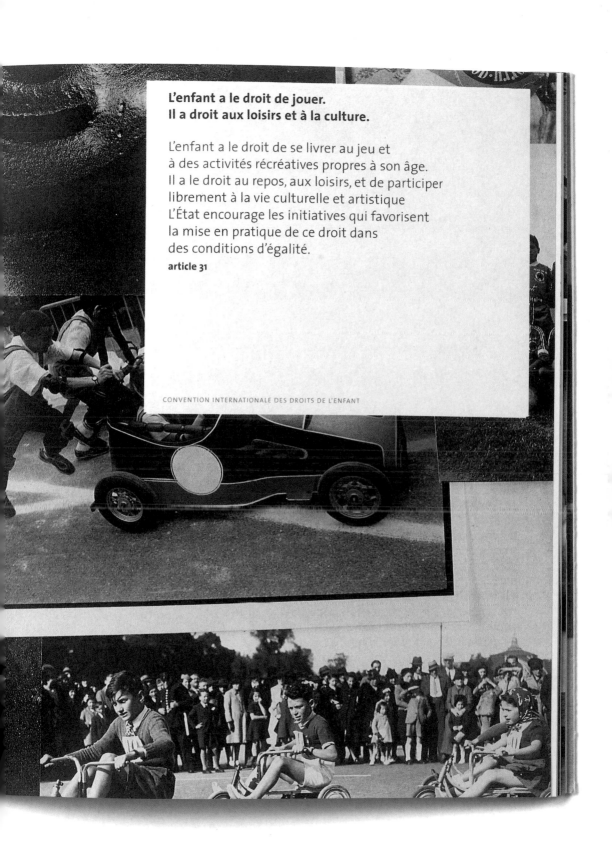

**L'enfant a le droit de jouer.
Il a droit aux loisirs et à la culture.**

L'enfant a le droit de se livrer au jeu et
à des activités récréatives propres à son âge.
Il a le droit au repos, aux loisirs, et de participer
librement à la vie culturelle et artistique
L'État encourage les initiatives qui favorisent
la mise en pratique de ce droit dans
des conditions d'égalité.
article 31

CONVENTION INTERNATIONALE DES DROITS DE L'ENFANT

Un nom pour être quelqu'un.
un prénom pour être quelqu'un d'autre

« Le nom propre d'un homme n'est pas comme un manteau qui pend autour de lui et qu'on peut tirailler et arracher, mais c'est un vêtement parfaitement adapté, quelque chose comme une peau, qui l'a recouvert entièrement et qu'on ne peut gratter ou écorcher sans le blesser lui-même. »
Johann Wolfgang von Goethe (1749-1832)

Être touché pour se sentir bien dans sa peau soi-même.

Le droit d'être élevé par ses parents et de vivre en famille.

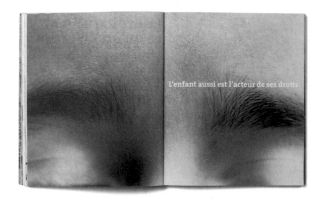

L'enfant aussi est l'acteur de ses droits.

L'enfant a le droit d'être protégé en toutes circonstances.

L'enfant doit être protégé contre toute forme de violence et de brutalités physiques ou mentales. Que l'enfant soit élevé par ses parents ou par d'autres personnes, **l'État doit prendre toutes les mesures nécessaires pour le protéger** des négligences et de l'abandon, des mauvais traitements, de l'exploitation et des violences sexuelles. Il a aussi l'obligation de mettre en œuvre des programmes de prévention. Dans les cas de mauvais traitements, il doit effectuer des enquêtes, un suivi, des soins à l'enfant et, le cas échéant, un recours à la justice.
article 19

Si l'enfant n'a pas de famille ou si vivre avec elle est contre son intérêt, l'État doit lui assurer une protection de remplacement en tenant compte de sa vie passée et de sa culture. Il est alors placé dans un foyer ou dans une famille d'accueil.
article 20

L'enfant ne peut être adopté que si c'est son intérêt et conformément à la loi. L'adoption d'un enfant par des parents d'un autre pays que le sien est possible si c'est la meilleure solution pour lui. Elle doit être effectuée par des autorités et des organismes compétents sans donner lieu à un profit matériel.
article 21

L'enfant réfugié ou demandeur du statut de réfugié doit bénéficier de la protection et de l'assistance humanitaire qu'il soit seul ou accompagné par ses parents ou d'autres adultes. Les États doivent collaborer avec les organisations compétentes pour assurer cette protection et rechercher ses parents ou sa famille s'il en a été séparé.
article 22

Des soins spéciaux et une éducation appropriée doivent être assurés à tout enfant handicapé physique ou mental pour lui permettre une vie digne et la plus autonome possible. Ses parents reçoivent l'aide de l'État afin qu'il bénéficie du droit aux soins de santé et à la rééducation, à l'éducation, à la formation professionnelle et aux loisirs. L'objectif est de favoriser son épanouissement personnel et son intégration sociale.
article 23

LARD Les comportements des différentes sociétés humaines à l'égard des enfants témoignent de leur degré de civilisation.

L'enfant a le droit d'être protégé par l'État contre toutes formes d'exploitation.
article 36

L'État doit prendre toutes les mesures qui protègent l'enfant de l'exploitation économique et veiller à ce qu'il ne soit astreint à aucun travail dangereux ou nuisible à sa santé, son éducation et son développement. L'État fixe l'âge minimum d'admission à l'emploi. Il prévoit une réglementation appropriée des horaires et des conditions d'emploi, ainsi que des peines et des sanctions afin d'assurer son application effective.
article 32

L'État doit protéger l'enfant contre la consommation de stupéfiants et des substances psychotropes et empêcher qu'il ne soit utilisé pour la production et le trafic de ces substances.
article 33

L'État doit protéger l'enfant contre toutes formes d'exploitation sexuelle et de violence sexuelle : incitation, contrainte, prostitution, spectacles ou matériel de caractère pornographique.
article 34

L'État doit prendre toutes les mesures pour empêcher l'enlèvement, la vente ou la traite d'enfants.
article 35

L'enfant a le droit d'être protégé par l'État contre toutes peines ou traitements cruels.
La torture et les traitements inhumains ou dégradants sont interdits à l'égard des mineurs, de même que la peine capitale et l'emprisonnement à vie. Les mineurs condamnés doivent être séparés des détenus adultes. Ils ont le droit de rester en contact avec leur famille et de faire appel à une assistance juridique.
article 37

L'enfant a le droit d'être protégé par l'État en cas de conflit armé.
L'enfant de moins de quinze ans ne doit pas être enrôlé dans les forces armées ni participer au conflit. Toutes les mesures doivent être prises pour que les enfants bénéficient, au même titre que l'ensemble de la population civile, de protection et de soins.
article 38

L'enfant victime a le droit de recevoir les aides qui lui permettront de se réadapter physiquement et psychologiquement et de se réinsérer socialement.
article 39

CONVENTION INTERNATIONALE DES DROITS DE L'ENFANT

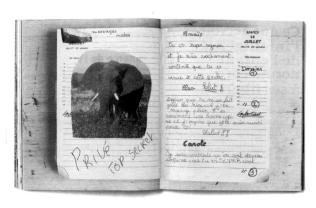

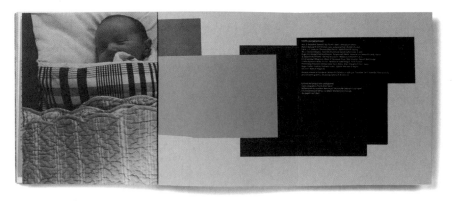

Secours Populaire Français

Logo for the aid organization Secours Populaire Français, 1981 Elements of a house style posters and brochures 2000 to date

Secours Populaire Français (SPF) is an independent aid organization whose field of work covers the whole gamut of society including the jobless, the handicapped and the elderly, and all forms of social intervention and cultural work. It operates on local, national and international levels and offers both emergency and more permanent aid. The attitude of the organization towards those receiving the help it gives is not paternalistic. It does not see the people it works with as passive victims nor as clients, but rather attempts to achieve what it calls a convivial relationship with them: a relationship of exchange, reciprocity and respect. *Respect, dévouement, solidarité* (respect, dedication, solidarity) are the core values by which Secours Populaire is guided. Those three words are underlined on the two posters designed by Bernard for the organization, one of which is discussed in greater detail on page 304 of this book. What the organization offers is not charity but practical solidarity: it creates alliances and is based on the ethic of the gift.

Secours Populaire Français depends on the work of volunteers. The organization came into being through an initiative of the communist labour movement. After the war, the SPF gradually distanced itself from this background (unlike its religious counterpart, Secours Catholique, which is still under the aegis of the French episcopate). The Marxist theory of class struggle as a source of inspiration was replaced by the Universal Declaration of Human Rights. The organization operates under the motto: 'All that is human is ours'. The members 'embrace all those of good will, children, young people and adults of all conditions, regardless of their political, philosophical or religious opinions, in the desire to develop together solidarity and all the human qualities associated therewith' (Article 1 of the statutes).

Secours Populaire has an extensive arsenal of resources: warehouses, lorries, holiday centres, homes for the elderly, educational facilities, second-hand shops, a training centre and a head office in Paris. Funding is mainly by private donations: the donor list numbers around a million names. Approximately 100,000 voluntary workers are supported by a national network with 600 paid employees. Based on a decentralized structure, the organization consists of local committees working together on a *département* basis in a federate structure. Secours Populaire is also active outside France: in 2003 it supported 162 development projects in 49 countries.

Secours Populaire operates in the public domain and was recognized by the State in 1985 as an 'institution of public utility' (*établissement d'utilité publique*). In some cases it receives supplementary subsidies from the government; financial independence, however, is seen as an absolute condition for it to be able to choose its own projects. Civil society organizations such as Secours Populaire demonstrate that the state and private organizations are no longer independent of one another, but that they interact.

The SPF's communication policy is as extensive and complex as the organization itself, functioning on many levels and in many ways. It does not regard itself primarily as an institution but as a collective of people who share the same values.

160

Strengthening their bonds is one of the aims of its communication policy. The SPF organizes conferences, festivals, movie screenings and auctions; it publishes magazines and bulletins to keep its volunteers, donors and partners informed of its activities and to inspire loyalty to the organization. In addition to strengthening its image as a reliable and efficient aid organization, another objective of communication policy is fund-raising and attracting new members.

When Grapus was dissolved in 1990, the work that the studio had done for Secours Populaire since the beginning of the eighties was continued by Alex Jordan and his design studio *Nous travaillons ensemble*. In 2000 Secours Populaire asked Bernard, who had designed the SPF emblem in 1981 (an analysis of this design can be found on page 17 of this book), to design new stationery, posters, forms and donor membership cards.

Given the decentralized character of the organization there was no need for a uniform house style, so he took the now familiar and widely accepted emblem and restored it to its original form. Greatly enlarged on posters or miniaturized and added to a page number, it now turns up, whether conspicuously or unobtrusively, in much of the printed matter produced by Secours Populaire.

Poverty, illness and other personal setbacks can make people despondent and ensnare them in a vicious circle leading to apathy, isolation and exclusion. Breaking this cycle and offering the chance of a better future is one of the goals of Secours Populaire. This calls for powerful images to counterbalance feelings of powerlessness. It is this principle that informs all the work of the Atelier de Création Graphique for the organization.

The corporate brochure of Secours Populaire Français is intended to present the organization to companies which are approached for financial support. This was the first such brochure for the SPF, which, as an organization with its roots in the labour movement, was little known in the business community.

On the cover the emblem replaces the name of the organization. The brochure looks like an illustrated magazine – the kind of thing one absorbs through casual perusal. It is not available in bookstores, nor is it sent out by post. It is an individual gift presented to those expressing an interest in offering their support.

Secours Populaire tells its story soberly and informatively, through carefully edited images and texts. Need and misery are certainly represented, but the emphasis is on the joy of life and the pleasure of human contact. Games, activities and recreation are introduced as an antidote to misery. The brochure tells of the opportunities people are given or may take, their perseverance and their resilience. The layout is characterized by modesty of means and structured on a fairly simple grid. SPF projects are explained in four columns, while more general information is given in two columns. With all its slender elegance the font used in the streamers, Typo-Simplette (designed by Fanette Mellier, who worked with Bernard on the design), has great simplicity. Variety is injected by adding colour to the text pages (for the general information) and colour photographs of the projects.

Bernard succeeds in bringing the dignity and equality of both givers and receivers to the fore. With comparatively modest resources he evokes the generosity and solidarity that are the bedrock of Secours Populaire Français.

With you everywhere in the world,
solidarity!
poster
Secours Populaire Français
80 × 60 / 1982

With you, always there –
the Secours Populaire Français
Solidarity in France and across the
world – join in!
Secours Populaire Français
poster
65 × 92 / 1980

SECOURS
POPULAIRE
FRANÇAIS

9-11 RUE FROISSART
75140 PARIS CEDEX 03
T 01 44 78 21 00
F 01 42 74 71 01

RECONNU D'UTILITÉ PUBLIQUE
GRANDE CAUSE NATIONALE 1991
AGRÉÉ D'ÉDUCATION POPULAIRE
ASSOCIATION ÉDUCATIVE
COMPLÉMENTAIRE
DE L'ENSEIGNEMENT PUBLIC

HABILITÉ À PERCEVOIR
LEGS ET DONATIONS

CCP 654 37 H PARIS

www.secourspopulaire.asso.fr
3615 Secours populaire (0,34 € / mn)

COMITÉ DE LA CHARTE
donner en confiance

TOUT CE QUI EST HUMAIN EST NÔTRE

Des familles citadines découvrent la technique de la greffe des arbres fruitiers à Saint-Clair-sur-Epte.

Visite au Sénat et découverte du patrimoine, août 2005.

Construction d'une école au Vietnam.

Premières vacances en famille

Accès à la santé : dispensaire au ghetto de Nadezhda, Sliven, Bulgarie.

Atelier d'insertion et culture biologique aux « Paniers de la terre », Le Guilvinec.

Libre-service de la solidarité à Nîmes, 2005.

Letterhead
Secours Populaire Français
29.7 × 21 / 2001

New Year card
Secours Populaire Français
15 × 21 / 2005

pp. 166-7
On holiday…
booklet for children
Secours Populaire Français
15 × 12 / 2003

Face à l'adversité: la force d'une relation d'égal à égal.

LE SECOURS POPULAIRE FRANÇAIS EST UNE ASSOCIATION DE SOLIDARITÉ FONDÉE EN 1945, ET RECONNUE D'UTILITÉ PUBLIQUE EN 1985.
IL EST PRÉSENT SUR TOUT LE TERRITOIRE FRANÇAIS AVEC SON ORGANISATION DANS CHAQUE DÉPARTEMENT, ET S'APPUIE SUR DES ANTENNES DANS DES QUARTIERS, DES ENTREPRISES AUTANT QUE DANS DES ÉTABLISSEMENTS SCOLAIRES, DES UNIVERSITÉS.

IL AIDE AUSSI EN LIEN AVEC PLUSIEURS CENTAINES D'ORGANISATIONS PARTENAIRES DANS LE MONDE DANS LE CADRE DE L'AIDE INTERNATIONALE.

PRÈS DE 80 000 MÉDAILLÉS ANIMENT CE GRAND MOUVEMENT DE SOLIDARITÉ POPULAIRE.

En France et dans une cinquantaine d'autres pays, l'aide apportée prend en compte les besoins des personnes dans la perspective de leur avenir.

> En fonction des nécessités et des conditions locales, de leurs désirs, savoir-faire et compétences, les équipes de bénévoles peuvent s'investir dans des actions de leur choix. Cette autonomie et cette souplesse de fonctionnement assurent la possiblité de réagir dans la proximité. Elle permet à l'ensemble de l'association de demeurer en prise sur les réalités vécues par nos contemporains les plus en difficulté, afin de les aider au mieux.

Partout où deux personnes décident d'agir pour la solidarité, une antenne* du Secours Populaire peut être créée. Depuis le quartier, l'école, l'entreprise, l'administration, l'université... où cette antenne* se constitue, elle est reliée à un comité* ou bien directement à une fédération*, instance départementale de l'association. >>>

*Antenne, comité, fédération : voir page 95

Les accompagnements quotidiens construisent l'avenir des personnes individuelles autant que celles des groupes sociaux.

Ci-dessus, en Bulgarie. L'aide à la scolarisation des Roms dans le ghetto de la ville de Sliven a été mise en place par la fédération de Corse.

Ci-contre, en peu partout en France. L'accompagnement scolaire des enfants est assuré par des bénévoles, au sein de la famille de l'enfant ou dans des locaux adaptés.

Grâce à des accords de partenariat avec un fournisseur d'accès Internet, des enfants découvrent le web en compagnie de salariés bénévoles.

6

Tout ce qui est humain est nôtre. Une vue d'ensemble.

Brochure about the organization
Secours Populaire Français
26 × 21 / 2004

168

Les efforts des bénévoles et des donateurs vont dans le même sens. Celui d'une main tendue à l'autre pour que la vie lui soit plus douce. Pour que, retrouvant ses moyens grâce à une solidarité chaleureuse, il s'autonomise et redevienne l'acteur de sa vie.

Les enfants aiment se rendre utiles. Solidaires de leur famille, ils sont tout prêts à s'investir aussi pour la cause des enfants de la planète. C'est ce que leur propose le mouvement Copain du monde. (page 54)

Les bénévoles ne sont pas des professionnels de la solidarité. Certains disposent de quelques heures par semaine ou de plusieurs jours, d'autres sont là en permanence. Leurs qualités humaines et leur empathie pour autrui créent un climat de confiance favorable à l'apaisement de l'angoisse des personnes en difficulté et à la restauration de leur situation. Chacun offre ce qu'il peut : disponibilité, savoir-faire particulier, force physique, acquis professionnels, idée et organisation d'une initiative, contacts intéressants pour le développement

de la solidarité, etc. Leur action est rendue possible par l'argent des donateurs. Outre quelques aides directes en urgence, celui-ci permet surtout à la solidarité... d'exister? L'espace solidarité où sont reçues les personnes aidées, le transport, la conservation, le stockage, la distribution des dons en nature (nourriture, vêtements, jouets et objets divers), les activités sportives et culturelles, les vacances des enfants et des parents, génèrent des charges que seules les sommes collectées permettent d'assumer. Sans toujours se connaître, bénévoles

et donateurs œuvrent de concert. Au-delà des droits reconnus par la société aux enfants, aux femmes et aux hommes, ils répondent présents à l'appel de la loi civilisatrice de la solidarité entre tous les êtres humains qui, elle, est inscrite dans les esprits et les cœurs.

Le Secours populaire : un mouvement au service de la solidarité populaire.

Conception éditoriale et textes : Nadia Menenger.
Coordination : Sophie Esbi.
Conception graphique : Atelier de création graphique, Fanette Mellier et Pierre Bernard, 2004.
Photographies : Pierre graphic. Imprimeur : Greg Pélissandre, Angers, 2004.

Numéro hors série de l'arc'enpierre, à l'occasion du 60e anniversaire du Secours populaire français.
N° 247 / Octobre 2005. Commission paritaire n° 0308I 8843.
Directeur de publication : Bernard Edfoy.

Crédits photographiques :
Cédric Colan : pages 17, 24 et 45 / David Carr : page 12 /
Hervé Chessebaume / Le Télégramme de Brest : page 46 / Melgin Colon : page 43 /
Jean-Luc Grzesic / le tur Journal : page 79 / Stéfane Reys : pages 23 et 69 /
Sylvie François : pages 12, 37, 58, 63, 62, 72, 73, 74, 75 et 95 / Didier Grimaud : pages 53 et 94 /
Benoît Jacoheli 40 : page 27 / Jean-Philippe Baudouin : pages 76 et 93 /
André Lepercq / le tur Pluriel : pages 34, 76 et 81 / Muriel Laroue : page 90 /
Josh Lamosa : pages 39, 89 et 94 / Marc Mariani / ess à pages du mouvement, les pages 9, 13, 14,
17, 21, 28, 29, 33, 47, 49, 50 et 52 / Olivier Pampero / le tur Pluriel : page 93,
Pages 11, 42 et 15 : pleine couverture du portfolio « première » phase de vacances » /
Laurent Pouget : pages 7, 16, 17, 19, 19, 35, 44, 65, 23, 56, 65, 89 et 92 /
Eric Prinvault : pages 7, 23, 24, 36, 57, 75, 59, 37, 36, 61, 66, 68, 22, 65, 38, 59, 59, 71, 60, 61,
84, 85, 89 et 95 / Franck Rozelé : page 51 / Jean Roy : page 78 / Yves Sichwski : page 67 /
Damien Edfoy : page 53 / Jean-Pierre Vallorani / le tur Pluriel : page 93,
18 : pages 65, 72, 73 et 66

Because poverty and precarity
are unacceptable: help us, let's act,
thank you
poster
Secours Populaire Français
176 × 120 / 2005

Respect, Dedication, Solidarity
poster
Secours Populaire Français
176 × 120 / 2005

~~inégalité~~

Secours populaire français, tout ce qui est humain est nôtre.

~~exclusion~~

Souvent, il y a urgence.   Manger, se vêtir, se chauffer… On est là.

~~injustice~~

Pour écouter et comprendre, pour apaiser, soutenir et construire. On est là.
Derrière l'urgence… Toutes les difficultés de la vie.
Pour rechercher, avec notre semblable en détresse, des solutions, faire des démarches…
On est là parce que la solidarité répare les êtres.

respect

Pour retrouver ce qui est dû à tous, ou bien y accéder pour la première fois : emploi, logement,
vie familiale, loisirs, culture, vacances…
Pour encourager les avancées.

dévouement

Aujourd'hui, demain, aussi longtemps qu'il le faudra. On est là,
pour que demeure le goût de vivre ou qu'il revienne ;
avec l'envie d'agir pour soi-même et pour les autres.

solidarité

SECOURS
POPULAIRE
FRANÇAIS

www.secourspopulaire.fr

Atelier de création graphique : Pierre Bernard 2005 – Photo : Nyl' Nandet – Rédaction : Nadia Montagne – RCS B 590 805 172

Cultural

The Salamander Theatre Company

Théâtre de la Salamandre
House style 1975–1982
Wordmark, posters,
news letters, stationery,
invitation cards,
programmes, brochures,
tour programmes, tickets,
stickers, advertisements,
postcards

In collaboration with
Gérard Paris-Clavel

The experimental theatre company Théâtre de la Salamandre, directed by Gildas Bourdet, was founded in 1969. In 1975 it was invited to the city of Tourcoing (pop. 100,000) in the north-west of France. There it became affiliated to the Centre Dramatique du Nord, then staging performances in thirty-three towns in the region. Bourdet invited other companies to join him in this enterprise, creating his own productions with La Salamandre in a former cinema and other venues in less central districts of the town. These performances attracted the attention of the national press and *Martin Eden* also had a successful run in Paris. By this time the Salamander Theatre Company had twenty full-time employees and a further thirty to fifty who were employed under annually renewable contracts. In the eighties, when the socialist government doubled the arts budget, La Salamandre was promoted to Théâtre National de la Région Nord/Pas-de-Calais and began to perform at Lille's premier theatre.

La Salamandre's performances and choice of repertoire were a reaction to prevailing French theatre practice. The plays the company performed were politically engaged, innovative and experimental, but also entertaining, anti-authoritarian and down to earth. 'Laughter from La Salamandre is a liberating weapon', *Le Monde* wrote, and: 'You can't take life too seriously: whatever happens, you won't come out of it alive.'

Despite national appreciation, La Salamandre continued to concentrate on establishing the theatre firmly in the region. In November 1976 we read in the *Journal du Théâtre de la Salamandre* (designed by Grapus) that the aim was to 'establish our work in a permanent and close rapport with the public of this region and to capture and retain a large and patient audience'. Bourdet saw the relationship with the theatre-going public as an ongoing dialogue. The theatre belonged in the heart of the city, for it was a *chose publique*. The company worked as a collective and wrote its own texts, but also performed repertory drama – some of it rewritten or adapted. 'Attempting to create our own theatre practice is to question our rapport with the world. It is, to paraphrase Ernst Bloch, to dream of the construction of a new world. Precisely because it is ephemeral, the theatre presents us with the first allegories of this new world.' [*Petit Journal* 1978].

At irregular intervals the theatre company published the *Petit Journal*, mailed free on request, designed by Grapus and printed by a local printer. Produced on four pages of newsprint, it appeared from 1977 to 1981, thirteen issues in all. The logo was red and yellow and was sometimes added to the newssheet as a sticker. The layout was based on two grids: one derived from Malevich (*Rostrum*, 1919), the other a regular pattern of squares. In either case the positioning of the text blocks sometimes does and sometimes does not adhere to the underlying grid, thus creating a contrast of order and disorder. In addition, the typeset texts contrast with pseudo-spontaneous handwriting in the margin. The layout was reinvented for each new issue. 'We disrupted the rules to find new ones', says Bernard. In the 1981/1982 season the group's enthusiasm for writing waned and Grapus even published an issue with blank columns.

In all, Bernard made about ten posters for the group. They all refer to something outside the picture they show: who is the man in the blurred photograph on the *Martin Eden* poster and what does he see? Who throws the tomato that explodes on the poster for a play by Labiche? From what heaven or hell are the shards hurtling down on *Les Précipitations*? Whose blood pollutes the gilded Versailles decor on the poster of *Britannicus*? What is the worker on the poster *Attention au travail* really doing, squatting down, his head on his arms, and his trousers around his knees? And who laced him up in coloured strings? Is he chained or does this colourful web suggest the force he will demonstrate as soon as he rises from his humble pose? The sex tragicomedy *Saperleau* lured the designer into a burlesque image that is unique in his oeuvre. What wrought-up character carries this megalomaniac and ridiculous dream of male potency in his briefs, a dream which, if you look at it more closely, is as fragile as an eggshell? What improbable love story brings together these two faces in a tender embrace on the *Derniers détails* poster?

What the posters for La Salamandre have in common is that they raise questions and give no answers; they are inviting and arouse curiosity. They are riddles for which the solutions can only be found in the theatre itself.

In 1975 the theatre was a new area for Grapus. The association with La Salamandre lasted until 1982. In all, Grapus worked for about twenty small theatre companies, but never for as long as with this one. 'As far as methods and goals were concerned, La Salamandre and Grapus had much in common', says Bernard: 'working as a collective, having a political and social conscience, thinking about and casting doubt on our own work, the playing and probing, the entertaining and questioning. With La Salamandre we weren't playing against the client but with them. At night we would go out fly-posting, it was like seizing the megaphone in the city. Today everything you see on the walls is institutionalized and conventional, there's money behind everything. In those days it was an investment of human energy and invention, and that came across to the passers-by who saw it.' [Boekraad 2006]

The major point of similarity was that the theatre company and the design collective saw their cultural work as a form of political activity in the public domain. In both cases there was a fading of the distinction between autonomous art and the performing arts. Both practised cultural productions as teamwork, for the Salamander Theater Company Bernard worked in close cooperation with Gérard Paris-Clavel. Grapus and La Salamandre regarded aesthetics and politics as falling within the ambit of the play: politics can not live without drama, and drama is always concerned with power. But in the theatre the power being wielded is not real, it is just an image of power and its effects. Compared with those who actually exercise power, actors and graphic designers tend to be subordinate, even if they are lords and masters within the boundaries of their own profession.

In the world of professional communication Grapus assumed the position of author, satirist, poet, polemicist or political commentator. In the wake of May 1968 actors too attacked the theatrical establishment. They began to write their own pieces, often as a collective, or they would undermine the dominance of the text on stage to reach a new balance of dramatic resources. In so doing they brought the

175

theatre close to the fine arts. Artists, in turn, discovered performance as a means of expression capable of abolishing the social isolation of both art and artists. From their socially marginalized position actors and designers were now able to comment on the world in which they and their audience lived, and to forge a bond with their audience, organizing them, albeit on a temporary basis, into a critical mass.

As observed above, what links graphic design and the theatre is the play. The play suspends reality. It creates an empty space in which the players can follow the logic of their questions, emotions and desires. They determine the stakes, the rules and the means by which the game is played. In a play a miniature society can be created which only exists in the time and space of the play itself. In the empty space of the play the players may become entangled or get lost, but they may also explore roles, trajectories and interactions that in the real world are blocked. It is this possibility of escaping factual reality that makes the play of language and image, of graphic design and theatre, so attractive and so indispensable. The play creates an illusion, but it is also a detour that sheds new light on the road followed so far and the road that can still be taken.

Was it coincidence that Grapus discovered the theatre world and found new congenial clients in about 1975, just when the prospect of real social change was declining? Theatre then offers a way of keeping alive a sense of hope.

Ten years earlier, in Poland, Bernard had observed in his mentor Henryk Tomaszewski (himself, as a teacher, a gifted actor) that theatre can act as a means of enduring a depressing sociopolitical reality. Tomaszewski's theatre posters threw off the strait-jacket of socialist realism and 'real' socialism. Many of Grapus's theatre posters fulfil a similar function, allowing us to escape the reality of real capitalism in which people flock to the fleshpots of Egypt.

Spring '80 Tourcoing
poster
The Salamander Theatre Company
113 × 75 / 1980

Théâtre de la Salamandre
Britannicus

Les clowns du Prato
La polka des saisons

Les tréteaux du midi
centre dramatique national
Dario Fo : "faut pas payer"

Jérome Deschamps
Les oubliettes

Jérome Deschamps
La petite chemise de nuit
(The little night shirt)

avec la collaboration de
la ville de Tourcoing

théâtre de
la salamandre
(20) 01 34 72
PRINTEMPS 80 TOURCOING

La Salamandre
magazine
The Salamander Theatre
Company
43 × 28 / 1976–1977

pp. 179-81
Petit journal de la Salamandre
newsletter, spread
The Salamander Theatre
Company
29.7 x 21 / 1978–1979

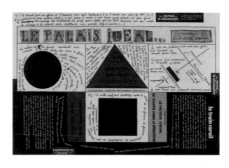

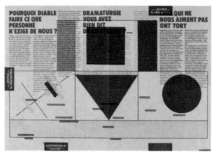

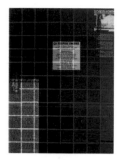

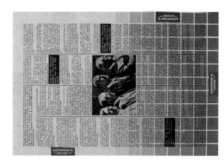

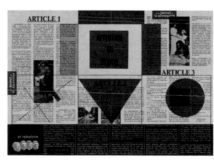

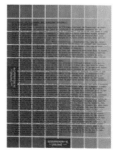

"(…) le travail fait ma gloire et l'honneur mon seul bonheur (…) A
Les visiteurs de mon palais idéal (…) ont peine à croire ce que leur
le ~~témoignage~~ témoignage des habitants du pays pour croire qu'u
le courage et la volonté pour construire un pareil chef-d'œ

LE PALAIS I

Le milieu de la façade représente une cascade. J'ai mis deux ans pour le faire, La petite grotte à côté, trois ans (…). A côté j'avais commencé un tombeau druide (…). J'ai mis quatre ans pour faire cette partie (…).

Le tombeau est dans le genre des temples hindous.

On y voit la vierge Marie, les quatres évangélistes, un calvaire, la mort et l'abandon, les pèlerins, des anges (…).

« S...
NS
L'OR,
...EVAL A ÉCRIT :

LE FACTEUR CHEVAL : « JE SU...

P.S - en mille n...
...jour au cimetière. Il con-
sacrera encore dix ans
à ce monument.

...de son

Ce n'est pas très clair ? Bon. Prenons un autre exemple : le Reader-Digest, Historia, le jeu des mille francs ou l'encyclopédie Alpha, c'est tout pour tous mais surtout tout pour moi si je réussis à en savoir plus qu'eux tous. Je vous le dis, le train corail c'est la possibilité d'envisager clairement et souverainement, si je le décide, ma responsabilité individuelle devant par exemple, et pourquoi pas, le travail, le chômage, la crise. Je n'ai pas peur des grands thèmes. Oui, je veux être seule, libre et coupable de la crise, comme on est seul face à la mort... Coupable mais responsable enfin.
Tiens, j'ai raté mon train. L'individualisme c'était à propos de « Martin Eden ». Il ne pourrait en aucun cas en être question dans un spectacle sur le travail.

combine, pour deve nir quelqu'un qui ne soit pas tout le monde

celui qui trouve la meilleure

LE FACTEUR CHEVAL

EST UN NASEAUCHISTE.

me suis-je dit (…)
…oient ; il leur faut
…omme ait pu avoir
…)

petit **journal** de **la salamandre**

Un moment de la préparation du prochain spectacle de la Salamandre sur le TRAVAIL : lecture commentée du Facteur Cheval.

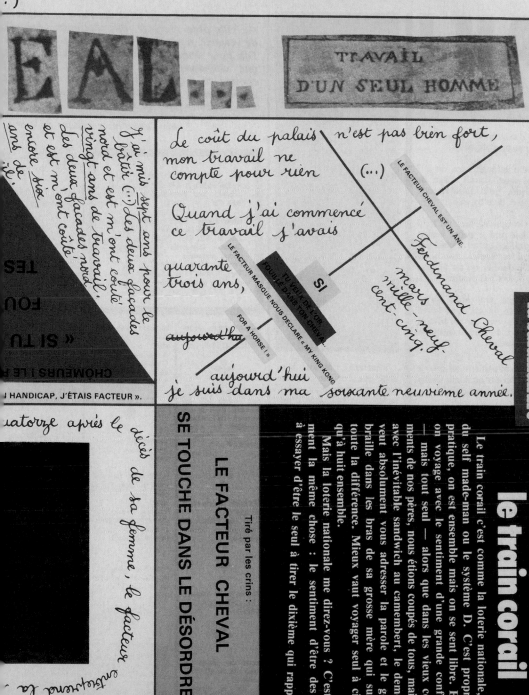

…EAL…

TRAVAIL
D'UN SEUL HOMME

J'ai mis sept ans pour le bâtir (…) les deux façades nord et est m'ont coûté vingt ans de travail, des deux façades nord et est m'ont coûté encore dix ans de …lé.

Le coût du palais n'est pas bien fort,
mon travail ne
compte pour rien   (…)

Quand j'ai commencé
ce travail j'avais

quarante
trois ans,

~~aujourd'hui~~

aujourd'hui
je suis dans ma soixante neuvième année.

LE FACTEUR CHEVAL EST UN ÂNE.

Ferdinand Cheval

mars
mille-neuf
cent-cinq.

LE FACTEUR MASQUE NOUS DECLARE « MY KING KONG

TU VEUX DE L'OR, FOUILLE DANS TON CHEVAL.

SI

FOR A HORSE ! »

TES

FOU…

« SI TU

CHOMEURS ! LE F…

J HANDICAP, J'ÉTAIS FACTEUR ».

…atorze après le décès de sa femme, le facteur

…entreprend la…

SE TOUCHE DANS LE DÉSORDRE

LE FACTEUR CHEVAL

Tiré par les crins :

petit **journal** de **la salamandre**

le train corail

Le train corail c'est comme la loterie nationale, le culte du self made-man ou le système D. C'est propre. C'est pratique, on est ensemble mais on se sent libre. En corail on voyage avec le sentiment d'une grande confraternité — mais tout seul — alors que dans les vieux compartiments de nos pères, nous étions coupés de tous, mais à huit, avec l'inévitable sandwich au camembert, le demeuré qui veut absolument vous adresser la parole et le gosse qui veut dans les bras de sa grosse mère qui sue. C'est toute la différence. Mieux vaut voyager seul à cinquante qu'à huit ensemble.

Mais la loterie nationale me direz-vous ? C'est exactement la même chose : le sentiment d'être des milliers à essayer d'être le seul à tirer le dixième qui rapporte des

millions. Quant au self-made-man, c'est la chance …

Martin Eden. Jack London
poster
The Salamander Theatre Company
109 × 73 / 1976

Focus on Labour
poster
The Salamander Theatre Company
152 × 107 / 1979

ATTENTION AU TRAVAIL

théâtre de
la salamandre

Le Saperleau
poster
The Salamander Theatre Company
77 × 101 / 1981

Brittanicus
poster
The Salamander Theatre
Company
78 × 113 / 1979

Last Details
poster
The Salamander Theatre Company
77 × 101 / 1981

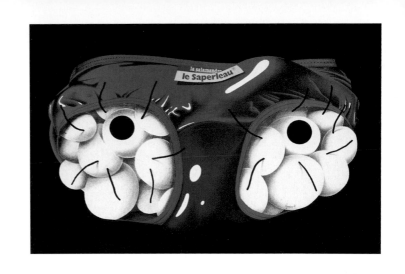

La Villette

House style for the
Parc de la Villette and
the institutions located
there 1984–1986
House style manuals, logo
posters, exhibitions, press
files and releases,
periodicals, programmes
invitations, invoices, order
forms, badges, key ring

The Parc de la Villette is one of the *Grands Travaux* undertaken under the presidency of François Mitterand (1981–1995). Continuing the French tradition of housing important public institutions in monumental buildings, they were also an attempt to give a massive boost to French cultural life and attune it to the requirements of the modern world. The notion of culture was expanded and defined as the sum total of 'the fine arts, music, science, technology and communication'. Design, then, is not listed as such, although it is implied.

As early as 1919, in the programme for the Bauhaus, Walter Gropius had taken the combination of technology, fine art and science as his point of departure for the new arts and design curriculum. [Wingler 1978] The modernist credo resonates in the ambitious cultural programme on which Mitterand's *Grand Travaux* were founded. Added to this credo was the new article of faith: communication. The city was defined as a medium of communication: the level, intensity and democratic content of communication were supposed to determine the quality of urban culture. Cultural politics became the vehicle of communication strategies.

A 1985 interim report proclaims that the *Grands Projets* 'create cultural, economic and scientific networks of communication across the entire territory of France. Therein lies the real importance of projects launched or supported by the State.' [*Grands Projets 1979–1989*, 1985]

The Parc de la Villette fits seamlessly into this concept. It combines a *Cité des Sciences et de l'Industrie* with a *Cité de la Musique* (which includes a conservatoire and a concert hall). The Park was designed to serve both experts and researchers and the public at large. The political intention behind the plan was to bring diverse groups together. The expectation that this would lead to a new definition of citizenship added a utopian dimension to it.

The Parc de la Villette was supposed to act as a link between the city and the suburbs to the north and east of Paris. The site was once home to a livestock market that had to be closed because of the ongoing urbanization of the area. Under the presidency of Valéry Giscard d'Estaing (1974–1981) the government had planned, for the site of the cattle market, an abattoir – a certain logic cannot be denied – and work on a gigantic concrete building had already started when Mitterrand was elected president. The new government of socialists and communists stopped the work on the public slaughterhouse and approved the creation of an entirely new urban amenity, a city park in which nature and industrial civilization, science and art, education and recreation were to be integrated.

In 1983 the Swiss architect Bernard Tschumi designed the ground plan for this area of 35 hectares. He based his plan upon point, line and plane, referring to the visual grammar outlined by Kandinsky in his book *Punkt und Linie zu Fläche* [1926/1955] [English translation *Point and Line to Plane*, New York 1947]. Kandinsky summarizes in this book part of his teachings at the Bauhaus, where he had been appointed *Meister* in 1922. Although the subtitle declares it to be a 'contribution to the analysis of the elements of painting', large parts of it are relevant to design disciplines, as Max Bill remarked in the preface of the 1955 reprint. The grammar of the Bauhaus, the first modern design academy (Bernard has often expressed his regret that it had so minimal an impact on French design), inspired Grapus in their invention of the visual identity of the Park.

The most important institutions in the park are the *Cité des Sciences et de l'Industrie* and the *Cité de la Musique*. The commissioning agency, the *Etablissement public du Parc de la Villette*, is the umbrella organization that is responsible both for these institutes and for the park. In 1984 it invited Grapus and five other studios, among them Pentagram (UK) and Total Design (Netherlands), to participate in the limited competition for the Park's house style.

For Grapus this project was a turning point in their design practice and a redefinition of their position in the public domain. Now the studio was moving away from a stance in the counterculture to work within the framework of the cultural policy of the State. By selecting Grapus, the commissioning authority was bringing the studio's oppositional visual language and communication strategies within the boundaries of official culture. As would become clear in the years that followed, not all members of the collective were happy with the new orientation. Apart from the political implications, the eventual rejection of this type of institutional communication commissions by Bernard's partners in Grapus may have had something to do with the working style which it forces upon the designer. For two whole years, a team of twelve Grapus designers spent two-thirds of their time working on the La Villette project (there was more to the job than just the four house styles). To lead a team like this for such a long period of time and simultaneously to deal with the commissioning authorities required an attitude and discipline, qualities and abilities quite different from what had been needed for the direct, short-term, often campaign- or event-oriented assignments which had been predominant in the group's output during its first decade. It was during the work on this commission that the first cracks in the collective began to appear, due to divergence on both political, organizational and professional matters. They did not become final, however, until Bernard accepted to work on another institutional project: the house style for the Louvre.

The house style for La Villette was designed to symbolize the politically desirable integration of the various institutions, each with its own operational independence, on a single site and under a single public entity. Accordingly it became a multi-layered identity programme on three levels: (1) the umbrella house style; (2) styles for the three individual institutes and (3) styles for the individual buildings with specific functions. The problem for the designers was finding a graphic system that assured a balance between La Villette as a whole and its component parts.

As his starting point for the logo Bernard took the typeface Michel Quarez had chosen for the park at an earlier stage, a somewhat angular architectural typeface that was both primitive and refined. Three letters of the word 'Villette' were replaced with the basic geometric forms of triangle, square and circle, in green, red and blue. The green triangle, which functions as a capital V, dominates by its size

187

and negates *en passant* the red, yellow and blue colour dogma of the Bauhaus. Bernard's team researched these elementary forms in depth, the results being assembled in compact and erudite visual essays which were presented to the client in support of the design proposal.

The three shapes represent the three components of La Villette: the Park (green triangle), the Cité des Sciences et de l'Industrie (red square) and the Cité de la Musique (blue circle). In the logo for La Villette as a whole the three geometric figures are all 'illuminated'. In posters announcing the activities of the various institutes, the logo always appears along one of the four edges, forming a constant framework for varying images and announcements.

For the individual buildings in the park, such as the *Géode* and the *Zénith*, Grapus designed separate symbols. The most famous of these became the symbol for the Great Hall, an improbably elongated cow that transplants the shape of the building into the animal kingdom and revives the collective memory of the old livestock market.

In modernist house styles the playful and creative element usually disappears completely in the final result. Efficiency, functionality and standardization seem to be incompatible with humour and poetry. The bureaucratic context in which they function and the instrumental rationality they serve and demonstrate do not invite unpredictable, subjective or expressive gestures. The house style for La Villette reconciles play and technology. The typographical code of the International Style is masterfully applied, but Bernard and his team escape its elegantly packaged rigour. At one stroke Bernard takes possession of the box of tricks of the late-modernist house style designer and casts it nonchalantly aside. Just as in the proposal for Rotterdam/Cultural Capital of Europe (1999) the geometric structure is first and foremost a trap for capturing living images.

It's here: La Villette
poster
La Villette
120 × 160 / 1985

Logotypes
La Villette Park
The Centre for Science and Industry
The Music Centre
Etablissement public de La Villette
1985

La Villette. Map of the site
Drawing by the La Villette Park Office
1994

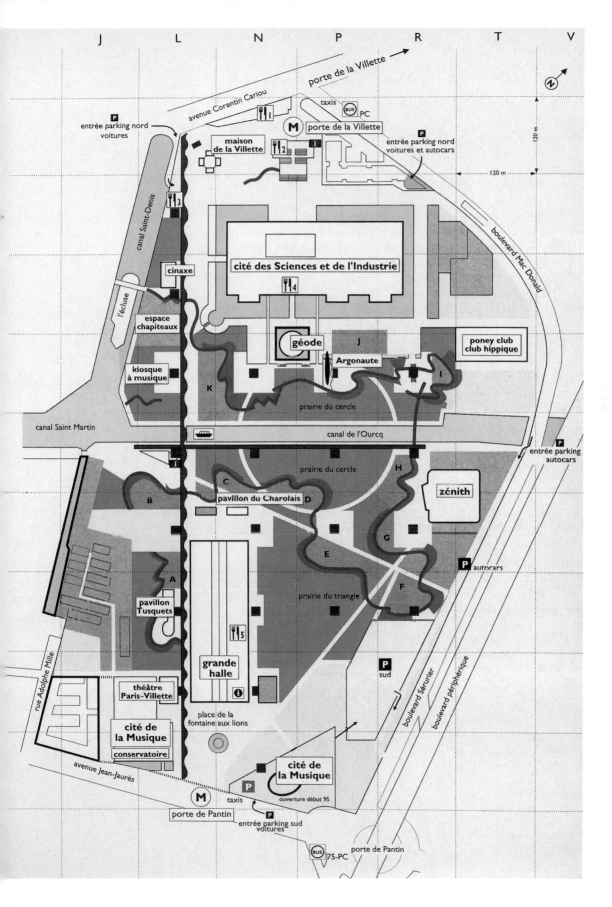

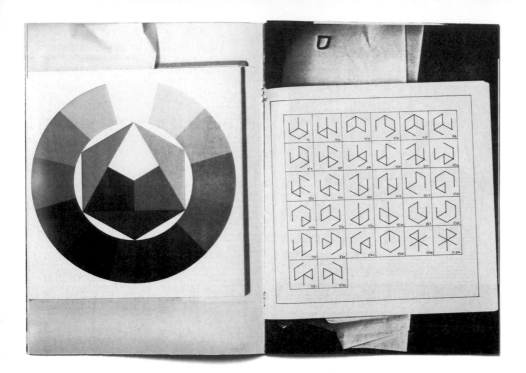

L'ESPACE UTILE

Spreads of three visual essays on the triangle,
the square and the circle
preliminary research for the logotypes of
La Villette
29.7 × 21 / 1985

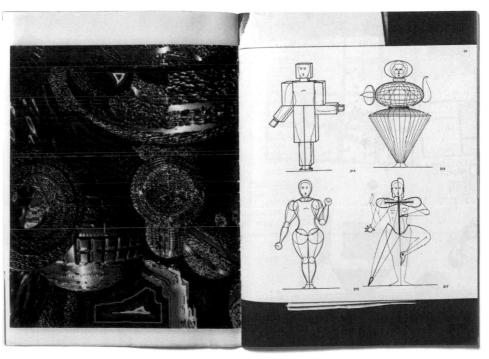

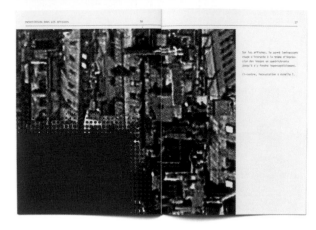

Design Standards Manual
cover and spreads
Centre for Science and Industry
29.7 × 21 / 1986

La Villette
project for a poster showing symbols designed for
all the different entities of the park
(independent production)
60 × 40 / 1986

pp. 196-7
Printed matter for the four institutes of La Villette

194

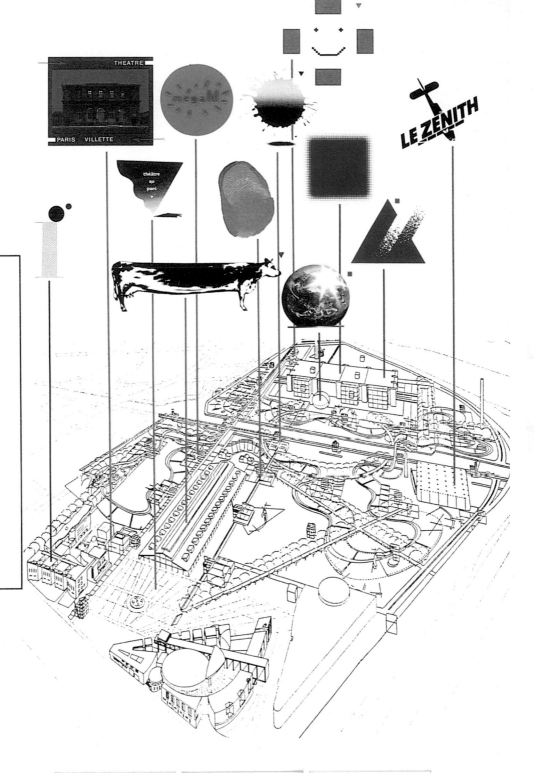

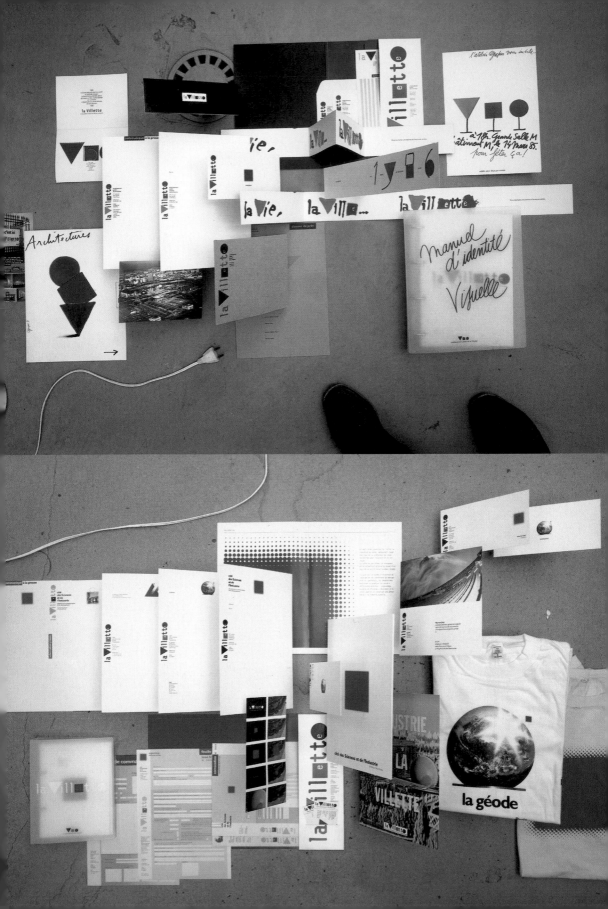

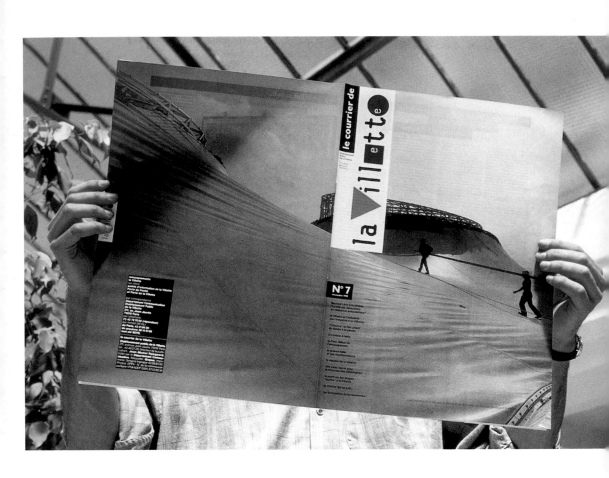

Le courrier de La Villette
magazine
42 × 29.7 / 1985

La Villette 1986
New Year card
7 × 21 / 1986

The Pompidou Centre

Graphic communication programme for the Pompidou Centre 2001–today Posters in various sizes, tarpaulin banners, admission tickets, invitations, New Year cards, programmes, exhibition folders, magazines and maps

The Pompidou Centre, officially named the Centre national d'art et de culture Georges Pompidou, housed in the famous high-tech building designed by Renzo Piano and Richard Rogers in the heart of Paris, opened its doors in 1977. The Centre is devoted mainly to the fine arts of the twentieth century but also presents such disciplines as architecture and design, photography and film, theatrical arts and literature.

The building has museum and exhibition spaces and a large library as well as cinemas, concert halls and theatres, lecture halls and children's workshops. Bookshops and restaurants are open to visitors. Renovation of the building and its immediate surroundings took place between 1995 and 2000. Currently the Centre attracts about six million visitors a year.

The emblem for the Pompidou Centre was designed in the mid seventies by Jean Widmer as part of a house style that was never applied as a coherent system. [Margot Rouard-Snowman 1995] The emblem is a graphic abstraction of the front facade in which six horizontal lines – the floors – are cut diagonally by the jointed double line representing the escalator.

Many other designers also worked for the Centre for shorter or longer periods: among them were Roman Cieslewicz (posters and catalogue covers), Ruedi Baur (signage) and Pierre Bernard (temporary house style and facade lettering during the renovation). For the reopening of the building in 2000 Baur designed the *typogram* of the Centre, a two-line composition of the wordmark in the sans serif DIN (Deutsches Institut für Normung). Developed in 1906 by Prussian railways for use on their rolling stock, DIN is a typical example of 'engineer's typography', a design that has neither echoes of the history of book typography nor any ornamental or representational ambitions. It suits the industrial character of a building that rebels against its historic surroundings, and a public institution that has an extensive and dynamic programme aimed at a very broad public. The wordmark consists of the words 'Centre Pompidou' placed one above the other, with the second line indented. It combines easily with the Widmer emblem, in which the diagonal also suggests an indentation. On posters only the wordmark is used as the Centre's signature.

In the spring of 2001 the Atelier de Création Graphique won the limited competition to design a graphic communication programme for the Centre. The programme, built on the emblem and the wordmark designed by Widmer and Baur, added a typographic programme, a colour wheel, a standard format, and photographic reproduction of artworks. The programme covered all the Centre's printed matter with the exception of stationery, internal documents and catalogues. Also outside the remit were signage, the website and exhibition graphics. In other words this is not an all-inclusive house style, something the Pompidou Centre never had. The publications, posters and invitations that did come under it were surveyed in a profusely illustrated eighty-page booklet, *L'Image du Centre* [2005], which clearly explains the intention and structure of the programme. I draw on this publication for quotations and factual information about the project, which has now been in progress for seven years.

For printed matter, Bernard extended the colour palette for the building's existing signage system with orange and purple. 'By giving itself six "crayons" the graphic aesthetic gains a new freedom and allows itself to use colour on all media', he says. In the programmes of the Centre colour is not just an aesthetic pleasure and ornamental addition, it is also a functional means of visualizing the passage of time over the seasons and years. Here colour provides orientation.

However, the axis around which the Centre's graphic identity turns is the condensed DIN. This extensive type family is characterized by functionality and monumentality. Its many sizes and weights make it possible to introduce a hierarchy into complex information, and to reserve certain categories for specific kinds of printed matter (all in all, the communication programme contains no fewer than twenty), without detriment to the stylistic unity of the whole. The monumental character of the typeface, which does not refer to cultural or social distinction, led the studio to ascribe to the printed matter set in it a 'harmonious authority'. The A5 format (21 × 15 cm) is a convenient size for both invitation cards and seasonal programmes.

In the treatment of images, the Atelier's attitude is strict. As a matter of principle it distinguishes between a work of art and its photographic reproduction. This allows the typography to run through or over the image where this is necessary or desirable – something that many still see as sacrilege.

This extensive programme was the first project in which Bernard used typography to create an institutional communication system. All printed matter emanating from the Pompidou Centre is recognizable as coming from the same institution. That it doesn't drown in monotony is due to the sophistication with which the system is employed, and to the functional but sometimes unabashedly decorative use of colour. In the preliminary and final pages of publications the Atelier is particularly fond of using colour gradients, which can give an air of luxury to an otherwise functional presentation of information. However, the risk of monotony is avoided primarily by the wealth of pictorial matter. The graphic identity of the Centre acts as a stage on which a never-ending parade of persons, images, events and activities appear before the footlights. It is they who create, in their colourful succession and variety, the true identity of the Centre.

The typographic system is a kind of recipe, with which a range of delicacies can be prepared. Some standardization in the design of institutional printed matter is unavoidable, given the volume of information it carries. Where the flow is channelled through clear editorial formulas, the systematic application of graphic variables is not a sign of laziness or looking for easy graphic solutions but more a matter of tailoring the design to suit the way the information will be used by the

201

laissez
Centre passer
Pompidou

New Year card
Pompidou Centre, Paris
21 × 15 / 2004

Museum pass
Pompidou Centre, Paris
5 × 8.5 / 2002

reader. Legibility varies with the purpose and the nature of the text. Giving printed matter a graphic identity facilitates the task of the reader to make a choice from such an extensive menu.

Within this system, Bernard makes a distinction between informational and communicative documents. In informational documents such as quarterly programmes, educational booklets and periodicals like *Revues parlées*, *Cinéma* and *Spectacles vivants*, it is the typography of the text that plays the leading role. In these publications, in which the information function is paramount, a standardized layout prevails with no interaction between text, reproductions and white space.
The content is structured by an editorial format, the form by a typographical grid. Where editorial format and grid are well matched, constantly changing information and data can be presented in a manageable and clear manner. Within the grid, the pictorial matter functions as visual information. The typographical system delivers a repeatable and programmable format whose content is periodically renewed. The specific application of this system can be entrusted to the studio staff in a prearranged division of tasks.

Communicative documents – posters, invitations and banners on the facades of the building – are different, both in character and function. These elements are a smaller but vital component of the programme. In documents of this kind a strong and characteristic image plays the main role, to which the typography (e.g. the name of the artist or exhibition title) is adjusted. Here we do have an interaction between text and image. The text is integrated differently in each design in a manner based on subtle, content-driven choices of colour, colour gradients, transparency, position and size. Typographically, on the posters the DIN capitals play the main role. But they dont 'contaminate' the image. Through a clever play of different degrees of transparency they may be in the foreground, or partially disappear into the space of the image. On the Max Beckmann poster the painter's name is clearly in front of the self-portrait; on Jean Dubuffet's self-portrait the lettering of the name is partly hidden by hatched parts of the figure. On other posters (e.g. Nicolas de Staël) the texture of the painting's surface shows through the letters. The colour of the DIN capitals sometimes contrasts with a background and sometimes blends into it (e.g. Cocteau, Alors La Chine).

The distinction between communication and information is relevant from the point of view of the designer, but not pertinent theoretically. As Robin Kinross has demonstrated with telephone books and railway timetables, even information that seems to be purely factual has its rhetorical side. [Kinross 1985] Of the means of persuasion identified by classical rhetoric – *ethos* (character), *pathos* (emotion) and *logos* (reason) – the first two at first sight do not play a role in informational printed matter. The speaker's character as perceived by the audience, the style and emotional charge of personal speech are absent. Ethos and pathos are not missing however, even if they are not related to a natural person but to a legal person: the institution offering the information. The informational printed matter designed by the Atelier de Création Graphique really does create an image of the Pompidou Centre: it convinces the visitor that he is entering an efficiently and rationally run public institution for which values such as openness, diversity, continuity and dynamism are of the highest importance.

The Surrealist Revolution
tarpaulin banner
Pompidou Centre, Paris
1200 × 900 / 2002

LA RÉVOLUTION
SURRÉALISTE

Centre
Pompidou

www.centrepompidou.fr

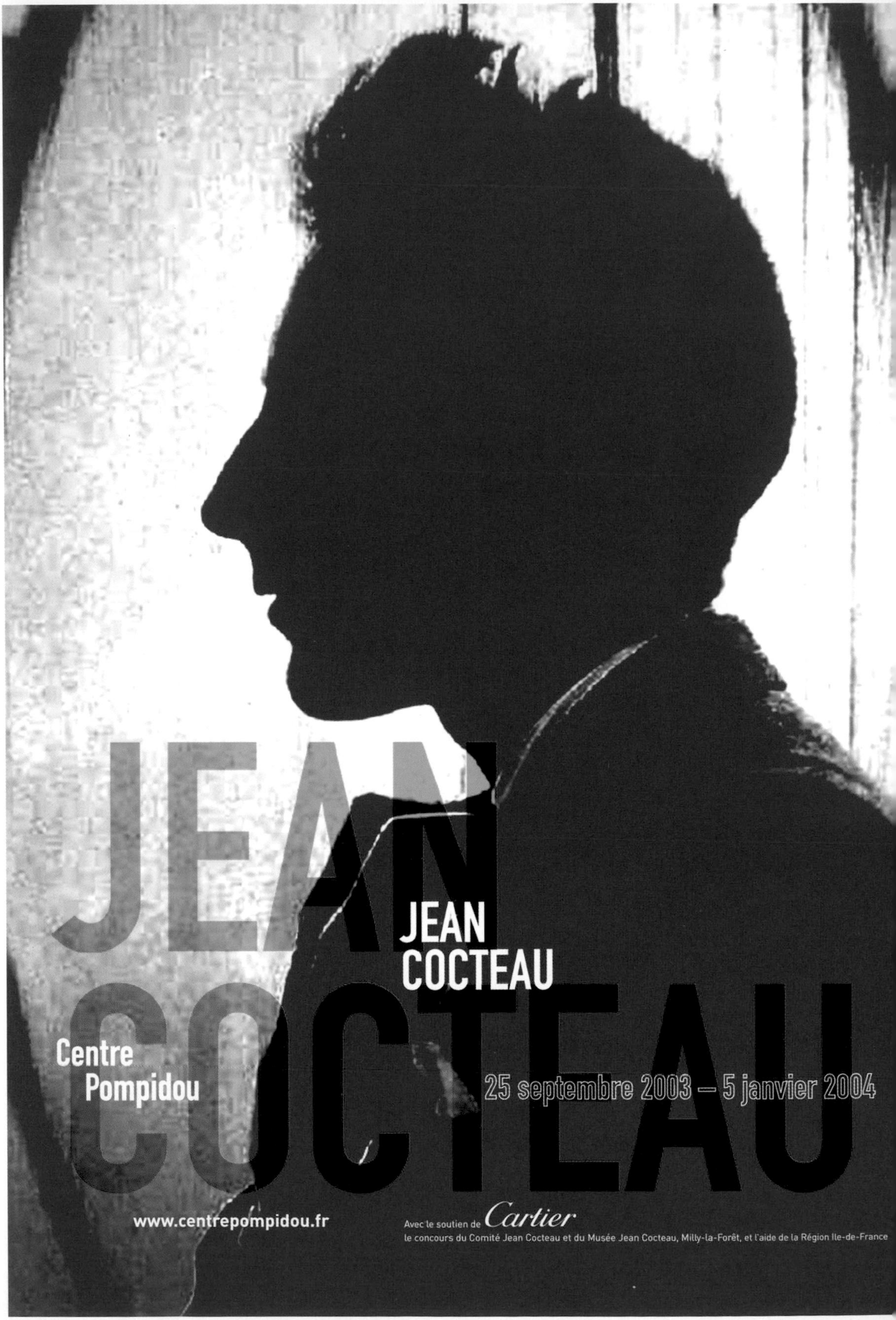

JEAN
COCTEAU

JEAN

COCTEAU

Centre
Pompidou

25 septembre 2003 — 5 janvier 2004

www.centrepompidou.fr

Avec le soutien de *Cartier*
le concours du Comité Jean Cocteau et du Musée Jean Cocteau, Milly-la-Forêt, et l'aide de la Région Ile-de-France

Jean Cocteau
poster
Pompidou Centre, Paris
176 × 120 / 2003

Invitation cards
Pompidou Centre, Paris
21 × 15 / 2003–2004

JEAN
DUBUFFET

CY
TWOMBLY

MARLENE
DUMAS

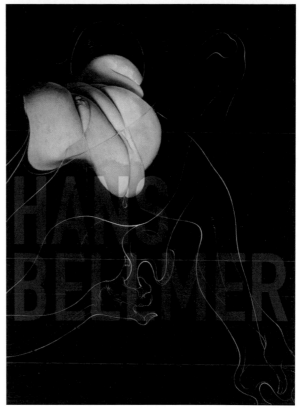

Invitation cards
Pompidou Centre, Paris
21 × 15 / 2003–2004

pp. 210-11
What's next, China?
poster
Pompidou Centre, Paris
300 × 400 / 2004

209

ALORS,
LA CHINE?

25 juin – 13 octobre 2003

mai
juin
juillet
Centre août 2003
Pompidou

novembre
Centre décembre 2002
Pompidou

p. 214
Exhibition folders
Pompidou Centre, Paris
21 × 15 / 2001–2005

Forthcoming events
Front and back covers
Pompidou Centre, Paris
21 × 15 / 2002–2003

p. 215
Banners
Pompidou Centre, Paris
2800 × 180 / 2003–2004

212

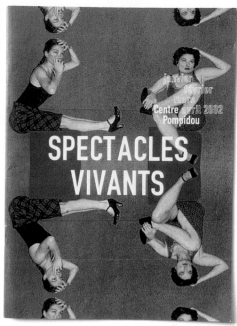

SPECTACLES VIVANTS

À VENIR
SEPTEMBRE-NOVEMBRE

ANDREI TARKOVSKI
RÉTROSPECTIVE INTÉGRALE

MICHAEL SNOW

RUTH BECKERMANN
DANS LE CADRE DU MOIS
DU DOCUMENTAIRE

L'ÉCRAN DES ENFANTS

LES CINÉMAS DE DEMAIN
TECHNO WEB

TOUR DU MONDE DU WEB:
JAPON
17 OCTOBRE

FILMS DE DANSE
5 SEPTEMBRE
3 OCTOBRE
7 NOVEMBRE

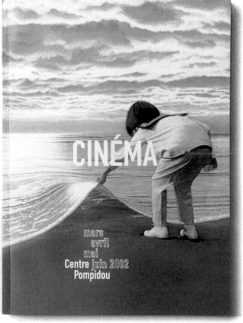

CINÉMA

mars
avril
mai
Centre juin 2002
Pompidou

213

National heritage

The Louvre

House style for the Louvre
Museum, 1989–1993
Logotype and graphic
identity programme:
stationery, publications,
catalogues and posters

In collaboration with
Dirk Behage and
Fokke Draaijer

Housed in the former royal palace in Paris, the Louvre Museum with its collection of 350,000 works is the most important national museum in France, and the third largest in the world. In 1989, the year in which Bernard designed the house style, it received more than four million visitors. Four out of five were tourists, the majority from other countries. To channel this enormous stream of visitors, a new entrance was opened in 1987: the spectacular glass pyramid designed by architect I.M. Pei which leads to a large underground entrance hall. On the occasion of its bicentenary in 1993 the museum was extended with the Richelieu Wing, formerly used by the Ministry of Finance.

In 1983 the Grand Louvre became an independent public institution, under the authority of the Ministry of Culture. This created greater autonomy and necessitated an internal reorganization: a central management was created above the seven department directors under the leadership of Michel Laclotte. The managerial reorganization was the first step in the expansion and restructuring of the Louvre, one of Mitterand's *Grands Projets*.

Grapus was invited to enter a limited competition for a new logo. Behind closed doors there was fierce argument about this commission, which some of the group's members were reluctant to accept. Bernard was the only one to speak in favour of the proposed assignment: 'Unlike other members of the group who only wanted to design for political causes, I believed that graphic communication could be an instrument for social change when applied to cultural institutions. … I didn't want to support the cliché that the Louvre was a place of order, reverence and boredom. I wanted to claim the wealth of the museum as the property of the French people, not the property of a cultural elite'. [Vienne 1999, p. 62] This difference of opinion hastened the disintegration of Grapus. In 1991 Bernard founded a new studio, the Atelier de Création Graphique, with two Dutch designers, Dirk Behage and Fokke Draaijer. They continued the work for the Louvre until 1993. By the time the project ended Bernard and his associates had carried out several other design commissions for the museum.

Before the contract was awarded to Bernard, the wayfinding system for the museum had been designed by the American agency Carbone Smolan Associates. The desirability of integrating signage and identity programme – standard practice when it comes to house styles for such institutions – was seemingly not obvious to the Louvre, despite the international level on which it operates. Ironically enough, Ken Carbone was a member of the panel that selected Bernard to create the museum's graphic identity.

The present logo with the clouds was the second design by the studio. A first version, a double equilateral triangle, inspired by but not identical to the triangle of Pei's pyramid, was vetoed by Pei. The architect had had it written into his contract with the Louvre that only *his* triangle could be used in the museum's representation.

The logo is a photographic image of clouds in grey, black and white, combined with a monumental typeface that refers to a classic French font, Granjon. In the heart of the wordmark, invisibly caught between the U and the V, it is still possible to discern the rejected triangle of the first design. Pei's pyramid is also present in another way: not its own form but the reflection of the cloudy Parisian sky in its glass panels inspired the design of the logo.

The cloudy sky is a section of a larger whole. It is a symbolic and indexical sign. It makes reference to Romantic art in which clouded skies were seen by such figures as John Ruskin as the very essence of painting, and at the same time to an indetermination and the passage of time, to dreams and fragility. The airiness of the photographic image contrasts with the monumentality, historicity and solidity of the letters. The logo is an impossible figure: letters that have been carved in or out of clouds. It is this paradoxical connection, which we might call volatile marble, that gives the emblem its poetic power.

In the stationery the cloud is used twice over: it floats as it were over the paper which is marked by the logo. The cloud is both sky and sign in the sky, background and figure at once.

On the calling cards of employees of individual museum departments a corner is cut out of the rectangular logo to indicate that they are attached to a part of the museum rather than to the central organization. In this way an asymmetry is introduced by which the classical formal language of the wordmark is broken again.

In publications of the Louvre, a combination of Granjon and Univers typefaces was used. In the catalogues, guides, brochures and posters the formal typography contrasts conspicuously with the playful disposition of the images. In this clear typography we discern the influence of Dutch graphic design, in the person of Dirk Behage.

The house style of the Louvre is characterized by a diversity of representational forms, depending upon the communicative objectives. Thus the *Petit Quoniam*, the small guide intended to offer a simple introduction for the general public and the least expensive booklet produced by the Louvre, was designed with particular care. The high quality of this mass product reflects Bernard's aim of presenting cultural wealth as attractively and accessibly as possible. The strict organization of the grid determines the position of the texts, while the images float freely across the spreads. The positioning of the images creates tension between them: they regard one another, as it were, and enter into dialogue. The *mise-en-page* becomes a *mise-en-scène*. The logo figures prominently on the cover, with masterpieces from the museum collection distributed around it like diamonds in a sky.

Other representational forms of the Louvre are seen in the brochure of 1990 in which the most famous painting in the museum, the *Mona Lisa*, is depicted within the format of the logo. Inside, the organizational structure of the museum is shown in a chart, the building both in isometric plans and on a panoramic photograph which shows its urban surroundings. On a postage stamp the logo is combined with a photograph of the building.

The 1991 poster for promoting a pass for young people is constructed from four images on which four verbs are printed diagonally: 'connaître, partager, découvrir, aimer' (know, share, discover, love). These words concisely summarize the museum's objectives. They also describe the values affirmed in the house style.

Bernard: 'If I work for a large institution like the Louvre, the idea of grandeur is at stake. As a designer I try to arouse that feeling in the public. I find it very interesting to arouse that feeling of grandeur and luxury that can be stimulated by considering works of art. The observer's eyes receive an impression of visual wealth, an emotion that has no connection with his or her own economic situation. The wealth with which I confront the public can be appropriated by that public. This wealth refers to desire and pleasure, to the possibility of happiness. … you introduce them to a particular imaginary world and invite them to use their imagination.' [Boekraad 1993, in: He 2006, p. 191] Bernard's redefinition of wealth has a double purpose. He dismisses the aesthetics of poverty that for a long time was common in leftist circles, and polemicizes against a puritan tradition, particularly strong in northern Europe, that elevates sobriety to a virtue and condemns wealth as a source of waste and seduction.

In Bernard's eyes, the *petite histoire* of the Louvre's house style reveals the distance between the potential of graphic design and the actual role that it plays in French culture: 'The house style of the Louvre gives us an insight into French design culture. In countries that have a developed design culture, the commissioning of a house style and its establishment in a manual, its implementation and its maintenance, are phases of a single process. In France it is different. Once the house style has been designed and used in a few productions, the matter is closed; the house style as such is no longer a live issue. From this we may deduce that graphic design is not really accepted and integrated into French culture. If you go to the Louvre now, fifteen years later, you won't see much of the house style. Only certain components are still functioning. Now there are gigantic reproductions of paintings defacing the front of the building, even more gigantic than the usual advertisements in the city. As a result the Louvre no longer sets itself apart as a prime example of a public institution.' [Boekraad 2006]

Logo of the Louvre Museum, Paris
1989

LOUVRE

Business cards and note cards
Louvre Museum, Paris
5.8×9 and 10×21 / 1989

Stationery
Louvre Museum, Paris
29.7×21 / 1989

MINISTÈRE DE LA CULTURE DE LA COMMUNICATION DES GRANDS TRAVAUX ET DU BICENTENAIRE

LOUVRE

Département

des Arts Graphiques

MINISTÈRE DE LA CULTURE DE LA COMMUNICATION DES GRANDS TRAVAUX ET DU BICENTENAIRE

LOUVRE

Administration Générale

Mu
34
750
Télé
Télé

Musée du Louvre
34-36 Quai du Louvre
75058 Paris Cedex 01
Téléphone (1) 40 20 50 50
Télécopie (1) 42 60 45 42

Isometric plan of the palace
Based on a drawing by the
communications
department of the Louvre

Winckelmann,
An art history
invitation to a conference
Louvre Museum, Paris
10×21 / 1990

Corporate brochure
Louvre Museum, Paris
22×21 / 1990

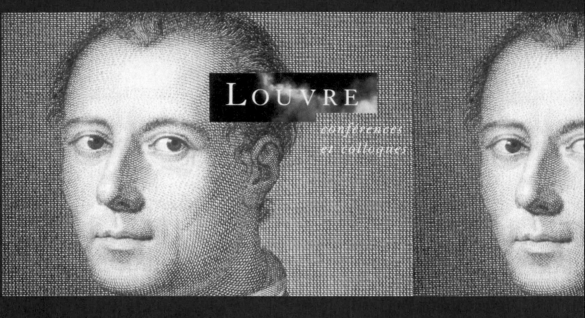

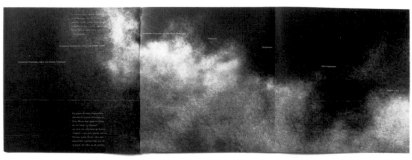

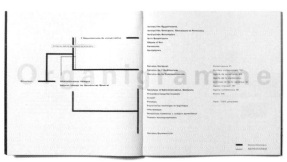

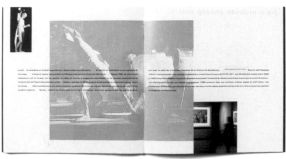

Previous small museum guide, the *Petit Quoniam*
design: Bruno Pfäffli
Louvre Museum, Paris
18.1 × 18.5 / 1983

New museum guide, the *Petit Quoniam*
Louvre Museum, Paris
22 × 21 / 1989

— Préparez votre visite avec nous

LOUVRE 40 20 51 77
Service culturel

Prepare your visit with us
poster
Department of Cultural Promotion
of the Louvre Museum, Paris
60 × 40 / 1989

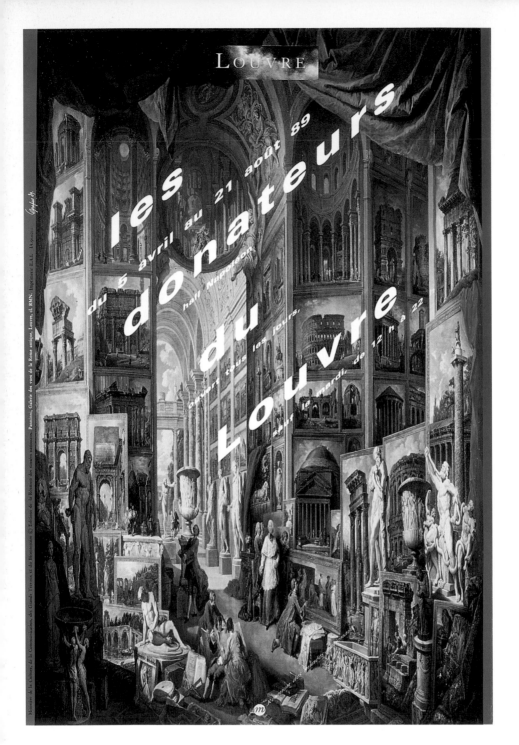

The Benefactors of the Louvre
poster
Louvre Museum, Paris
150 × 100 / 1989

Know, Share, Discover, Love
poster promoting a museum pass
for young people
Louvre Museum, Paris
150 × 100 / 1991

National Parks of France

House style 1989–1996
Emblem, stationery, folder
maps, wayfinding system
information panels,
pictograms, flags, badge,
uniform

In collaboration with
Dirk Behage and
Fokke Draaijer

In 1960 the French parliament decided to establish national parks. In so doing
the State recognized the exceptional quality of some of the country's unspoiled
environment and assumed responsibility, with local communities, for maintaining
their quality. The first national park was inaugurated in 1963; there are now seven,
with three more in preparation. The national parks come under the Ministry of the
Environment and have their own scientific staff.

These natural monuments are considered, like historical monuments, to be part
of the national heritage. The primary objective of the parks is the protection and
conservation of the biodiversity of the landscape and its flora, fauna and eco-
systems. However, it is also part of their responsibility to manage and maintain the
cultural heritage, helping inter alia to combat depopulation, promote traditional
skills and crafts and create environmentally friendly tourism. Also included in their
task is educating the public to develop a responsible and careful attitude towards
nature.

France's national parks function as a model for the country's nature conservation
policy. In addition to the seven national parks, about forty regional parks have been
established. In 2004 the government recognized the Environment Charter (*Charte
de l'environnement*), which in ten articles sets out the rights and duties of French
citizens and institutions regarding the environment. The Charter will eventually be
incorporated into the constitution of the Republic.

The creation of the seventh park, La Guadeloupe, in 1989, prompted the desire to
create a common visual identity to represent the national parks as a coherent
ensemble. The limited competition was won by the Atelier de Création Graphique.

A remarkable feature of this house style is its scope. Not long after the successful completion of the comprehensive house style of the Musée d'Orsay by Jean
Widmer and Bruno Monguzzi (1983–1987), the Atelier de Création Graphique
succeeded in transforming the original assignment – seven logos for seven parks –
into a house style in which the parks' public relations, wayfinding system, printed
matter and objects all combine to create a whole. Bernard took Massimo Vignelli's
graphic identity system for the US National Park Service as a professional benchmark to convince the client of the desirability of an integrated approach. The
implementation proceeded in phases and the design process was completed in
1996 with a three-volume manual. Part 1 addressed the emblem, logos and
stationery, part 2 the publications, clothing and objects, part 3 the wayfinding
system. Since then the ACG has designed the national parks' annual calendars.

Bernard's approach to this commission was characteristic of his design method.
Rather than coming up with prefabricated proposals, he first familiarized himself
thoroughly with the parks and gained an understanding of the organization's culture
by talking to those who worked for it. He analysed their communication problems
and needs, and used the self-image, expertise, skills and attitudes of the employees
as a guideline for the design. His starting point was the rich iconography of the flora
and fauna of the parks. He carefully studied the photographic records kept by both
scientific and non-scientific staff in order to understand their way of seeing things,

their interpretation of the qualities of their professional surroundings. In the presentation of his proposals, he showed the famous tapestries of *La Dame à la Licorne* (The Lady and the Unicorn) in the Musée de Cluny, a series of paradisiacal representations of nature from the fifteenth century in which its wealth and mystery are beautifully portrayed. We recognize these elements in the emblem that the Atelier designed for the parks.

The extraordinary spiral emblem and its unusual features are discussed in the notes on the images at the beginning of this book (p. 22). The archetype of the spiral is an appropriate choice as a symbol for areas that have been inhabited for millennia. The spiral evokes the notion of continuous motion. Both the expansive and cyclical character of natural processes can be projected on it as well as the semantic values of continuity within change. These ideas also tie in with the intergenerational perspective of sustainability that is the core of ecological values.

The emblem is the opposite of an unequivocal logo. Without being an illustration or pictogram, it evokes the parks' exceptional biodiversity. As a supersign it embraces and absorbs the many sub-signs of which it is composed: the silhouettes of animals and plants. The effect of this absorption is that the individual silhouettes lose what makes them unique: their immediately recognizable contours. Note too that the logo is monochromatic and in no way imitates the colours of the fauna and flora. Legible as either form or counter-form, it emphasizes its character as a graphic symbol, but it is far removed from the geometric visual language and typographic styling that dominated logotypes in the Swiss style. It underlines the universal rather than the national values of the parks. On flags and on the badge worn by the park rangers a reference to the French flag is created by placing the emblem on a blue background and adding an upright red bar. This endows it with a dimension of grandeur and legal authority which, by itself, it entirely lacks.

In the designers' thinking this emblem would only be used outside the parks, since inside the parks visitors are already surrounded by the wealth of nature that it evokes. In practice it is now being stuck onto virtually everything, even inside the parks, so that it has effectively been degraded to the status of a trademark. Bernard: 'In the [job for the] parks we tried to create a complex emotional image in which one could lose oneself – just as one can lose oneself in pictures of our own planet. We then put this emotional vision into a context which is totally functional, to allow as many people as possible to have the great emotional pleasure of visiting the parks.' [Poynor 1991, p. 12] Brief and to the point, Bernard identifies the two dimensions of this house style: symbolic representation and functional efficacy.

The house style uses a combination of two fonts: Sabon and the sans serif Mol. The logo of each park is made up of the emblem, its own name in Mol and the subtitle 'Parc National' in Sabon. Once again the emblem is in black and white, but the name of the park is printed in the Pantone colour decreed by the house style. The brochure in which the new style was launched claims that the seven Pantone colours evoke the diversity of colours in nature. This assertion falls somewhat short when it comes to its factual basis. It could only have come from a city-dweller and it gives the palette too much credit. Pantone colours are as far from natural colour as is the monochrome of the emblem. Otherwise, for a design proposal of this complexity, the brochure is a model of sober and convincing presentation.

The elegant Sabon was designed in 1966 by Jan Tschichold, who took his inspiration from Garamond. It is used for the parks as a whole, as an institution in the public domain. Mol is used for signage, creating functional cohesion in the wayfinding system inside the parks. A modern, highly legible and easy-to-reproduce font, Mol was designed by the Dutch type designer Gerard Unger for the Amsterdam metro. Its rounded forms are easily incised by drill into the material of the objects which have to carry the text. In the parks it is used on small signs in a shade of yellow rare in nature, and cut into the same kind of laminate material used by the Memphis group for some of their furniture. The colour of these signs contrasts sufficiently with the surroundings to be easily visible, whereas the rough wooden posts on which the signs are placed merge into their surroundings. The wayfinding system is augmented by a handsome set of pictograms that politely but firmly regulate visitor behaviour.

Like Vignelli, Bernard devoted a great deal of attention to cartography. The printing of maps and hiking guides was entrusted to a specialized firm with which a long-term collaboration was established. The values achieved in this printed matter are those of an encyclopedia: logical arrangement, easy consultation and accessibility for the millions that visit this public domain every year.

On the signs and in the information folders we see a clear and attractive functionalism that was characteristic of public communication in the Netherlands in the seventies and eighties. This house style may be said to be a striking synthesis of a French and a Dutch design tradition.

Les Parcs Nationaux de France ont une nouvelle image

Il en va d'une image comme de la nature: elle existe 'comme ça', posée comme
un élément indiscutable qui se révèle au fur et à mesure de sa découverte.
En 1989, le septième parc national a été créé. Simultanément la nécessité d'unifier
ces espaces dans une image universelle s'est imposée.
Dépositaires du mouvement, de la richesse et de la complexité de la vie, lieux de
découverte des mystères du monde animal et végétal, espaces du patrimoine vivant
protégés par l'homme, espaces pluriels, singuliers et unis, sources de rayonnement
d'une richesse à elle seule éloquente, les parcs nationaux avaient besoin d'un système
d'identité graphique contemporain.
L'Atelier de Création Graphique – Grapus a créé cet emblème qui porte la diversité
biologique des parcs, leur volonté de s'identifier culturellement. Il intègre
naturellement les prochains parcs nationaux sur des espaces comme la forêt, les zones
humides, la montagne et les rivages marins. Enfin, cet emblème est le label d'espaces
d'aventure, de pérennité et de paix, dans la diversité de la nature intacte.

● **Ministère délégué auprès du premier ministre chargé de l'environnement
et de la prévention des risques technologiques et naturels majeurs**

Améliorer la qualité de la vie quotidienne, assurer la qualité
de l'air, de l'eau, maintenir les équilibres biologiques, lutter contre
les pollutions, gérer les ressources tout en préservant la richesse
et la diversité des espaces naturels, telles sont, avec la prévention
des risques naturels et technologiques, ses responsabilités.

● **Direction de la protection de la nature**

Elle favorise la connaissance du patrimoine naturel. Elle propose
et met en œuvre toute mesure pour protéger la faune, la flore
et les milieux naturels concernés par la vie sauvage. Au-delà,
son action s'étend au domaine de la chasse, de la pêche et
à la mise en valeur de l'espace naturel.

● **Service des espaces naturels**

Il identifie les espaces à protéger. Il instruit la création des
protections réglementaires, foncières ou contractuelles
(parcs nationaux, réserves naturelles, parcs régionaux, etc...).
Il élabore leur politique de gestion à long terme en liaison avec
la recherche scientifique. Il favorise la protection de la montagne
et du littoral.

● **Parcs Nationaux de France**

Territoires exemplaires pour la politique des espaces naturels, leur
vocation est de protéger la nature, les paysages et les sites, assurer
la diversité biologique dans leurs territoires, mettre leur patrimoine
à la disposition du public, le transmettre aux générations futures
et participer au développement de comportements respectueux
de la nature et de ses équilibres.

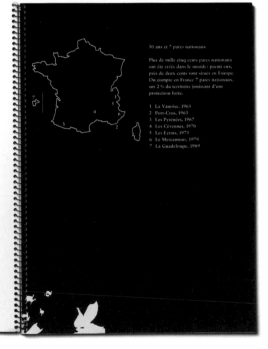

30 ans et 7 parcs nationaux

Plus de mille cinq cents parcs nationaux
ont été créés dans le monde: parmi eux,
près de deux cents sont situés en Europe.
On compte en France 7 parcs nationaux,
sur 2 % du territoire jouissant d'une
protection forte.

1 La Vanoise, 1963
2 Port-Cros, 1963
3 Les Pyrénées, 1967
4 Les Cévennes, 1970
5 Les Ecrins, 1973
6 Le Mercantour, 1979
7 La Guadeloupe, 1989

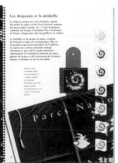

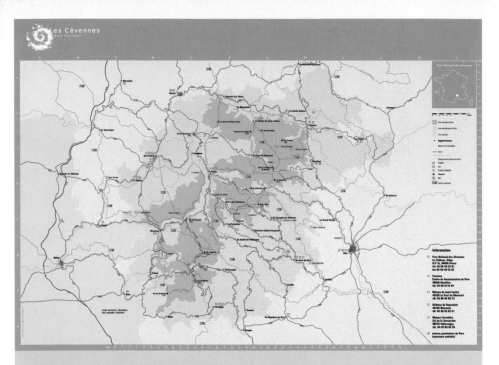

Réglementation du Parc national (Zone de protection)

Un parc national est un territoire d'exception, ouvert à tous sous la responsabilité de chacun.
Il est protégé par une réglementation. Merci de la respecter.

- **Chiens en laisse**
ils perturbent la faune sauvage et
les troupeaux.

- **Ni cueillette, ni prélèvement**
respectez tous végétaux sauvages ou cultivés.

- **Emportez vos déchets**
ils souillent toujours, ils blessent parfois.

- **Pas de feu**
ses marques sont irréversibles, ses dégâts
catastrophiques.

- **Ni camping, ni camping-car, ni caravaning**

- **Pas de tout terrain en vélo, moto ou auto**
circulation interdite en dehors des voies
autorisées.

- **Ni bruit ni dérangement**
pour la quiétude de tous.

- **Pas de sports aériens**
le survol du parc est interdit à moins de
1 000 mètres du sol.

- **Respectez les clôtures, refermez les barrières**

Dispositions particulières
- Les activités agricoles, pastorales et
forestières continuent de s'exercer. Plans de
gestion et conventions règlent la sylviculture.
- Une chasse dirigée permet le maintien des
équilibres agro-sylvo-pastoraux.

- La pêche s'exerce dans le cadre des
règlements nationaux.

*Pour davantage d'information,
renseignez-vous auprès des Maisons du Parc.*

*For further information,
contact the Park Visitors' Centers.*

Signpost
National Park Les Ecrins
12.8 × 40 and 9.6 × 40 / 1995

Badge for park rangers
enamelled metal
5.1 × 5.8 / 1990

Welcome panels
National Park La Vanoise
National Park Le Mercantour
108 × 75 / 1993

p. 243
30th anniversary of
the French National Parks
poster
120 × 80 / 1993

Parcs Nationaux de France

Science

CNRS

Proposal for a house style
for the Centre National de
la Recherche Scientifique
(National Centre for
Scientific Research) 2003
Internal publication of
the Atelier de Création
Graphique presenting a
non-implemented design
project, 80 pp.
29.7 × 21 / 2003

In collaboration with
Jacqueline Kübler,
Fanette Mellier,
Gregoire Romanet

The National Centre for Scientific Research was founded in 1939 by the French government as an institute of fundamental research and is currently made up of six departments: biosciences, information and communication, nuclear physics, environment and energy, nanotechnology and space research. 30,000 people work in 1260 research units and general services.

Since the eighties the emphasis of the research has shifted to become more interdisciplinary in character, and requests from business and social organizations now play a greater role. The CNRS comes under the Ministry of Research and maintains contacts with higher education, industry and defence, as well as regional and international institutions. It produces its own publications but also contracts work out to commercial publishers.

This was a limited competition with the Atelier de Création Graphique as one of the participants. Before any decision could be made, however, new management scrapped the entire project. What is shown here are the fragments of a model that was never built. 'The organization wanted to replace its old logo, to create a stronger identity and a more coherent communication and publication policy', says Bernard. 'We were asked to develop a house style for an organization that is concerned with the production of high quality knowledge. The character of this house style should be as far removed as possible from brand names and markets. After all, the organization itself isn't oriented to the market but rather to a forum of scientists and researchers. Our aim was to make the diversity of the research fields visible and treat them as members of an extended family. The design had to show a balance between similarity and difference. Each department received its own colour and its full name was added to the logo.' [Boekraad 2006]

There is no colour in the logo of the CNRS: it is *une couleur non-couleur*, i.e. black or white, as opposed to the colours of the departments. This neutrality of colour reflects the public character of the organization and of science in general. The logo represents the exactitude and certainty of scientific knowledge on the one hand, the openness and uncertainty of scientific research on the other. It also makes reference to the infinite and the infinitesimal of the objects studied by the CNRS. The images of the visual essay with which the studio's internal publication on the house style opens also refer to these extreme leaps in scale: they are borrowed from the 1968 film *Powers of Ten* by Charles and Ray Eames, in which photographic images taken at regular distances are shown in two series. One series moves from man and ends in the macrocosmos; the other moves in the other direction, from man to micro-cosmos, ending with the photo of a carbon atom.

As the institutional typeface for the house style the design team proposed Interstate since it shows no traces of any origins in script. In CNRS publications Interstate is combined with Times New Roman. The designers explored and demonstrated possibilities for using series of scientific images in varying layouts in the publications of several research institutes and departments. 'My source of inspiration', says Bernard, 'was the exceptionally high quality and variety of scientific photographic, digital and microscopic images that scientists themselves

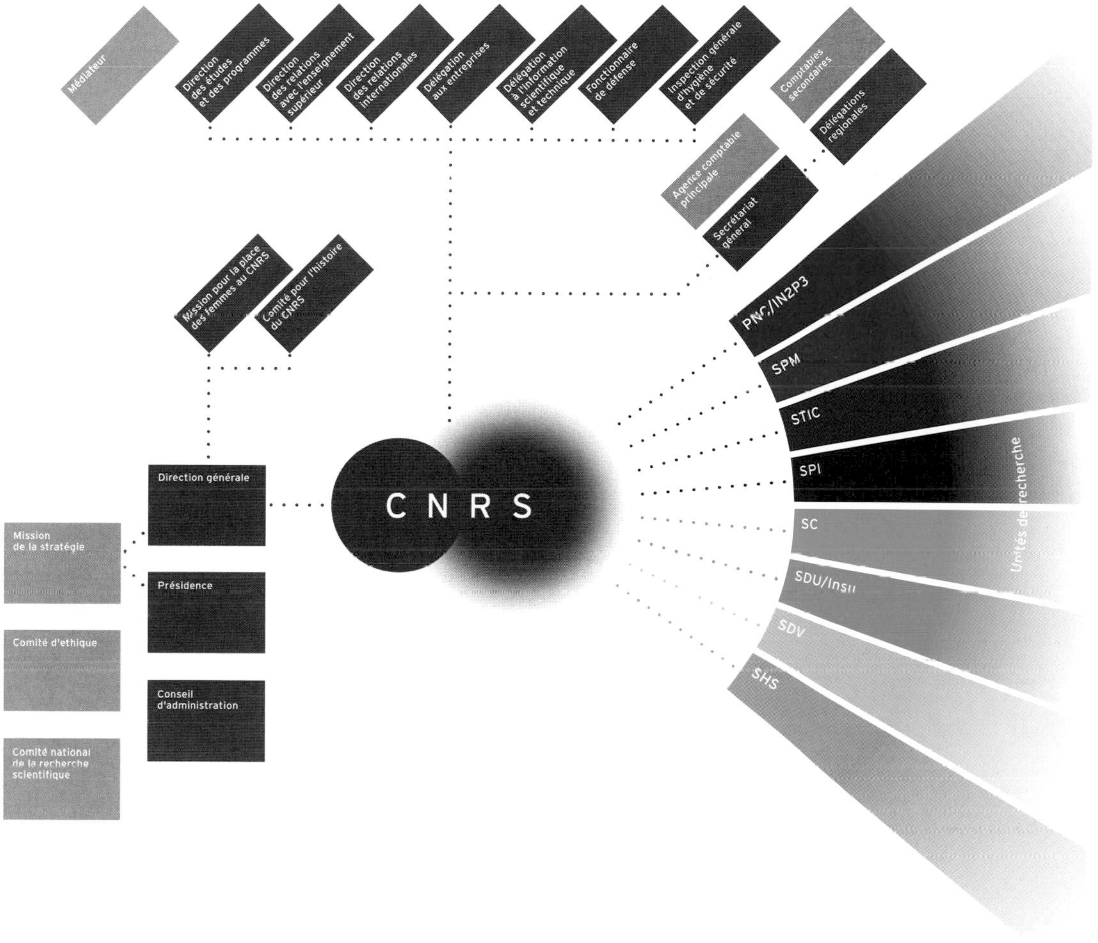

Médiateur

Direction des études et des programmes

Direction des relations avec l'enseignement supérieur

Direction des relations internationales

Délégation aux entreprises

Délégation à l'information scientifique et technique

Fonctionnaire de défense

Inspection générale d'hygiène et de sécurité

Comptables secondaires

Délégations régionales

Agence comptable principale

Secrétariat général

Mission pour la place des femmes au CNRS

Comité pour l'histoire du CNRS

Direction générale

Mission de la stratégie

Présidence

Comité d'éthique

Conseil d'administration

Comité national de la recherche scientifique

C N R S

PNC/IN2P3

SPM

STIC

SPI

SC

SDU/INSU

SDV

SHS

Unités de recherche

... de notre propre galaxie

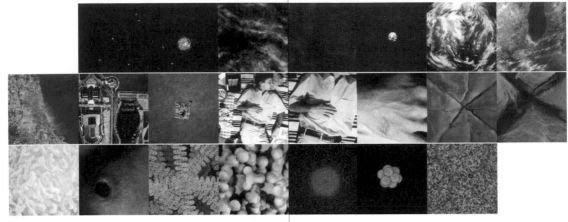

au noyau d'un atome de carbone...

Images extraites du projet « Powers of ten »
de Charles et Ray Eames.

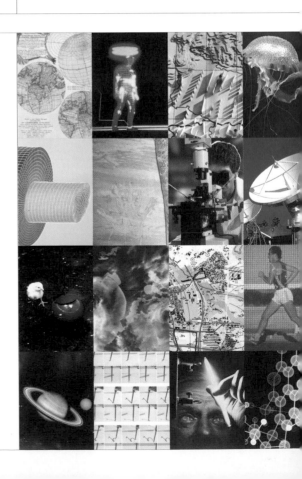

science
connaissances
recherche
découverte
rigueur
intelligence
exploration
savoir
excellence
dynamisme
innovation
valorisation
performance
compétitivité
société
citoyenneté
humanité
débat
progrès
retombées sociales et économiques
partenariat
éthique
expertise
réactivité
initiative
prospective
expertise
évaluation
fédérateur
référence
label
ouverture
rôle d'animateur de la communauté scientifique française
organisation et structuration de la recherche
interdisciplinarité / pluridisciplinarité
tranversalité
réseau
europe
espace européen de la recherche
international
interface avec le monde socio-économique
transfert

produce as part of their research.' Each cover for the CNRS's *Journal* combines the logo with a new image.

This proposal envisaged a systematic way of presenting knowledge and examined new forms and images instead of the commonplace geometric abstractions that were in vogue for the covers of scientific publications. Bernard strove for unity in the appearance of all CNRS publications while at the same time diversifying the visual material. This was an ambitious plan because the CNRS works with several publishers, all accustomed to distributing scientific publications through commercial channels. Had the Atelier's proposals been put into practice they would most likely have run into opposition in the market, which, as a rule, prefers working with familiar forms. Bernard's designs valorize the production of knowledge, not the identity of the publisher or distributor. 'The presentation of scientific information calls for design that also results from research and innovation, i.e. of the codes of communication', says Bernard. 'If we had won the competition, we would have had to face reality and would have been forced to modify our proposal to take the established practice in science publishing into account. But we do not have to wait for an ideal world in order to introduce real improvements.'

The initiative to renew the house style and publications policy of the CNRS was remarkable at a time when the genre of the scientific and academic book was – as it still is – under pressure. Almost all French publishers are seeing the contribution made by scientific and academic publications fall, in terms of both titles and sales. This project is an expression of the utopia of the public domain – or at least of a significant segment of it – in which the distribution of knowledge would be organized and designed according to the logic and method of science itself, without regard to current practices. The design proposal by the Atelier de Création Graphique passes grandly by the alliances of government and market players in the distribution of knowledge and is itself a form of fundamental research by a design studio. To carry through such an enterprise would take the acuity and perseverance of a Diderot.

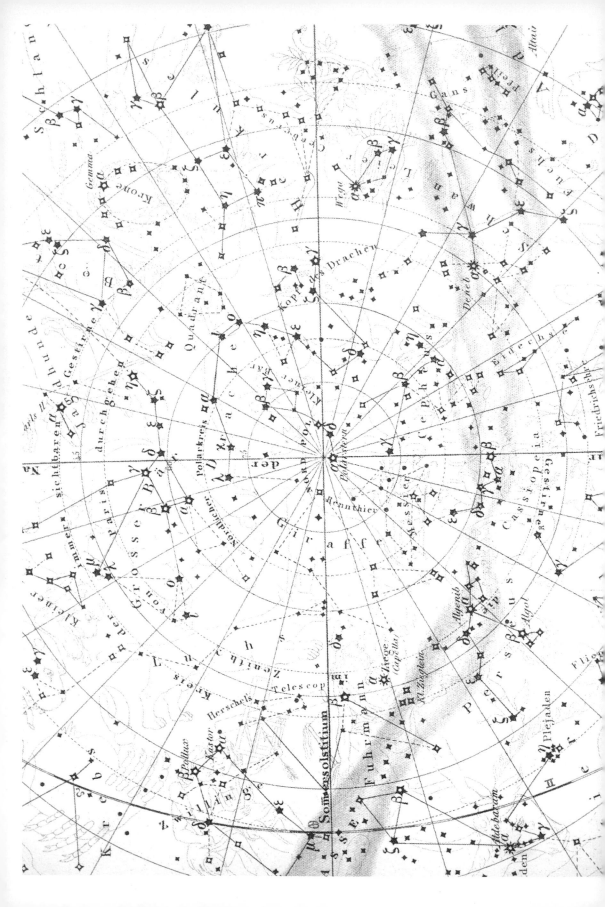

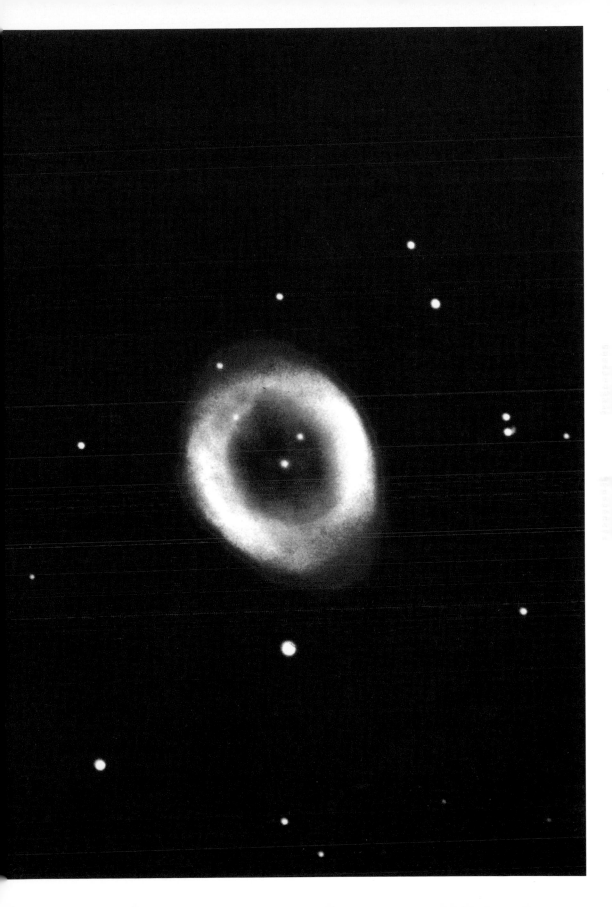

CNRS

Département
Physique nucléaire et corpusculaire /
Institut national de physique nucléaire
et de physique des particules

Département
Sciences physiques et mathématiques

Département
Sciences et technologies
de l'information et de la communication

Département
Sciences pour l'ingénieur

Département
Sciences chimiques

Département
Sciences de l'Univers /
Institut national des sciences de l'univers

Département
Sciences de la vie

Département
Sciences de l'homme et de la société

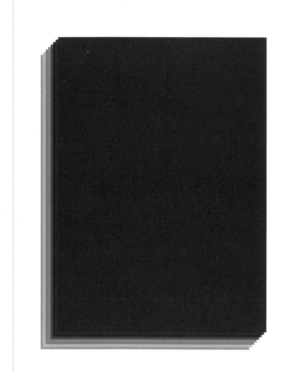

Sciences de l'homme et de la société
Lettre des départements scientifiques du CNRS
n°39 mai 2004

Physique nucléaire et corpusculaire
Lettre des départements scientifiques du CNRS
n°15 septembre 2003

Sciences et technologies de l'information et de la communication
Lettre des départements scientifiques du CNRS
n°50 juin 2004

Sciences de l'univers
Lettre des départements scientifiques du CNRS
n°30 janvier 2004

Sciences de la vie
Lettre des départements scientifiques du CNRS
n°26 octobre 2003

Sciences physiques et mathématiques
Lettre des départements scientifiques du CNRS
n°17 février 2004

Sciences chimiques pour l'ingénieur
Lettre des départements scientifiques du CNRS
n°15 avril 2004

le Journal

le Journal

le Journal

le Journal

le Journal

le Journal

Preventive archaeology

By signing the European Convention on the Protection of the Archaeological Heritage, otherwise known as the Malta Convention, in 1992, France joined other countries in pledging to have archaeological surveys carried out before any earthworks are undertaken, whether in the countryside or in urban areas. Subsequently the task of preventive archaeology was also regulated by law. In his introduction to this booklet, the president of the Institut National de Recherches Archéologiques Préventives (INRAP) cites the law: 'The State shall ensure the reconciliation of the requirements of scientific research, heritage conservation, and economic and social development'. He concludes that preventive archaeology (usually known in Britain as rescue archaeology) is a permanent compromise between these three necessities. The image this brings to mind is of an archaeologist with shovel and digging stick, probing for relics of ancient times with a developer's bulldozer at his heels. But let us put that caricature aside and examine the reality of modern archaeology.

The commissioning authority for this project was INRAP, a public body set up in 2002 under the aegis of the two ministries of Research and Culture. Its primary task is to gather and disseminate knowledge about the archaeological heritage of France and contribute to its preservation. The institute carries out surveys and excavations for natural persons and companies involved in developing and exploiting land for the construction of roads and housing: construction companies, quarry and gravel pit operators, developers etc. It does the same for public bodies such as local councils, regional authorities and the French railways. Research at archaeological sites involves everything from soil surveys to the publication of scientific reports on the results of excavations.

2004 saw the publication of what is now a standard work, *La France archéologique, vingt ans d'aménagement et de découvertes*, with INRAP as one of the publishers and the Atelier de Création Graphique as the designer. The small spiral-bound book presented here, *Vingt ans de découvertes*, is an abridged version of that manual and describes the salient features of the research methods and subjects of preventive archaeology. More than ten thousand copies of this summary were distributed to contractors, developers, local councillors and other representatives of the people – in France, every municipality is required by law to develop an archaeology policy – as the activities of these private and public parties have a direct impact on the nation's archaeological heritage.

The area in which preventive archaeology is active in France is enormous. The database of identified sites now numbers some 400,000 – a figure that is only three to five percent of the estimated total. On the average, each square kilometre of French soil contains about twenty archaeological sites.

Archaeology, a discipline whose practitioners were mainly amateurs up to about 1970, has changed in character. The excavations themselves are no more than a link in the long chain of archaeological work. The artefact as an isolated and spectacular object – the treasures of Troy, for example – is no longer the main issue. The focus today is on the traces and patterns of human society at any given location. For

Vingt ans de découvertes (Twenty years of discoveries) Publication of the Institut National de Recherches Archéologiques Préventives (INRAP) (French National Institute for Research in Preventive Archaeology) Book with spiral binding 144 pp. 20 × 16.2 / 2005

In collaboration with Grégoire Romanet

example, bone fragments, pollen, pottery shards and charcoal allow us to reconstruct our forebears' nutritional habits and ancient techniques of farming and animal husbandry. Excavations also lead to research into land ownership and use, long-term changes in climate patterns and vegetation, and the general evolution of a given site.

Archaeology is now an interdisciplinary science. It covers an enormous time span, from the Palaeolithic to the present. Archaeologists collaborate with anthropologists, historians, zoologists, botanists, sedimentologists: the list is endless. Indeed, today they also call upon specialists from the design disciplines: architects, draughtsmen, cartographers and photographers. In short, archaeology no longer simply concentrates on showing us a picture of the past: it is involved in the intensely scientific processing of that past. It defines heritage not primarily as something that is dead and gone but as a factor that even now helps define the identity of local communities, and as a treasure that must be handed down to generations yet to come.

This booklet covers a period of half a million years, divided into eight periods. Each period and each chapter in which it is treated is given its own colour. The chapters open with a photograph of a characteristic object for the period concerned, serving as an identifier. Together these icons make up a small visual code which is presented on the front cover and explained at the back of the book.

The project descriptions are grouped in columns with a differently coloured background for each chapter. The texts are a constant element, interacting with images that vary in format and character. The visual material includes maps, panoramic views and details, objects and collections of objects, aerial and site photographs. The whole is a transparently structured stream of images and texts. Despite its modest format and size, then, this booklet is a gold mine of information.

This publication illustrates what intelligent editorial design is capable of. Not only are its contents of public benefit, so too is its design. In this booklet INRAP gives a concise, clear and instructive insight into the aims and results of rescue archaeology. It provides not only a surprising picture of the way it works but also experiments with a particular form of public communication. The logical and visually attractive presentation of the information sets a benchmark for public communication in a democracy. The design makes it possible for citizens to understand INRAP's objectives and endorse them. While providing factual information the booklet is above all a plea to the reader. The graphic designer acts as a visual rhetorician, offering a professional contribution to the quality of public administration by not only informing the reader but also persuading him to approve of a particular policy. Any law is only effective if the public are convinced of its justice.

Les temps des
chasseurs-cueilleurs

Le Paléolithique et le Mésolithique

L'homme est apparu d'abord en Afrique, il y a six millions d'années, avec les Australopithèques. Leur succèdent, il y a deux millions d'années, les *Homo erectus*, qui taillent les premiers outils et maîtrisent bientôt le feu. Ce sont eux qui, les premiers à quitter l'Afrique, pour atteindre l'Europe. Ils apparaissent en France il y a environ un million d'années, leur cas correspond le Paléolithique, subdivisé en trois périodes. Le Paléolithique inférieur correspond à l'arrivée des *Homo erectus* sur notre territoire, le Paléolithique moyen débute vers −300000, avec l'homme de Neandertal, et enfin le Paléolithique supérieur correspond à l'apparition de l'homme actuel, *Homo sapiens sapiens*, vers −35000.

C'est à des Français que l'on doit la définition du Paléolithique, d'abord à Jacques Boucher de Perthes dans les années 1840, puis à Denis Peyrony et à l'abbé Breuil, enfin, dans la seconde moitié du XXe siècle, à François Bordes et à André Leroi-Gourhan. Ce dernier met au point une nouvelle méthode de fouilles, sur une large surface, permettant de mettre en relation les objets.

Premiers bergers
et paysans

Le Néolithique

L'apparition de l'agriculture et de l'élevage, la sédentarisation, la guerre et les inégalités sociales qui en ont résulté sont si importantes pour l'histoire humaine qu'on a appelé cette période la « révolution néolithique ». Ce processus vient du Proche-Orient par deux voies distinctes, l'une au sud, longeant le bord de la Méditerranée (vers −6000), l'autre par le Danube, entrée sur notre territoire par le nord-est (vers −5000). Les deux courants se sont rejoints sur notre sol, apportant chacun sa culture.

Le Néolithique doit beaucoup à l'archéologie préventive qui, en traitant de vastes surfaces, a permis de fouiller des villages entiers et été comprendre l'organisation. Dans le Midi, on fait le creusement préalablement tous les grands travaux d'autoroutes et de lignes de TGV. Les sites nous renseignent sur ces premiers agriculteurs, qui élèvent chèvres, moutons, bœufs et porcs, cultivant le blé et l'orge qu'ils broient sur des meules en pierre, creusent de profondes fosses pour entreposer les céréales et sont entre les aliments sur de grands emplacements circulaires. Les poteries portent des décors faits.

Métallurgistes, guerriers
et agriculteurs

L'âge du Bronze

Les sociétés de l'âge du Bronze, et notamment les « chefferies », sont assez semblables à celles du Néolithique final. Seule la découverte du bronze (alliage de cuivre et d'étain) permet un progrès dans la technologie des armes, puis des outils.

On distingue trois périodes : le Bronze ancien (−2200 à −1600), le Bronze moyen (−1600 à −1350) et le Bronze final (−1350 à −800). Deux principales zones culturelles se partagent le territoire, l'une dite nord-alpine, l'autre atlantique. Toutes deux, sauf fortement hiérarchisées au départ, comme en témoignent les tombes monumentales remplies de parures et de vaisselle d'or et d'argent. Au Bronze moyen, la fabrication des objets métalliques se fait en série, notamment celle des haches, des lourds bracelets et des jambières. Les bras enfants font leur apparition, sait en pleine terre, soit dans des urnes placées sous un tertre. Au Bronze final, les innovations techniques s'intensifient. Haches à ailerons, faucilles, rasoirs apparaissent. Vers la fin de la période, à côté des fermes isolées se développent des habitats groupés, souvent en hauteur et fortifiés.

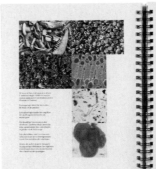

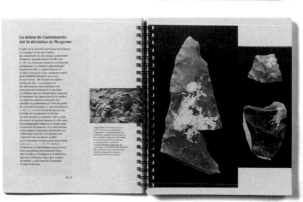

Un habitat du Paléolithique à Rueil-Malmaison

Le site du Closeau à Rueil-Malmaison (Hauts-de-Seine), sur le tracé de l'autoroute A86, était occupé il y a environ 12000 ans par les derniers chasseurs de l'époque glaciaire, au moment du réchauffement climatique. Ce réchauffement s'accompagne d'un changement progressif de l'environnement : le cerf succède au renne, entraînant de profondes modifications des pratiques de chasse. Les Aziliens succèdent aux Magdaléniens avec des outils de pierre plus grossiers, un armement en os ou en bois de cervidé moins développé, des expressions artistiques moins fécondes, mais néanmoins une culture matérielle élaborée. Il s'agit du plus vaste gisement du Paléolithique supérieur en Europe (28000 m²). Les chasseurs venaient y guetter les troupeaux d'herbivores, s'approvisionner en eau et en matières premières à tailler, et installer leurs campements saisonniers. Les petites occupations peu structurées du niveau le plus récent tranchent avec les habitations circulaires du niveau ancien, encore dans la tradition magdalénienne avec leur foyer central près duquel se trouvent les vestiges de taille du silex, d'utilisation des outils, d'entretien du foyer… L'intérêt de ce site est d'avoir pu montrer une filiation entre Magdalénien et Azilien ancien. Une majorité d'ossements de chevaux et de cerfs ont été découverts dans le niveau ancien. La chasse de ces deux espèces a donc été privilégiée lors des deux passages saisonniers, l'un au printemps, l'autre à l'automne. Plus étonnante est la présence du sanglier, dont on pensait qu'il n'apparaissait que plus tard ; il s'agit des plus anciens sangliers de la fin du Paléolithique.

Les chasseurs du Closeau vivaient dans des habitations circulaires d'environ 6 m de diamètre, dont subsistent de gros blocs de pierre qui en marquent la forme. Autour du foyer central, on retrouve les restes de diverses activités.

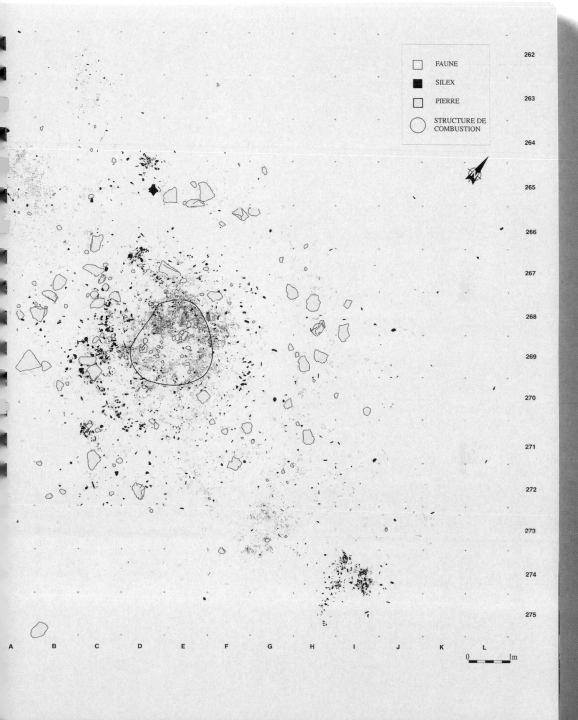

≃ −800 → ≃ −50
Le temps des Gaulois

L'âge du Fer

Pas davantage que celle du cuivre, l'invention du fer n'a véritablement révolutionné la société protohistorique. Il se répand en Europe au 1er millénaire avant notre ère mais demeure un métal rare. Le véritable phénomène de l'époque est plutôt l'affinement croissant des cultures méditerranéennes (grecque, romaine, phénicienne, carthaginoise) à travers les comptoirs implantés sur nos côtes pour y acquérir matières premières et esclaves.

Notre pays n'est pas alors la Gaule mais qu'ont décrite, par nationalisme, les historiens du xixe siècle, mais une mosaïque d'États qui diffèrent entre eux par la langue, les coutumes, les lois « (César). L'âge du Fer se divise en deux périodes: le Hallstatt (–750 à –480) du nom d'un cimetière autrichien, et La Tène site –189 à la conquête de la Gaule en –125, tiens d'un site suisse.

Dans la partie nord de la Gaule, l'archéologie préventive a mis en évidence des centaines de fermes comme celle de Chézy-d'Onnes, soit l'époque de l'ordre Trévoa, tant que de véritables petites forteresses.
28/28

≃ −120 → ≃ 400
Le temps des villes
et des campagnes

La Gaule romaine

À la partie méridionale conquise en 120 avant notre ère, devenue province de Narbonnaise, César ajoute en –52 le reste de la Gaule jusqu'au Rhin. Ce territoire ne s'est pas romanisé du jour au lendemain après le défaite d'Alésia. L'archéologie prouve au contraire que les romanités se réinsérant commence dès la fin du xie siècle, au xe siècle au à travers des contacts commerciaux nombreux, entre Celtes et Romains. De plus, Rome, dès la Conquête, s'occupe la bienveillance des élites qui confisent le élite de citoyen romain très nécessaires gaulois, qui reçoivent des charges. Renouvel des constructions et dressant les meilleurs propagateurs du romanité.

À partir d'Auguste (–43 à 14), Rome organise administrativement sa conquête, tout en respectant habituellement les anciens découpages des peuples gaulois, qui deviennent des « cités ». Le pays est, outre la Narbonnaise, divisé en trois provinces : la Lyonnaise, l'Aquitaine et la Belgique. La paix d'aucuns États, au xie siècle de notre ère, l'Empire subit une grave crise économique, sociale et politique, aggravée par des invasions. Il faut attendre le xe siècle
72/73

≃ 350 → ≃ 1000
Héritages antiques
et temps nouveaux

Le haut Moyen Âge

Au xe siècle de notre ère, les grandes invasions vous incitent à lire l'oubli de l'Empire romain et laissez place à une mosaïque de royaumes « barbares » (Wisigoths au sud, Burgondes à l'est, Francs au nord). Ainsi fini l'Antiquité et commence le Moyen Âge, traditionnellement scindé en deux époques : le haut Moyen Âge, du baptême de Clovis, vers 496, jusqu'à l'arrivée au pouvoir d'Hugues Capet, en 987, et le Moyen Âge classique, jusqu'à la mort de Louis XI, en 1483.

Contrairement aux fabriques qui distinguent une période mérovingienne et une période carolingienne, les archéologues considèrent que les résultats les plus déterminants ont eu lieu au xe au xie siècle, un seule même de l'époque mérovingienne. Longtemps ces siècles ont été considérés comme une période sombre, barbare et troublée. On les vestiges réalisés que les premiers temps du Moyen Âge traient encore empreinte de culture antique. Les campagnes restent romaines, et quelques celles disparaissent au aussi, au xie siècle. D'aucunes restent, telle la richissime ville du Liené, en Picardie, occupée jusqu'à la fin de l'époque
86/87

≃ 1000 → ≃ 1500
Châteaux, bourgs
et cathédrales

Le Moyen Âge classique

Longtemps considéré comme obscurantiste, le Moyen Âge bénéficie aujourd'hui d'un autre intérêt de la part des chercheurs qui, au-delà de l'histoire événementielle, mettent en constante enquête une nouvelle répartition des rôles dans une société essentiellement fondée sur les pouvoirs religieux, administratif, politique, pratique ce répartissent entre le clergé et les villes civiles. De ce monde, naturel en quelques siècles des progrès techniques déterminants : routes le moulin de l'énergie hydraulique, l'usage banalisé de la charrue et du moulin, l'amélioration de la métallurgie et des industries de transformation. Cette dynamique économique accompagne le développement des villes, souvent à partir de centres antiques, dès le xie siècle.

Ce sont des quartiers de nos villes médiévales que l'archéologie préventive a mis au jour. À partir des années 1980, où qui des aménagements des centres urbains. Ces fouilles ont amont bouleversé l'image traditionnelle du Moyen Âge, elles furent aussi autant de laboratoires pour la mise au point de méthodes et de techniques de recherches en archéologie préventive.
100/101

264

Archéologie de la Grande Guerre dans la région d'Arras

Depuis une quinzaine d'années, dans les régions de l'Est et du Nord, les archéologues sont confrontés aux vestiges de la Grande Guerre et la région d'Arras, un secteur qui fut au cœur des combats, est exemplaire du développement de cette archéologie. C'est à partir de 1990, à l'occasion de recherches sur des carrières de pierre des XVe et XVIe siècles de la ville d'Arras, que se développe l'intérêt archéologique pour les vestiges de la Grande Guerre car ce réseau souterrain fut aménagé par les Britanniques afin d'accueillir plus de 24 000 hommes. Il fut donc le cantonnement de soldats français et britanniques ; une démarche archéologique a permis une nouvelle approche de leur vie quotidienne.

Ailleurs, sur les champs de bataille, les corps de combattants déclarés disparus sortaient de terre. Ainsi, l'archéologie prenait en charge ces sépultures, livrant des informations de première main sur des pratiques funéraires « d'urgence », peu décrites dans les récits des combattants.

L'archéologie permet, par l'analyse des habitats et par l'étude des objets de la vie quotidienne, d'éclairer nos connaissances sur des aspects qui ont peu fait l'objet de commentaires : le logement des troupes, leurs aménagements non réglementaires dans des conditions de vie très précaires. Les dépotoirs apportent leur lot d'informations sur les habitudes alimentaires et sur l'utilisation d'ustensiles hétéroclites, sur l'artisanat de tranchée.

Cliché aérien où se reconnaissent des tranchées sinueuses de la Grande Guerre venant couper les murs d'un bâtiment romain.

Fosse contenant les corps de vingt soldats britanniques appartenant au 10e Lincolnshire et originaires du même village.

Public space

Tourist information system for motorways

Tourist signs
Silkscreen on
aluminium plate
630 × 315 / 1991

In the second half of the twentieth century, in France as elsewhere, the national road system was expanded with a system of motorways. The French State operates a number of these autoroutes, but an increasing share has been concessioned to private companies. As a result, a collective good is partially removed from the public domain and made an object of private profit and personal consumption in return for cash payment.

A peculiarity of the French administrative system is that transport and tourism are under the authority of one ministry. France was the first country to add tourist information to its motorway signage system. Anyone who has driven through France will be familiar with the brown and white signs on which this tourist information is displayed. The toll operator not only promises the motorist safe passage on the roads but also addresses him as a tourist, recreation-seeker and consumer.

Between 1972 and 1978 Visuel Design, the agency of Jean Widmer, a Swiss designer who trained in Zürich, designed 550 pictograms for 2500 km of autoroutes. Each pictogram is presented on a brown panel and complemented with a similar text panel in one font, Frutiger. They inform motorists of the tourist sites, recreational possibilities and products of the region he is driving through. The signs constitute an integrated system. They inform, identify, orient, represent and valorize: all the functions of graphic design are fulfilled in this communication system. It is a paradigm of the Swiss modernistic approach to communication in public space.

In her monograph on Jean Widmer, Margot Rouard-Snowman [1995] describes the objective of Widmer's tourist information system as a form of animation: 'The idea was to break the rigid monotony of long distances, while respecting the cultural environment, and to stimulate the curiosity of the motorist for the nature and heritage of the various regions: cultural, architectural, urban and commercial.' This system of artificial landmarks can certainly be considered an enrichment of a modern transport system, but to some extent these claims lack credibility. The impressive system of France's autoroutes may be efficient, but inevitably it causes a loss of contact with and of personal observation of the landscape, villages and towns. Widmer's system of pictograms seems to have an additional function as a peace offering: it stands in the place of what has actually been sacrificed. The price the motorist pays for the greater functionality of the transport system is a loss of sensory perception, and this sensory deprivation is perpetuated in the compensating system itself. The pictograms make reference to concrete objects and situations, but abstract these to insert them into a uniform system of iconic signs.

The visual language of Widmer's pictograms goes back to the symbols of the picture statistics developed by Otto Neurath in the nineteen-twenties and thirties in the *Gesellschafts- und Wirtschaftsmuseum* in Vienna. Neurath wanted to make the complex relationships between modern society and economics accessible to broad segments of the population by translating facts and figures into picture statistics. He invited the German artist Gerd Arntz to design the symbols for this pictographic language. Between 1928 and 1956 Arntz designed 4,000 graphic symbols, which are of uniform size and can be combined in series. Their visual language is greatly simplified to make them easily understood. Over the course of the years their form, size and colour were standardized. They are intended to present quantitative information. [Gerd Arntz 1979]

Widmer invented a similar pictogram system and some of his symbols bear a striking similarity to Arntz's, although Widmer's are intended for the presentation of qualitative rather than quantitative information. The result is a contradiction between the diversity of the regional cultures and the uniformity of the formal language. For example, Widmer's architectural pictograms seem to represent architectural types rather than real buildings. He wanted to stir curiosity and to make his system like a game. But this game has the structure of a quiz: the answer to the meaning of each pictogram is given a few hundred metres later on a text panel. The images per se, though very well drawn, are unintriguing: all ambiguity has been removed from them. They give some information, but they fail to stimulate, exhort or excite the passive motorist.

In the sixties Bernard was a student of Widmer at ENSAD, the national academy of applied arts in Paris. They met again in 1991 as competitors for the job of designing a tourist information system for the autoroutes in the Rhône-Alpes region. The selection of Albertville as the venue for the Olympic Winter Games in 1992 had led the authorities to launch a campaign to make the region more attractive, and the competition was part of that effort. It was organized under a public-private partnership by two road operators: the private company AREA and the government authority Direction Départementale de l'Equipement (DDE). The brief was for some 200 signs to be set about five kilometres apart. Brown and white were mandatory, as was the Frutiger. The themes were decided in consultation with local authorities and the national commission for tourist signposting.

Bernard interpreted the brief as follows: 'The purpose of these tourist signs is clear: it is a matter of marking out a route to make it less boring, to evoke memories, to question reality, to probe the geography. It has a wake-up function in a highly codified and repetitive environment.' [Corbin, p. 21] He based his proposal on Widmer's system, but with a difference: the panels, silkscreen on aluminium plate, are in two halves, like dominoes. The visual information is provided not by signs but by images, which, with a single exception, are in the top half of the domino. One is struck by the lavish use of upper-case letters in the texts. Bernard abandoned the uniformity of the pictographic code and with his associates created images that vary greatly in terms of content, technique and expression. This gives them a certain unpredictability that adds to the effectiveness of their wake-up role. Each sign, like a domino, is at once autonomous and a link in a network. The poster-maker gives himself away by fitting unique text/image combinations into an information system. The result is a visual enrichment of this kind of communication. Bernard explained the designers' method like this: 'We multiplied our stylistic approaches by combining unusual forms with relatively familiar contents. ... In creating each sign it was a great pleasure to go to the site, search for books and documents, talk to the locals and steep ourselves in the place, drawing and taking photographs.' [Corbin, p. 23] As in ZUP!, the design was based on talking to local people.

Bernard's system's design takes account of the impact of visual culture on the man in the street and his increased visual competence. The images are related to their theme not so much descriptively as allusively. 'This partial or more playful character can nonetheless be quickly deciphered because the icons are based on visual clichés that motorists are familiar with from the media.' This reasoning, found in the notes to the design for the DDE, is particularly interesting given that, compared with the Widmer code, it is based on the visual competence and expectation of the observer rather than on formal aesthetics. The images are visual, emotional and sensual interpretations of the theme, whereas Widmer's pictograms are linear, conceptual, schematic mental images, all in the same style. The images of the Atelier are diverse: sometimes they zoom in and focus on a detail as a *pars pro toto*. The key word here again is richness, not just of the images but also the richness of the historical and local reality to which they refer and of the experience they offer to the public.

Widmer and Bernard apply two different principles of legibility in the same type of commission. Widmer designed a system which is legible because of the application of an optical grammar that requires images to be constructed according to a limited set of rules. Bernard, by contrast, relies on achieving legibility through the differential design of text and image, and the interaction of the images inside the information system and in the visual culture at large. His typography of the text also follows a code and offers a pedestal on which the image is anchored. At the same time he allows the images as much variety as possible. Widmer's approach is motivated by the tenets of system theory, and relies on concepts. Bernard's approach is rhetorical, and is based on the coexistence of convention and invention. The series of images and the rhythm that develops as the spectator travels along the autoroute create a dynamic relationship between the spectator and the message. The images address the motorist in constantly changing ways and appeal to his associative and interpretive abilities.

Bernard's conception of communication as a rhetorical, dialectical and dialogical process goes back to his vision of society and the social role of the graphic designer: 'The further I go in my graphic practice, the more I think that our job is about articulating and harmonizing the extremes that are characteristic of the social conditions in which we live: order and disorder. It is a matter of organizing the contrasts. In total disorder, contrast no longer exists, but of course in universal and permanent order there is even less of it!' [Corbin, p. 24]

← Abbaye de Tamié, 17e et 19e S.

Confluent de l'Arc et de l'Isère

Eglise de Chamousset 18e S.

← Château de Miolans, Forteresse 11e S.

↑ Le Mont Blanc

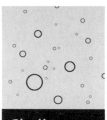

↗ Massif de la Chartreuse, e Granier

↖ Eglise Romane de Clery 11e et 12e S.

Vignobles de Savoie

Challes les Eaux, thermalisme

La Combe de Savoie

Sensation
Image

Sens
Texte

Domino system
Presentation on cardboard
for tourist sign system
in the Rhône-Alpes region
60 × 30 / 1991

273

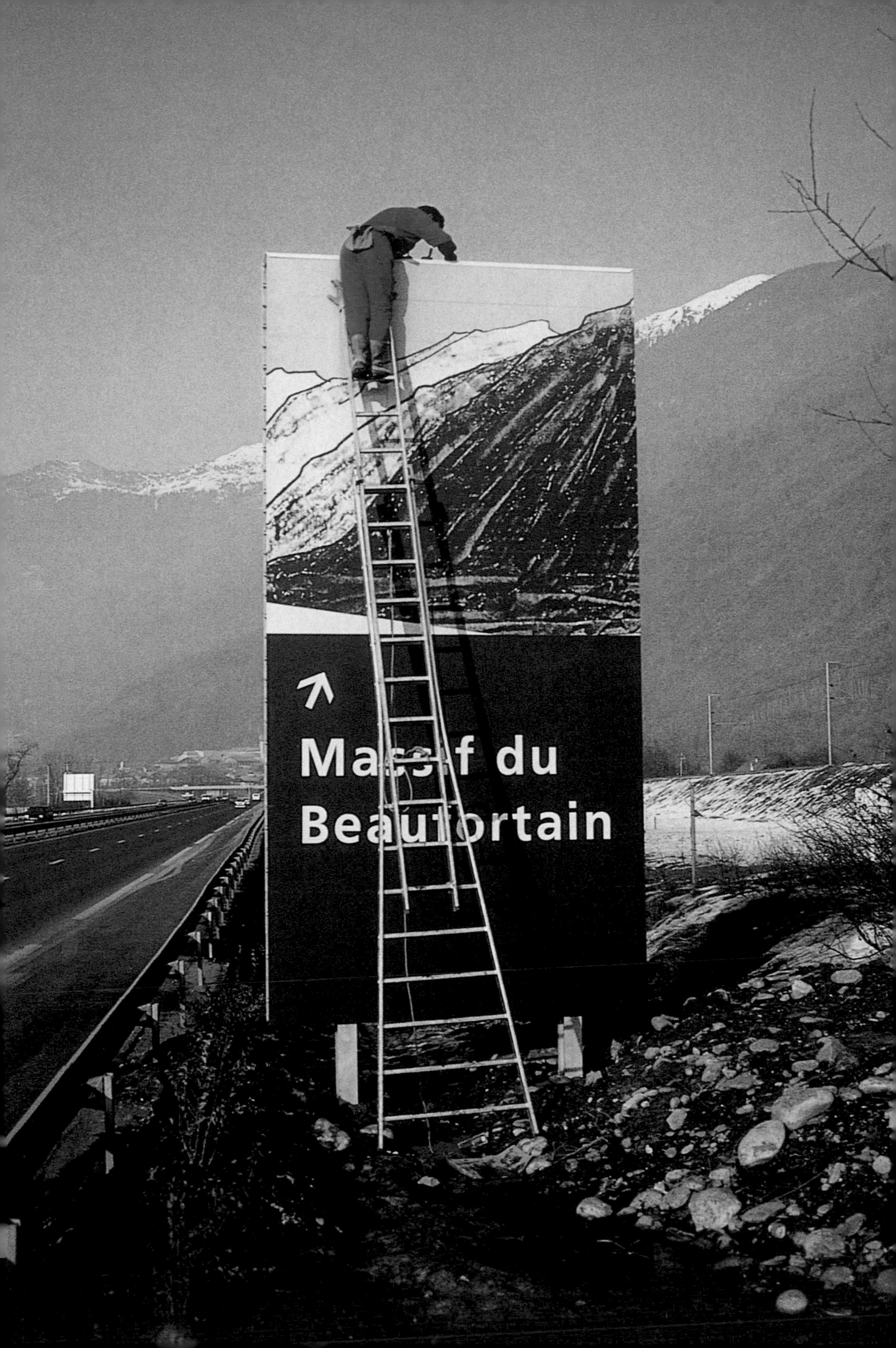
Mass f du
Beau ortain

Tourist signs along
the motorways in the
Rhône-Alpes region:
Massif de Beaufortain;
Graphite industries and
special alloys;
Le Pays de Romans
(shoes manufacture);
The Vercors, centre of
Resistance in Second
World War;
Bâthie Roselend
underground power station

pp. 276-7
Mont Blanc
630 × 315 / 1991

↑ Le
Mont Blanc

Renovation of the Pompidou Centre

Printed matter and facade lettering for use during the renovation of the Pompidou Centre 1995–2000 based on an alphabet designed in two versions Barré and Barré de couleur

When the Pompidou Centre opened in 1977, it was estimated that there would be 5,000 visitors a day, but the thirst for art turned out to be greater than had been anticipated. The building was a magnet that attracted tourists from far and wide, and by 1995 the flow of visitors had swollen to 25,000 a day. The area around the building had not been designed for such numbers, with the result that it was degenerating in quality and was no longer fit for its purpose. A large-scale renovation of the building and its immediate surroundings was necessary. The Pompidou Centre and the city of Paris decided to ask Renzo Piano, one of the building's two architects, to draw up a new plan. The Ministry of Culture, the city and the parking garage operator acted as co-financiers.

The renovation started in 1995. In the first phase of the project the facade and immediate surroundings would be renovated (1995–1997); in the second, the inside of the building: the entrance hall, exhibition spaces and technical installations (1998–1999).

In 1995 François Barré, president of the Centre, informed local residents in a newsletter: 'It is above all a matter of harmonizing the "urban landscape" and correcting the problems that have become apparent to us all.' One of the objectives of the renovation was 'to rebalance the pedestrian flows outside the Centre, particularly on the piazza'. The changes that he announced included the re-arrangement of street furniture and lighting, a tree-planting programme and repaving of the squares and pavements. Brancusi's studio, which had been in a building on the front plaza, was given a new lodging designed by Piano. And the Centre itself needed attention: the steel pipes on the outside walls needed anti-corrosion treatment and had to be made more fire-resistant. This work was to be finished in 1997 in time for the twentieth anniversary of the building's opening. The building and facilities of the Centre would remain open to the public during this period and its activities would, as far as possible, continue as usual. In the second phase, during which the interior was to be refurbished, the Centre would have to close its doors to reopen in grand style in the millennium year. The architecture of the construction site was entrusted to Patrick Rubin of Bureau Canal, who surrounded the building with a white steel fence.

Pierre Bernard and the Atelier de Création Graphique were invited to design the information about the renovation, starting with the leaflets for local residents and visitors. For this Bernard designed his first font, Barré, which has no lower-case letters, only capitals and numerals. Named after the client, Pompidou Centre president François Barré, it became the core of the temporary house style until 2000, for all institutional information about the activities in and around the building: newsletters, leaflets, a wall newspaper, notices and signage (for this purpose a couple of substantial arrows were added to the font). The designer wanted to create a typeface that gave expression to the transformation of the Centre as it headed into the twenty-first century.

In the typographical research for this project neither legibility nor functionality were major concerns. What was more important was the relationship between the shape of the characters, the high-tech nature of the building and its urban surroundings. Bernard took as his starting point the numerals and letters of French car number plates, which he described as 'down to earth, urban and deeply French ..., technical, a *typographie d'ingénieurs*, ... neither on the side of literature nor [of] fashion.' [Held 1999 in: He 2006, p. 216] The number-plate letters and numerals were redrawn digitally, accentuating precisely those formal characteristics that are considered by book typographers to be imperfections: the very small counter of the A for example, and the rounding of angles inside a letter where two straight lines meet, as in W and N.

Choosing this typographical zero point as his point of departure Bernard followed the path set out by Adrian Frutiger and Hans-Jürgen Hunziger twenty years earlier when for the Centre's first house style they designed Beaubourg, a font inspired by the IBM typewritter letter. Barré and Beaubourg are both mechanical in character: characters without variation in thickness and without any trace of or reference to handwriting. Both are part of a modern visual culture to which the public at large is accustomed without being aware of it. Transposition from the traffic system to a cultural context changes not only the environment of a typographic code but also its function. Projected onto the facade of a museum it acquires a new value and role in the visual culture of the city.

Barré attracted attention when it was used on the facade of the Centre in 1996, but it had already been used a year earlier in the newsletters informing about the renovation. Even the running text is set in Barré, in smaller capitals. The text is arranged in blocks that are separated by extra space and colour bars, and has indentations marked by arrows. The Chinese characters (for the word 'welcome') in one of the folders are also drawn in the Barré idiom: in strokes of even thickness.

Initially the museum wanted to camouflage the building during the work with gigantic reproductions of works of art. Bernard came up with another solution: 'For me, art is inside the Centre. As soon as you put it on the facade, it becomes decorative.' [Held 1999, p. 64] He suggested a typographic solution instead. During the renovation a white corrugated steel hoarding encircled the building and one corner was covered from top to bottom by a gigantic white panel. He wanted to use this surface, 40 metres high, as a notice board for the entire exhibition programme for a year and a half, listed in black Barré. This had an interesting side effect: 'Many people discovered the variety of the Centre's activities, even regular visitors to the Centre didn't know the entire programme. It was almost contradictory: the cladding was a revelation of the Centre.' [Held 1999, p. 65] At the end of each successive exhibition the titles were not removed but crossed out, so that this typographical calendar acted as a sort of countdown leading up to the closing of the building. Crossed out with red, blue and yellow stripes but still legible, the announcements reminded visitors of recent events they had either been to or missed. Visually, the letters that were struck through had greater presence than their black equivalents. This crossing-out attracted attention in another way: it was done by professional mountaineers painting lines through the letters while suspended on ropes.

The colour, length and position of each stripe were precisely defined for each character in order to achieve a certain rhythmicality in the whole.

This transformation of Barré into Barré de couleur was based on a play on words. As already observed, Barré was the name of the president of the Pompidou Centre who had fired the starting shot for the renovation. But in French his name can also be read as the past participle of the verb *barrer*: to deny access or cross off. This wordplay led to the pictorial typography described here.*

The visual quality of the characters was enhanced because they were modified by the declination of bars of varying length, direction and colour. The original clarity, objectivity and technical look of the characters was altered by this intervention so that they took on the appearance of fabric. This effect was even more noticeable when Bernard expanded the colour range of the bars to twelve and even more in a secondary adaption of Barré de couleur (p. 310).

The bars, placed at different angles in relation to the vertical axes of the letters, introduce a rotating movement into the static signs. The typography takes on movement, is animated and assumes the temporal character of the events it announces and subsequently writes off. The appearance of the calendar changes with time. The museum, the building and the typography are all work in progress.

*

There is another meaning of the word *barré* that is relevant here because it plays a role in the prehistory of graphic design. It is a term from heraldry, the Medieval semiology of the distinctive signs of aristocratic families and of a region, a city or a state. In this strictly coded language *barré* is said of a coat of arms in which the field has diagonal bars.

Heraldry describes the signs and figures with which the usually coloured shields of medieval knights were covered. Of course, the function of this feudal sign system is diametrically opposed to the administrative function and typography of a vehicle number plate. That cannot be said of Barré de couleur. On the facade of the Pompidou Centre it did act as a blazon proclaiming the identity of the institution. I would not have mentioned the heraldic meaning of the word *barré* – which played no role in the design of the typeface – if there were not a striking similarity of form between the heraldic Barré and Barré de couleur.

p. 281
Facade lettering of the exhibition programme
Pompidou Centre, Paris
1996

A B C D E F G H I J K L M
N O P Q R S T U V W X Y Z
(» . , ; : / – ! ? * - + «)
→ 0 1 2 3 4 5 6 7 8 9
É Ê È Ç À Ü Î  ←

A mountaineer keeps the
programme up to date by
crossing out past dates and
events
Pompidou Centre, Paris
1996

Typeface Barré
1995

French vehicle number plate.
This lettering was the model
for Barré

283

CAJARC / CÉRET
CHALON-SUR-SAÔNE
COLMAR / DÜSSELDORF
HELSINKI / LONDRES
LYON / MADRID
MARSEILLE / MEXICO
MILAN / NANTES
NEW YORK / NICE
NÎMES / OSAKA
ROUEN / SAINT-ÉTIENNE
TOULOUSE
VILLENEUVE-D'ASCO

MAX ERNST
6/5/98 → 27/7/98

Notice of Max Ernst
exhibition during the
renovation, outside the
building
Pompidou Centre, Paris
1998

pp. 286-7
Entrance
Lettering on the white steel fence
surrounding the building
Pompidou Centre, Paris
1995

Biography
Bibliography

Pierre Bernard

1942
Born in Paris.
1964
Graduated from the Ecole Nationale Supérieure des Arts Décoratifs (ENSAD) in Paris.
1964-5
Student in the studio of Henryk Tomaszewski at the Academy of Fine Arts in Warsaw, Poland.
1965-6
Graphic designer, and later art director of the magazine *Jeune Afrique* in Paris.
1967-8
Studies Animation at ENSAD
1968
May-June takes part in the strike and occupation at ENSAD and designs posters in the school's studio, the so-called 'atelier populaire no 2'.
1969–71
Research student at the Institut de l'Environnement, Paris. Graduation project: the image in political propaganda in France in 1936 and 1958.
1970
Co-founder of the graphic design collective Grapus, with François Miehe and Gérard Paris-Clavel.
1971–5
Teaches the course 'materials and textures', and from 1973 'visual communication' at ENSAD.
1970–90
Co-director of Atelier Grapus. Jean-Paul Bachollet joins the executive team in 1974, Alexander Jordan in 1975. François Miehe leaves the group in 1978.
1987
Member of Alliance Graphique Internationale (AGI).
1990
The four leading members of Grapus end their collaboration.
1991
Co-founder of Atelier de Création Graphique, with Dirk Behage and Fokke Draaijer. Fokke leaves the Atelier in 1995 and Dirk in 1997, each to found his own studio. Until now Bernard has sole artistic responsibility for the Atelier.
1992-4
Graphic design lecturer, Jan van Eyck Academy in Maastricht, Netherlands.
1993–2007
Lecturer, graphic design and visual communication, ENSAD.
2002
Artistic co-director of the International Poster Festival at Chaumont, France.

Awards

1968
Bronze medal, social posters class, 2nd International Poster Biennale, Warsaw, Poland.

Grapus

1978
Silver medal, social posters class; RSW Prasa-Ksiazka-Ruch Prize, 7th International Poster Biennale, Warsaw, Poland. Grand Prix, 8th Biennale of Graphic Arts, Brno, Czechoslovakia.
1979
Alain LeQuernec presents the Golden Mussel award, Galerie Saluden, Quimper, France.
1980
Gold medal, social posters class; Silver medal, cultural posters class, 8th International Poster Biennale, Warsaw, Poland
Gold medal; Silver medal; Bronze medal; Pressfoto Publishers Prize, 9th Biennale of Graphic Arts, Brno, Czechoslovakia.
1981
First Prize, cultural posters class, 4th Poster Biennale, Lahti, Finland.
1982
Silver medal, 10th Biennale of Graphic Arts, Brno, Czechoslovakia.
1983
Award of honour, 5th Poster Biennale, Lahti, Finland. First Prize, 3rd International Poster Festival, Fort Collins, Colorado, USA.
1988
First Prize, culture and society class, 2nd Poster Triennial, Toyama, Japan.
1991
Grand National Prize of the Graphic Arts, France.

Atelier de Création Graphique

1993
First Prize, International Poster Exhibition, Chaumont, France.
2002
First Prize 'Europe 2020', Pan European Poster Competition, Zagreb, Croatia.
2003
Second Prize, cultural posters, 1st International Poster Biennale, Hangzhou, China.
2006
The Erasmus Prize is awarded to Pierre Bernard for his graphic work in the public domain, Netherlands.

Exhibitions of Grapus

1975
Massy, France, Works council of CGE Alsthom.
1976
Moscow, USSR, *The Contemporary Poster in France 1965–1975*, exhibition organized by the Centre of Industrial Design, Pompidou Centre (group exhibition).
1977
Aubervilliers, France, *Les Murs ont la Parole*.
1978
Chatillon-sous-Bagneux, France, Works council of Aérospatiale.
1979
Quimper, France, Galerie Saluden.
Grenoble, France, Maison de la Culture, *l'Image politique, sociale et culturelle* (Cieslewicz, Gesgon, Grapus).
1980
Düsseldorf, Germany, *Visuelle Agitation*.
1981
Athens, Greece, Art group+ Gallery, *The Floating Image, Grapus*.
Allonnes, France, *Défense d'Afficher* (group exhibition).
Amsterdam, Netherlands, Stedelijk Museum, *Grapus*.
Paris, France, Ecole Estienne, *A la tienne, Estienne*.
Zagreb, Yugoslavia 'ZGRAF 3, International exhibition of graphic design and visual communication' (group exhibition).
1982
Pecs, Hungary, Pécsi Gallery.
Mons, Belgium, Musée des Beaux-arts, Second Triennial of the European Political Poster (group exhibition).
Budapest, Hungary, Dorottya Gallery.
Zurich, Switzerland, Kunstgewerbemuseum.
La Rochelle, France, *Art Socio-Critique* (group exhibition).
Paris, France, Musée de l'Affiche et de la Publicité, *Grapus 100 affiches de 1976 à 1982*.
1983
La Courneuve, France, Fête de l'Humanité, *Grapus POLI-TIQU-ARTS*.
1984
Aspen, Colorado, *Grapus*.
Montreal, Canada, Museum of Contemporary Art, *Grapus*.
1985
Breda, Netherlands, De Beyerd, Museum for Graphic Design, *Grapus 85 Various Different Attempts* (also in De Zonnehof, Amersfoort, Netherlands).
1988
Jerusalem, Israel, Museum of Contemporary Art.
Lahti, Finland, Julistemuseo, *Grapus Posters*.
Delft, Netherlands, TU Delft Department of Industrial Design, *Graphic Design Grapus*.
1989
Paris, France, Couvent des Cordeliers, *66 Affiches pour les Droits de l'Homme et du Citoyen* (group exhibition).
1990
Rostock, Germany, Kunsthalle Rostock, *Plakate aus Paris*.
Tokyo, Japan, Gallery Alpha Cubic World, *Grapus + Makoto Saïto*.

Exhibitions of the Atelier de Création Graphique

1991
Orleans, France, Institut d'art visuel, *Demain se décide aujourd'hui*.
Paris, France, Pompidou Centre, *Parcs Nationaux de France, un emblème, une identité*.
1992
Rio de Janeiro, Brazil, Museum of Modern Art, *30 Posters on Environment and Development* (group exhibition), United Nations Rio conference.
1993
Paris, France, Pompidou Centre, *Identité graphique du Musée du Louvre*.
1994
Chaumont, France, Jesuit Chapel, *Atelier de Création Graphique*.
2000
Osaka/Tokyo, Japan, DDD and GGG Gallery, *Pierre Bernard: Be Reasonable, Ask The Impossible*.
2003
Hangzhou, China, Exhibition at the 1st Chinese International Poster Biennale.
2006
Amsterdam, Netherlands, Stedelijk Museum, *Pierre Bernard: Erasmus Prize 2006*.
The Hague, Netherlands, Museum for Communication, *Pierre Bernard, 6 Designs, 6 Postage Stamps*.

Bibliography

Publications by Pierre Bernard

'Du bonheur en papier', in: *L'Affiche contemporaine en France 1965–1975*, Paris (Pompidou Centre) 1976.
'Raconter le design. Grapus: design engagement', in: *Art press* (1987) 7, pp. 30-32.
'Social concerns in graphic design', in: Frascara, J., *Graphic Design, World Views. A Celebration of Icograda's 25th Anniversary*, Tokyo 1990.
'Plus que jamais "choisir l'arbre de la vie contre la spirale de vente"', in: cat. *Mois du graphisme d'Echirolles*, 1990.
'Pierre Bernard/carte blanche', in: *Le Dauphiné Libéré*, 3ème mois du graphisme d'Echirolles, 1992, p. 4.
'The grass is always greener on the other side', in: Boekraad, H.C., Hefting, P. (eds.), *The boundaries of the postage stamp*, Amsterdam/Maastricht (De Balie/Jan van Eyck Academy) 1993, pp. 54-57.
'The choice of… Pierre Bernard', in: *Affiche* (1994) 11, pp. 26-27.
'The social role of design', (lecture 1991) in: *Essays on design 1 – AGI's Designers of Influence*, London 1997.
'People/money', in: *Adbusters* (1999) 27.
'Faire du graphisme, c'est faire le graphiste', in: *Dans la rue. Franse affiches*, Amsterdam (Stedelijk Museum, cahier 19) 2000.
'Be realistic, demand the impossible', in: *Design Korea* (2002) 283
'Graphic design: in search of a territory', in: *étapes international* 02 (éditions pyramid) 2005 (conference 2003).
'La Chine, la France… c'est mon pays', in: *Hangzhou-Paris*, Paris 2005.
'Cassandre', in: Sauvage, A-M. (ed.), *A.M. Cassandre. Oeuvres graphiques modernes 1923–1939*, Paris (Bibliothèque Nationale de France) 2005.

Publications about Pierre Bernard

Aknaï, T., 'Poster guerillas: the Grapus Group', in: *Interpress Grafik* (1982) 2
Alexandre, A., 'Grapus', in: *Novum Gebrauchsgraphik 50* (1979) 8, pp. 3-10.
An., 'Le groupe Grapus', in: *B.A.T.*, August 1978.
An., 'Longwy vivra, Solidarité', in: *Antoinette* 174, June 1979.
An., 'Graphic stars', in: *Designer*, May 1980.
An., 'Grapus', in: *Sugestie*, October 1980.
An., 'De l'or pour Grapus et la Charte 77', in: *ATAC Informations* (1980) 111.
An., 'Grapus et la Charte 77', in: *Révolution*, 1 August 1980.
An., 'La vie d'artiste en 82', in: *Arts*, June 1982.
An., 'A Grapus Csoport', in: *Modszertani Fuzetek* (1982) 2.
An., 'Instant design', in: *Design World* (1989) 17, pp. 76-81.
An., 'What's true in design?', in: *Creative Review* 10 (1990) 5, pp. 85-88.
An., 'Auf der Suche nach der sinnlichen Darstellung', in: *Form* (1990) 132, pp. 56-59.
An., 'Glasgow Congress-Plakate', in: *MD* (1993) 11, p. 44.
An., 'Pierre Bernard', in: *Idea* 41 (1993) 240, pp. 30-31.
An., 'Show offs', in: *Creative Review* 13 (1993) 8, p. 33.
An., 'Pierre Bernard awarded the Erasmus Prize 2006', in: *LINO Magazine* (2006) 14, pp. 18-21.
Banholzer, C., 'Festival d'Affiches de Chaumont', in: *Novum Gebrauchsgraphik* 65 (1994) 11, pp. 44-49.

Barré, F., 'Grapus, ou la traversée du réel', in: *L'Expo-journal* nr 2 (1979) (Maison de la Culture de Grenoble), reprint in: *Projekt* 130, August 1979.
Barré, F., 'Grapus, un collectif d'affichistes', in: *Graphis* (1981) 213.
Bertaux, L., 'Bernard', in: *Hot Graphics International* (1992) 13, p. 28.
Blum, M., 'The poster as message: all signs point to Grapus', in: *New York Herald Tribune*, 14 January 1983.
Boekraad, H.C., 'Entretien avec Pierre Bernard', in: Boekraad, H.C. (ed.), *The new academy*, Breda (St. Joost Academy) 1997, pp. 16-27.
Boekraad, H.C., 'Graphic design: functionalism and subversion. Pierre Bernard interviewed by Hugues Boekraad', in: *Prix de Rome 1988*, The Hague 1988.
Boekraad, H.C., 'The redefinition of wealth', in: Boekraad, H.C., Hefting, P. (eds.), *The boundaries of the postage stamp*, Amsterdam/Maastricht (De Balie/Jan van Eyck Academy) 1993, pp. 58-71.
Boekraad, H.C., Interviews with Pierre Bernard, 2006 [audiotapes, unpublished].
Braunstein, C., 'Grapus: design engagement', in: *Art Press* (1987) 7, pp. 30-32.
Cato, K., Hindsight, Sydney 1998.
Corbin, A., 'Notre métier, c'est articuler l'ordre et le désordre', in: *Parce que* 2 (n.d.) pp. 20-23.
Curzi, L., 'Mille images, un combat: Grapus', in: *l'Humanité*, 11 april 1977.
Dossier de presse *Le livre des droits de l'enfant*, Département Seine-Saint-Denis 2001.
Emanuel, M., 'Fous d'images', in: *Print* 35 (1981) 2, March/April, pp. 58-63.
Faeti, A., 'Grapus – A heart bursting with graphic throbs', in: Anceschi, G. (ed.), *Prima Biennale della Grafica*, Milan 1984.
Flugge, M., 'The Grapus group of graphic designers/die Grafikergruppe Grapus', in: *Bildende Kunst* 31 (1983) 4, pp. 160-163.
Forde, G., 'Stamp and the public interest', in: *Eye* 3 (1993) 9, pp. 83-84.
Fukuda, S., 'Posters for "Design Renaissance": the International Design Congress Glasgow 1993', in: *Idea* 42 (1994) 242, pp. 64-67.
Gauthier, N., 'Du graphisme à la signalétique', in: *Le moniteur architecture* (1993) 38, p. 65.
Harper, L., *Radical Graphics/Graphic Radicals*, San Francisco 1999.
He, Jianping, *Pierre Bernard*, Singapore 2006.
Held, U., 'Public works', in: *Eye* 8 (1999) 32, pp. 64-65.
Heller, S., 'Grapus', in: *Graphis* 44 (1988) 257, pp. 48-57.
Heller, S., 'Master class', in: *Applied Arts* 17 (2002) 5, pp. 19-24.
Henrion, F.H.K., 'Grapus', in: *TOP Graphic design* (1983).
Jones, M., 'Hot air in Rio', in: *Design* (1992) 524, pp. 38-41.
Junek, D., 'Grapus', in: *Vytvarny Zivot* 32 (1987) pp. 51-53.
Knoll, M., 'A l'Estienne: Grapus', *Estienne Information Spot* (1981) September.
Macdonald, N., 'Timeless cast of characters', in: *Eye* 8 (1998) 30, pp. 74-75.
Matsunaga, S., 'The 5th International Graphic Arts Competition: Festival d'affiches de Chaumont 1994', in: *Idea* 43 (1995) 248, pp. 72-77.
Mermoz, G., 'Grapus: The "Floating Image"', in: *Idea* 29 (1981) 166, pp. 100-113.

Naggar, C., 'Un collectif de graphistes, 15 ans d'activité de la Maison de la Culture du Havre', in: *Zoom* (1977) 47.

Nelson, L., 'The changing face of French graphic design', in: *How* 11 (1996), pp. 28-33.

Pavec, J-P. Le, 'Grapus la lune, avec parfois le soleil', in: *Révolution*, 30 April 1982.

Pelta, R., 'Grapus: diseno con vocacion social', in: *Diseno Interior* (2000) 101, pp. 75-76.

Peshet, B., 'Exposition Grapus', in: *Bretagne Nouvelle*, 18 February 1979.

Pieters, D., *Grapus affiches*, Amsterdam (Stedelijk Museum, exhibition folder) 1981.

Poulet, J., 'Grapus s'affiche', in: *ATAC Informations* (1978) 96.

Poynor, R., 'Pierre Bernard', in: *Eye* 1 (1991) 3, pp. 8-16.

Pupin, M.A., 'Communication visuelle dans le secteur social' (Pour choisir un métier), Avenirs/Onisep (1978).

Quernec, A. le, 'La 8e Biennale de l'Affiche', in: *B.A.T.* (1980) 28.

Risbeck, P., 'Third Colorado International Poster Exhibition: Colorado '83', in: *Graphis* 40 (1984) 229, pp. 24-37.

Roberts, C., 'Profiles: Jeanne Verdoux', in: *Graphics International* (2001) 85, pp. 38-39.

Stuber, J., 'Mais qu'est-ce qu'ils veulent?', in: *Itinéraire* (1982) 90 (Théâtre de Sartrouville), pp. 4-8.

Taborda, F., 'Posters on environment and development', in: *Novum Gebrauchsgraphik* 63 (1992) 7, pp. 24-29.

Taborda, F., '30 something', in: *Hot Graphics International* (1992) 12, pp. 42-43.

Taylor, R., 'Grapus', in: *Direction* (1987) March, pp. 18-21.

Telford, A., 'Atelier de Création Graphique', in: *Communication Arts* 35 (1994) January/February, pp. 72-81.

Towndrow, J., 'Mellow rebel', in: *Graphics World* (1987) 69, pp. 69-71.

Twemlow, A., 'On peut post bills ici', in: *Print* 58 (2004) 5, pp. 76-81.

Vienne, V., 'Pierre Bernard: staying true to the Frenchman in him', in: *Graphis* 55 (1999) 320, pp. 60-71.

Walters, H., 'The star report', in: *Creative Review* 19 (1999) 2, pp. 53-55.

Watano, S., Matsuzaki, Y., 'L'Atelier de Création-Grapus: Pierre Bernard', in: *Idea* 39 (1991) 227, pp. 40-47.

Weidemann, B., 'Letter from Paris', in: *Design Statements* 7 (1992) 3, pp. 18-20.

Weil, A., 'La grafica francese oggi: tra affiche e pubblica utilità', in: *Quattro stelle – graphic design in Europa*, Milan 1993, pp. 9-21.

Weil, A., 'Grapus', in: *Création* (1991) 8.

Wesselius, J., Weringh, K. van, *Grapus 85: verschillende andere pogingen/différentes tentatives différentes/various different attempts*, Utrecht 1985.

Wlassikoff, M., 'Parce que c'était eux, parce que c'était lui. L'Atelier de Création Graphique 1992', in: *Signes* (1993) 8, pp. 28-31.

Wlassikoff, M., 'What's left… ?', in: *Affiche* (1993) 7, pp. 36-47.

Yew, Wei (ed.), *Atelier de Création Graphique. The works of 12 European Community graphic designers*, Quon Editions 1993.

Zagrodzki, C., '100 French posters in Saint Petersbourg', in: *Idea* 41 (1993) 237, pp. 34-41.

Zeyons, S., 'Pour que les mûrs aient des idées d'aujourd'hui', in: *La vie ouvrière*, 27 November 1978.

Exhibition Catalogues

cat. *Grapus*, Quimper (Galerie Saluden) 1979.

cat. *l'Image politique, sociale et culturelle*, Grenoble (Maison de la Culture) 1979.

cat. *Grapus*, Pecs (Pécsi Galéria) 1982.

cat. *Grapus au Musée de l'affiche*, Paris (Poster Museum) 1982.

cat. *Grapus*, Warsaw (Muzeum Plakatu Wilanowie) 1984.

cat. *Grapus 85: verschillende andere pogingen/différentes tentatives différentes/various different attempts*, Breda (De Beyerd) 1985.

cat. *Grapus*, Tokyo (Alpha Cubic World) 1990.

cat. *Es war einmal Grapus. Plakate aus Paris*, Rostock (Zentrum für Kunstausstellungen der DDR) 1990.

cat. *Pierre Bernard*, Tokyo (Ginza Graphic Gallery) 2000.

cat. *Pierre Bernard*, Hangzhou (First China International Poster Biennale) 2003.

cat. *l'Image du Centre – Atelier de Création Graphique*, Paris (Pompidou Centre) 2005.

cat. *Pierre Bernard, 6 Designs, 6 Postage Stamps*. The Hague (Museum for Communication) 2006.

Other Literature

Actes du symposium international (Université de Montréal 8–11 mei 1991). Special edition of *Informel*, Montreal 1993.

Anceschi, G. (ed.), *Prima Biennale della Grafica. Propaganda e cultura: indagine sul manifesto di pubblica utilità dagli anni Settanta ad oggi*, Milan 1984.

Arntz, G., Broos, K., *Symbolen voor onderwijs en statistiek. 1928–1965 Wenen-Moskou-Den Haag*, Amsterdam 1979.

Barthes, R., *Mythologies*, New York 1971 (Orig. Paris 1957).

Baur, R. (ed.), *Das Gesetz und seine visuellen Folgen*, Wettingen 2005.

Benjamin, W., 'The Work of Art in the Age of Its Technological Reproducibility', in: Walter Benjamin, *Selected Writings*. Vol. 3, *1935-1938*. Ed. by H. Eiland and M.W. Jennings, Cambridge 2006 (Orig. 1936).

Bobbio, N., *Democracy and Dictatorship: the Nature and Limits of State Power*, Cambridge 1989.

Boekraad, H.C., 'Dutch Design. Hoe bestaat het?', in: *Vormberichten* (1994) 5, pp. 2-5.

Boekraad, H.C., 'Graphic Design as Visual Rhetoric', in: Gruson, E., Staal, G. (eds.), *Copy Proof. A New Method for Design Education*, Rotterdam 2000.

Boekraad, H.C., 'Rotterdam 2001. Five Design Proposals for a House Style', in: Lauwen, T. (ed.), *Identiteiten. Identities*, Rotterdam 2001.

Bolten, J., *Het Nederlandse bankbiljet en zijn vormgeving*, Amsterdam 1987.

Broos, K., Hefting, P., *Grafische vormgeving in Nederland. Een eeuw*, Amsterdam/Antwerp 1993.

Buchanan, R., 'Wicked Problems in Design Thinking', in: Buchanan, R., Margolin, V. (eds.), *The Idea of Design*, Massachusetts 1992, pp. 3-20.

Calvet, L-J., *Roland Barthes, 1915–1980*, Paris 1990.

Calvet, L-J., *Roland Barthes, un regard politique sur le signe*, Paris 1973.

cat. *The Great Utopia: The Russian and Soviet Avant-Garde 1915–1932*, New York (Solomon R. Guggenheim Museum) 1992.

cat. *High & Low. Modern Art and Popular Culture*, New York (The Museum of Modern Art) 1991.

cat. *Images d'utilité publique*, Paris (Pompidou Centre) 1988.

cat. *l'Image des mots*, Paris (Pompidou Centre/CCI) 1985.

cat. *Politisch/soziales Engagement & Graphik Design*, Berlin (Neue Gesellschaft für Bildende Kunst) 2000.

cat. *"qu'est-ce qu'une campagne publicitaire?"*, Paris (Pompidou Centre/CCI) 1975.

cat. *Henryk Tomaszewski*, Amsterdam (Stedelijk Museum) 1991.

Cohen, L., Arato, A., *Civil Society and Political Theory*, Massachusetts 1992.

Damisch, H., *A Theory of Cloud: Toward a History of Painting*, Stanford 2002 (Orig 1972).

Demoule, J-P., 'Introduction', in: *Vingt ans de découvertes*, Paris 2005.

Findeli, A. (ed.), 'Promothée éclairé. Ethique, technique et responsabilité professionelle en design', I, II, III, IV, in: *Informel* (Montreal) vol. 3 no.2, 1990; vol. 4 nos. 1/2, 1991; vol. 5 no.1, 1992.

Glaser, M., Ilić, M., *The Design of Dissent*, Gloucester (Mass.) 2005.

Graafland, J.L.M., Stalins, A., *Encyclopédie Héraldique/ Heraldische Encyclopedie*, The Hague 1932.

Gurvitsch, G. *La vocation actuelle de la sociologie*. Vol. 1 *Vers une sociologie différentielle*, Paris 1950.

Habermas, J., *The Structural Transformation of the Public Sphere*, Cambridge 1989 (Orig. 1962).

Habermas, J., *The Theory of Communicative Action*, Boston 1984 (Orig. 1981).

Heller, S., Ilić, M., *Handwritten: Expressive Lettering in the Digital Age*, London 2004.

Hofland, H.J.A., *Een teken aan de wand. Album van de Nederlandse samenleving 1963–1983*, Amsterdam 1983.

Hollis, R., *Swiss Graphic Design. The Origins and Growth of an International Style 1920–1965*, London 2006.

Huygen, F., Schmidtt-Siegel, H., 'Die Niederlande – fast ein Designer-Paradies', in: *Form* (1985) 108/109, pp. 52-59.

Internationale situationniste 1958–69, (reprint) Amsterdam 1970.

Jaquet, C., *Das Staatsdesign der Schweiz –Zustand und Reform*. Analyse des Erscheinungsbildes der Bundesverwaltung und Empfehlungen für seine Vereinheitlichung, Bern 2004.

Kandinsky, W., *Point and Line to Plane*, New York 1947 (Orig. 1926).

Keane, J. (ed.), *Civil Society and the State*, London 1988.

Kinross, R., 'The Rhetoric of Neutrality', in: *Design Issues* 2 (1985) 2, pp. 18-30.

Krimpen, H. van, *Boek. Over het maken van boeken*, Veenendaal 1986.

Lipovetsky, G., *Le bonheur paradoxal. Essai sur la société d'hyperconsommation*, Paris 2006.

Lootsma, B., 'Mentalities Instead of Objects', in: Lootsma, B., Staal G., Baan, C. de (eds.), *Mentalitäten, Niederlandisches Design*, Bremen (Securitas Galerie, catalogue) 1995.

Lupton, E., Miller, J. Abbott (eds.), *The ABCs of Triangle, Square and Circle. The Bauhaus and Design Theory*, London 1993.

Marquand, D., *Decline of the Public*, Cambridge 2004.

Miège, B., *La société conquise par la communication*, Paris 1989.

Mission de coordination des grands opérations d'architecture et d'urbanisme, *Grands Projets 1979–1989*, Paris 1985.

Neurath, O., *Modern Man in the Making*, New York 1939.

Open, cahier over kunst en het publieke domein, 4 (2005) 8.

Osborne, D., Gaebler, T., *Reinventing Government: How the Entrepreneurial Spirit is Transforming the Public Sector*, Reading (Mass.) 1992.

Papanek, V., *Design for the Real World. Making to Measure*, London 1972.

Pessers, D., *Big Mother, over de personalisering van de publieke sfeer*, The Hague 2003.

Pessers, D., 'De symbolische legitimaties van de constitutionele monarchie', in: Elzinga, D.J. (ed.), *De constitutionele monarchie in Europees perspectief*, Amsterdam 2006 (English translation forthcoming).

Rouard-Snowman, M., *Jean Widmer graphiste. Un écologiste de l'image*, Paris (Pompidou Centre) 1995.

Ruskin, J., *Modern Painters*, London 1860.

Sauvage, A-M. (ed.), *Cassandre. Oeuvres graphiques modernes 1923–1939*, Paris 2005.

Sennett, R., *The Fall of Public Man*, New York 1974.

Sennett, R., *The Conscience of the Eye: the Design and Social Life of Cities*, New York 1990.

Skolos, N., Wedell, T., *Type, Image, Message. A Graphic Layout Workshop*, Gloucester (Mass.) 2006.

Sontag, S. (Introduction), *A Barthes Reader*, London 1982.

Spitz, R., *hfg Ulm. The View Behind the Foreground. The Political History of the Ulm School of Design 1953–1968*, Stuttgart/London 2002.

Staal, G., Wolters, H. (eds.), *Holland in Vorm; Dutch design 1945–1987*, The Hague 1987.

Starobinski, J., *L'invention de la liberté 1700–1789; suivi de: 1789 Les emblèmes de la Raison*, Paris 2006.

Supiot, A., *Homo Juridicus. Essai sur la fonction anthropologique du droit*, Paris 2005 (English translation forthcoming).

Teunissen, M., 'Dutch Railways', in: Staal, G., Wolters, H. (eds.), *Holland in Vorm; Dutch design 1945–1987*, The Hague 1987, pp. 45-49.

Verhoeven, C., *Folteren om bestwil*, Baarn 1977.

Vico, G., *On the Study Methods of our Time*, Ithaca/ New York 1990 (Orig. 1709).

Weintraub, J., Kumar, K. (eds.), *Public and Private in Thought and Practice. Perspectives on a Grand Dichotomy*, Chicago 1997.

Wells, C., 'KLM, a history of the future', in: Bos, B., Hefting, P., Henrion, F.H.K. (eds.), *The Image of a Company*, London 1990, pp. 125-134.

Wingler, H.M., *Bauhaus: Weimar, Dessau, Berlin, Chicago*, Cambridge 1978 (Orig. 1975).

Wlassikoff, M., *The Story of Graphic Design in France*, Amsterdam 2006 (Orig. 2005).

Wunenburger, J.-J., *Imaginaires du politique*, Paris 2001.

Yazamikhammer, D., Fillinger, G., Ughetto, B. (eds.), *Pour les droits de l'homme. Histoires Images Paroles*, Paris 1989.

SOS-Kinderdorf

Poster for
SOS Children's Villages
95.4 × 84 / 1998

Established in Austria in 1949, SOS-Kinderdorf has since grown into a worldwide organization that builds villages for orphans in war zones and developing countries. Here the children are accommodated in a family environment offering security, education, healthcare and social services so that they have a prospect of rebuilding their lives. The organization, which is dependent upon donations, regularly invites a graphic designer to create a poster about its aims and activities.

On this poster Bernard reduces the village to a house, drawn in a single unbroken line. This archetypal symbol is placed in the centre of the image. The facade is divided into four triangles, each in its own colour as if the facade were one large painted shutter of a European farmhouse. Its diagonals are extended to the space around the house, creating four sections, each with its own colour and theme.

The poster is the schematic representation of a war child's cosmology. Starting with the horizontal axis of the image, the triangle to the left of the house is the space of the past. It is an unattractive region, strewn with black smudges and various sorts of mechanical vehicle drawn as if by a child. On this side the house is closed, but the black that dominates this blasted terrain nevertheless penetrates the adjacent section of the house. The area to the right of the house is in quite a different key: open, bright, and relatively undefined. It is populated by a throng of sensuous, voluminous, drifting clouds. On this side the house is open.

Now for the picture's vertical axis. The space above the house is dominated by a blaze of yellow specks and warm red hearts rising from the chimney. Spreading out like a plume of rising smoke, the hearts demonstrate a law of human perception, becoming larger with decreasing distance. Below the house is the natural world, inhabited by a bird of prey and a fabulous creature that the designer has conjured out of his top hat. Blurring the boundary between two species it is – whether by turns or simultaneously – a stubborn donkey and a cuddly rabbit. Bernard adds this creature to the realm of imaginary animals, but haven't we been familiar with it all our lives?

The whole picture, including the path to the door of the house, is seen through the eyes of a child. The path and hearts draw a diagonal that articulates the poster in yet another way. The path, winding through the world of nature, bears the name of the organization. It leads to the security of the house, finding its extension in the heart-smoke rising from the chimney.

The cheerful, optimistic tone of the poster contrasts with the seriousness of the topic. Sunny, bright colours and forms dominate, not denying the negative side of reality but capturing it in a frame in which it remains a memento. The image as a whole promises security, trust and love.

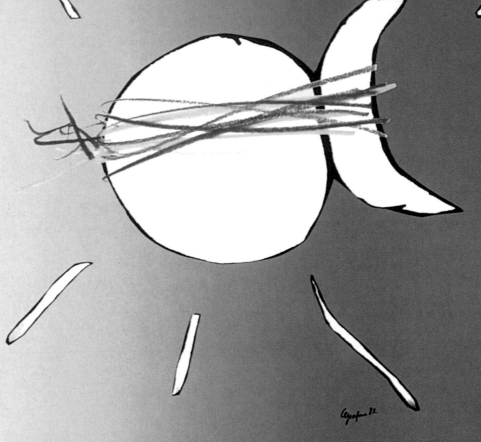

10 juillet...

...7 août

Avig*Avignon* 82.

location : bureau du Festival, 84000   tel. (90) 86 24 43

Avignon 82

On this poster, time passes from left to right, from light to dark, from day to night, from 10 July to 7 August. The sun and moon, symbols of day and night, are tied together and appear as one celestial body on a background that changes from light to dark grey. The title is duplicated: positive and negative at the bottom of the poster. Everything is black, grey or white; the only colour is in the threads. Sun and moon are colourless and their rays too are white, except at the very tips where flecks of red or yellow can be discerned. Where they touch, the sun and the moon flatten each other, as if the sun is carrying the moon on its back.

The inspiration for this image was a song by Charles Trenet: 'Le soleil a rendez-vous avec la lune, mais la lune n'y est pas et le soleil l'attend' (the sun has a rendez-vous with the moon but the moon's not there and the sun is waiting for it). Here the failed meeting in the song has become a solid union, but the keynote remains melancholic. Sun and moon are inseparable: they have been removed from the natural world and transplanted in the world of humans, where human emotions and relationships are projected onto them. The union is ambiguous: it can be read as stemming from affection and mutual attraction, but also as the locking together of two opposing entities.

Represented as an animal, a fancy goldfish or bird moving through the air, the sun/moon is an overdetermined creature. This metaphorical image visualizes the definition of the metaphor itself as an ontological mistake, a jump from one order of being to another. Man is a wolf to man, the sun is a lover to the moon. This image demonstrates the surrealistic definition of the metaphor: the uniting in one image of two signs/meanings that are in reality as far removed from one another as possible.

For one of France's most important cultural festivals Bernard creates a symbolic image that not only surprises but, like every symbol, is open to interpretation. The poster illustrates just one of the festival's characteristics – the intermingling of day and night – but it is also a reference to the sultry atmosphere of the southern French summer, to fleeting liaisons and amorous attachments.

Without involving the studio, the client used the festival emblem on other printed matter such as leaflets, as well as items of merchandise, e.g. wine labels and T-shirts. The emblem was an unqualified success, but Grapus's commission was not renewed the following year. Even a professionally run festival like Avignon can evidently fail to see the importance of having a graphic design studio as a long-term partner.

Grapus Posters

Poster for a Grapus
exhibition in Lahti, Finlan
70 × 50 / 1988

An autumn evening in Finland. Grapus has an exhibition in Lahti where the biennial poster festival is taking place. The moonlight casts the shadow of the name 'Grapus' on the floor of the exhibition room. Bernard is struck by the projection of the word framed in the distorted perspective of the window. Unable to resist the temptation to play a part in this shadow theatre he magically produces the silhouette of an animal between the glazing bars of the window, below the name. Turn the image through ninety degrees and you can see how the head of a camel or horse is formed by the shadow of his body, elbow and hand.

This scene is then recorded in a photograph in which not only the silhouette of the 'puppeteer' but also the shadow of the photographer is recorded. In other words, the photo records not just the surprising image itself but also the way it was made. Thanks to the moonlight and the laws of optics on which photography is based, the image is created by two people, reminding us of the collaborative aspect of all Grapus designs.

This poster is an invention in two phases. The discovery of the word Grapus on the floor led to the staged photograph of the shadow play. Second, the picture was manipulated through the addition of a décor of the heavens in which a spiky moon lights up the night sky. Onto this dark sky a poster is drawn, a black surface filled with scratchy lines. This poster within the poster lies somewhere between the moon, the camera lens and the pointing hand of the designer. Flanking it are the handwritten words *Grapus* and *affiches*, the latter with letters that have been thickened, filled in or distorted.

Seen against this composite background, the pointing gesture of the illuminated hand becomes an ambiguous sign. The hand plays the age-old game of intercepting the light, but at the same time its gesture acquires an indexical function. The finger points not at the poster but at the moon alongside or above it, thereby visualizing the expression *Quand on montre la lune, l'imbécile regarde le doigt* (point at the moon, and the imbecile looks at the finger).

This poster is an ode to graphic art, a play of black, white and grey. Lit by the moon, the grey floor becomes a white background against which we see the murky figures of the photographer, the mythical animal and the shadow player. The dark grey background is trumped by the black rectangle, a generic image representing the posters on display in the exhibition. At the bottom of the poster a black bar gives information printed reversed out.

Also another linguistic association is at work in this image. There is a saying in French that inseparable friends are *comme l'ombre et le corps* (like shadow and body). It should be remembered that in 1988, when this poster was made, Grapus had already started to disintegrate. The black overpainting of the poster-within-the-poster is another sign that the designer realizes and laments that the collective's glory years, the results of which are shown in the retrospective exhibition in Finland, are over.

JULISTEMUSEO LAHTI Vesijärvenkatu 11   8. 10. – 11. 12. 1988   Avoinna päivittäin 10 – 18

ter for a conference
he International Council
Graphic Design
sociations in Glasgow
× 60 / 1993

Design Renaissance

We are familiar from Greek mythology with the image of Atlas bearing the world on his shoulders. Here the world is reduced to the size of a marble. Whereas in the poster Amériques Latines (p. 309) we see a continent at the heart of a flower, here the whole world is cradled in the palm of a hand. Once again Bernard combines two recurrent themes in his work: the hand and the world. The globe is executed in papier mâché and painted in ink, which leaves traces on the palm and fingers. The hand also functions as the medium for the message, with information about the conference and its title written on the skin in felt-tip pen, as if the designer happened not to have any paper to hand.

The photographic image is at once familiar and mysterious; the globe is sharp, the hand blurred. The globe appears to float, freeing itself from the skin onto which it casts a shadow. Taken with a Polaroid camera, the picture was originally intended as a sketch to show the professional photographer what was wanted. However, it proved impossible to match the expressiveness and atmosphere of the Polaroid with a professional camera.

The chiaroscuro around the hand creates an indeterminate space, isolating the hand from the body so that it becomes an independent symbol. Together, hand and globe invite participation, not just in the Icograda conference, but also in caring for the world. Given the freshness of the ink-stains, the hand must first have been closed around the globe, protecting the world and being its shelter. Since the hand is put in a vertical position, it symbolizes the power to act, or simply power per se. It gives a stop signal or warning: the earth is vulnerable, and its future lies in the hand of man. The values being appealed to here are responsibility and vigilance.

The significance of any image is to some extent determined by its context. Bernard designed this poster for the Icograda conference in Glasgow, Scotland, in 1993, under the noble-sounding but non-committal title of *Design Renaissance*. The poster subtly criticizes the vague progressiveness that the profession likes to evince at such well-attended international meetings. Besides offering a surprising image of the world, it gives us a picture of the designer's profession. The hand is covered with signs, the very stuff with which graphic designers fill the world. The profession is brought back to its graphic origins: saturating paper with ink. Indeed, the world is so full of ink that it leaves traces on the skin, creating a print which is, however, anything but perfect. We can still make out one or two continents, but on the inside of the fingers there is a chaotic archipelago, a *corps morcelé* of scattered signifiers. The Sartrian concept of dirty hands to which the poster alludes suggests that the designer is not free of blame.

Respect, Dedication, Solidarity

Respect, Dévouement, Solidarité
Poster commissioned by
French aid organization
Secours Populaire Franç●
176 × 120 / 2001

This poster was widely distributed by Secours Populaire Français, a volunteer organization that provides moral and financial support to those suffering or at risk of social exclusion. The poster presents and represents the organization in several ways: by its emblem, by a statement of its values, and by images of its activities.

The central element is a text area superimposed on the frontal image of a superb white pigeon. Placed seemingly at random and overlying three of six other images, the words state the core values of the organization. A diagnosis is made: the world is full of inequality, exclusion and injustice. The rejection of this state of affairs is indicated typographically by the lines that strike through the words as a thrice repeated 'No'. The same typographical element is used to *under*line a trio of positive values. Printed in a smaller size across the poster and more closely linked to the images, keywords identify the organization's objectives.

The positioning of images on the edges of the poster recalls the way people slip pictures into the frame of a mirror. The pictures show some of the SPF's activities: holidays for children led by volunteers, help for the sick and frail, the bringing together of children of various cultures. This loose constellation of images is grouped not just along the edge, but also around the centre. Through its activities as a civil society organization Secours Populaire mediates between the values of the public domain and the private world of people living precarious lives.

The central block of text confidently and deliberately proposes an alternative version of the values of the French Republic: liberty, equality, fraternity. Compared with the motto of the Republic, however, there is a shift: rather than the principles of the democratic constitutional State, the words *respect*, *dévouement* and *solidarité* denote human attitudes. Particularly striking is the term *dévouement* (devotion or dedication), which refers historically to feudal and family virtues and today to human goodness and emotional engagement with others. *Solidarité* is a class concept coined by the nineteenth-century workers' movement. *Respect* has to do with the way individuals treat each other, independent of political ideology or social status. The three concepts act as the coordinates of the ethic of reciprocity that the poster urges us to adopt, an ethic that transcends the framework of the principles of the constitutional State.

The unity of the poster image, divided into a series of rectangles, is created not only by the central text block but also by the dominant image of the dove on the vertical axis. This choice of image was probably informed by association with the wings in the emblem of the SPF. However, this particular bird is less gentle than what we are used to, its dark eyes contrasting sharply with the softness and purity of its feathers. This dove is very much alive, watching us alertly as if overseeing adherence to the values pinned to its breast. Its position high and mighty in the poster gives this friendly bird, this symbol of peace and constancy, a connotation of dominance and power – so much so that it almost appears threatening. This dove takes on aspects of the eagle, king of the skies.

SECOURS
POPULAIRE
FRANÇAIS

ENGAGEMENT

~~inégalité~~, ~~exclusion~~

MONDE

AVENIR

ACTION

~~injustice~~,

BÉNÉVOLAT

FRANCE

ENFANCE

JEUNESSE

respect, dévouement,

DROITS DE L'HOMME

solidarité.

CITOYENNETÉ

FRATERNITÉ

graphisme Atelier de Création Graphique 2001, photographe(s)de haut en bas et de gauche à droite: Bettina Rheims, Andrés Le Jarre, le Gar Floréal, Martin Parr, Marie-Paule Négre, Axel Rahamvololy, Mario Fostino, Dominique Delpoux.

first day of issue
eerste dag van uitgift.

60+30c
Nederland

dag van
uitgifte
8-9 1992
den haag
125 jaar
nederlandse
rode kruis

Nederland
70+35c

dag van
uitgifte
8-9 1992
den haag
125 jaar
nederlandse
rode kruis

NEDERLAND
80 + 40C

eerste

dag van
uitgifte
8-9 1992
den haag
125 jaar
nederlandse
rode kruis

NR 299

plaatsen waar levensgevaar dreigt   waar mensen in nood zijn   hulp behoeven

ued by the Dutch Post
fice on the occasion of
125th anniversary of the
tch Red Cross
×3.6 / 1992

Postage stamps

The postage stamps present three faces of the Red Cross: medical services to relieve human suffering; the emblem of the organization as used in the media; and the reciprocal relationship of people supporting each other – the Red Cross as a volunteer organization. The theme of individual suffering is evoked by a gauze dressing through which seeps a yellowish salve and against which the red cross contrasts sharply. Reproduced on a television screen or in a newspaper, the emblem loses its outline and colour. In situations where one person helps another the cross becomes transparent: the concrete gesture of aid shining through. Symbol and gesture blend and the institutional symbol becomes a metaphor for a certain kind of human relationship. In the words of Pierre Bernard: 'What really exists is the two arms. Where help is offered the cross disappears.'

Each of the three stamps exploits the tactile quality of cloth. The emblem is displayed on a flag. The pleated shirt of the aid worker can be seen through the transparent cross. The close-up photograph of the gauze is expressive: the fine mesh structure is not used ornamentally because of its repetitive pattern, but rather as a metaphor of closeness, as a second skin. The use of textile in these stamps is at odds with the post-modern predilection for decoration.

The word 'Nederland' and the face values are rendered in three different ways: in a sans serif font, a dot matrix font and handwriting. 'The form and position of the numerals and the name have been harmonized with the aesthetic of each image', says Bernard. The additional slogan is a variation on the well-known 'I love New York' rebus in which the word 'love' is replaced by a the pictogram of a heart. Here the cross has been substituted for the heart and New York has been replaced by an orange miniature map of the Netherlands. The rebus translates as: 'I personally participate in the Dutch Red Cross.' This commitment is illustrated by the handwritten indication of the number of members (*leden*) and volunteers (*vrijwilligers*).

These stamps incarnate two different forms of the public interest. The very choice of the Red Cross theme acknowledges the public interest in the Red Cross as a humanitarian organization. As a medium, however, stamps themselves represent a form of public interest, as they are an exponent of the national visual culture. In an interview given when the stamps were issued, Bernard emphasized this aspect of the stamp policies of national postal authorities. 'In France the choice of theme is dictated by a mania for commemoration. Year in year out the same stereotypes are repeated. They are never provocative and the result is a stereotypical national iconography. In Britain and Holland stamps are infinitely more adventurous. This attitude makes their stamps a window on the national culture. Above all, they show us different world-views. If you have a long-term policy of selecting good themes and designers, a very rich world opens up.' [Boekraad 1993]

307

Latin America's

Amériques Latines
Poster for a series of
cultural events devoted to
Latin America, in the
Pompidou Centre
176 × 120 / 1992

In 1992 Pierre Bernard and the designer Dirk Behage, his partner in the newly founded Atelier de Création Graphique, attended a UN conference in Rio de Janeiro. As they were leaving the conference centre, they were each presented with a flower by a Brazilian woman. Bernard kept his exotic bloom and the memory of the event came back to him a few months later when he was asked to design a poster for the Amériques Latines festival in the Pompidou Centre in Paris.

The design came about through the association of two images representing Latin America. As an indexical sign, the flower petal represents the continent from which it sprang. The cartographic image shows a continent by night, its major conurbations shining out in the darkness. Not only has the continent lost its relief, the customary orientation of the north-south axis is reversed: here the south is our north. The surprising image created by this combination is based on an enormous jump in scale. René Magritte once discovered a whole tree in the nerve structure of its leaf. Bernard goes a step further and discovers Latin America in the heart of one of its flowers.

The form of the saw-toothed coastline corresponds to the irregular outline of the petal. The rich colour of its upper part pales in the lower half, becomes brown and fades in the craquelure of parched, dried-out earth. Here geography becomes political commentary. The idea of projecting the continent onto the flower was triggered by the dark spot where loose fibres are a reminder of its separation from the stem. The suggestion of a violent break with the wealthy north, i.e. the United States, is found in the structure of the plant itself. Only a minor adjustment to the orientation of the strip of land linking North and South America was needed to imbue a botanical given with a political charge. Cutting the umbilical cord from the north causes the loss of colour in the south; the lifeless black, contrasting with the vibrant colours of the flower, becomes the sign of death and decay. The neutral map acquires the value of a symbol.

The typography is subtly positioned within the outline of the petal; the institutional information yields to the form of the flower, yet contrasts with it. The aesthetic of the typography responds to the modernist aesthetic of the Pompidou Centre itself, and in particular to the emblem designed by Jean Widmer: another play of horizontal and diagonal lines.

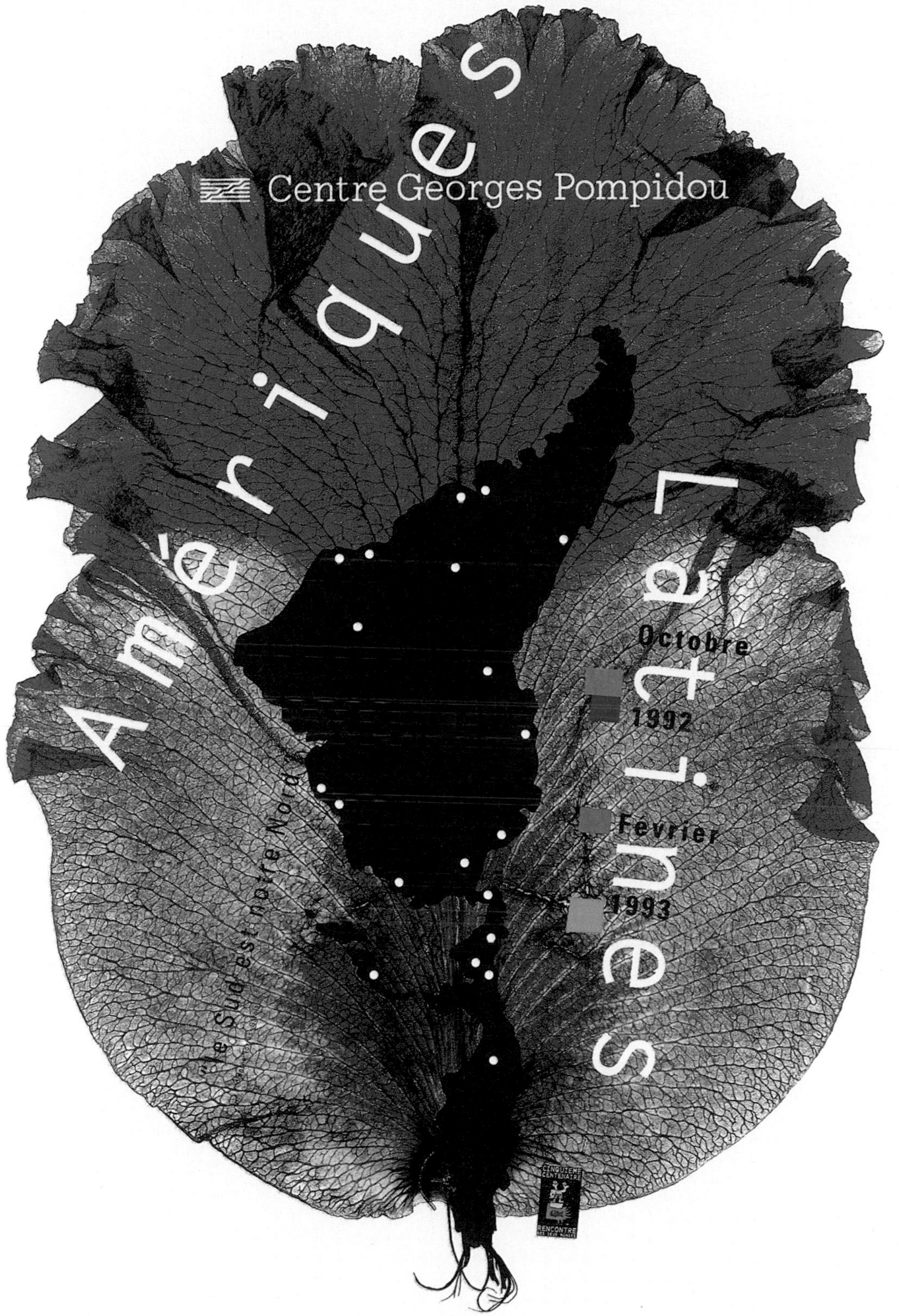

Amériques

Latines

Amériques

Centre Georges Pompidou

le Sud Est notre Nord

Octobre
1992

Fevrier
1993

Atelier de Création Graphique '92 - Grapus   Photo : Studio N Sérigraphie : Graphicn

TRACES DU PARADIS TERRESTRE ».

wo pages of the Atelier
e Création Graphique's
ew Year card, printed in
:rossed-out and colour-
riped typeface
ooklet, 8 pages in a cover
) × 14.5 / January 1996

Barré de couleur

Barré de couleur is an adaptation of Barré, the typeface designed by Bernard in 1995 for the site signage at the Pompidou Centre during the renovation that began that year (pp. 278-280). The print version of Barré de couleur was presented by de Atelier in a booklet sent to its clients and contacts as a New Year greeting. It was probably the first font in the world to have a stroke through each letter as an integral component.

Why do people cross words out, and what effect does crossing out have? Words can, of course, be struck through to make them illegible, e.g. to hide information in a document. *Horizontal* deletion of this kind arouses our curiosity or frustration about the text that has been withdrawn from view, and invests it with an air of mystery.

A *diagonal* stroke through a text can indicate that it has been dealt with, taken care of, or declared passé – that is how the past year's numbers are crossed off in this New Year card. Another function of crossing out is correction: the stroke indicates that the crossed-out passage has been rejected or must be rewritten. *Vertical* strokes can divide a text into segments, just as in musical notation the bars are indicated by bar lines (Barthes goes so far as to maintain in *S/Z* that a text is comparable in every way to a musical score). Finally, a diagonal stroke through a letter can also function as an extended accent, intensifying its presence.

In this New Year card it is not the words that are struck through, but the letters. This has been done in such a way that they remain legible, albeit with some effort. To the extent that the crossing out slows down reading, it increases the reader's attention. Here crossing out functions like underlining. The capitals are given pseudo-ascenders and descenders of equal width but varying length, thus breaking up the linearity of the text. Since the bars are placed at different angles relative to the vertical axis of the letters, a rotational movement results that undermines the static verticality of the typography. The colours modulate the binary black-and-white.

The strikethrough in Barré de couleur, which might appear to take something away from each letter, acts as a supplement adding variety, colour and rhythm to it. The strokes are correction marks in the sense that they cancel out the functional unambiguity of the black Barré. They bring music to the letters.

The text reproduced here consists of the last four words of a quotation from Emil Cioran, the Romanian philosopher and essayist who died in 1995. The full quotation is as follows: 'It is not without reason that in every era people believe they are witnessing the disappearance of the last traces of earthly paradise.' (C'est avec raison qu'à chaque époque on croit assister à la disparition des dernières traces du paradis terrestre.) It is a paradoxical statement. The last traces of paradise are not the last, they show up anew in every era, although not *sub specie aeternitatis* but as an effect of melancholy. Cioran's paradox confirms the indestructibility of hope. The image of Eden can be seen in every desert. It is that game of simultaneously disappearing and reappearing that the coloured stripes play with the letters. They cover up and illuminate in one and the same movement.

311

Information panel Tamié Abbey

Sign along Route national no. 90
630 × 315 / 1991

Tamié is a Cistercian abbey in Savoy whose history dates back to the twelfth century. Rebuilt in the seventeenth century, it is still inhabited by Trappist monks. On this sign the abbey is not presented as building but as a place devoted to the spiritual life: the Gregorian church music is a reference to the way of life of the monks who dedicate much of their day to prayer and song.

The selection of Albertville as the site of the 1992 Winter Olympics – Tamié abbey is quite close to the town – was seized upon by the local authorities as an opportunity to make the region more attractive. As part of that effort, a competition was organized for the design of a new tourist information system along the motorways in the region. The competition, in which Jean Widmer was also a candidate, was won by the Atelier de Création Graphique. This victory is remarkable bearing in mind that it was Widmer's studio Visuel Design that had designed the system of pictograms that provide tourist information along 2500 kilometres of French autoroutes.

So what is the difference between Bernard's information system, of which the sign for the abbey is a part, and Widmer's? Widmer presents the themes in a highly simplified, uniform picture language. He also physically separates image and text on two panels: a first sign shows the pictogram and then, a couple of hundred metres down the road, another carries the text. The Atelier de Création Graphique breaks with the uniformity of this visual language. Stylistically the iconography of the Atelier is flexible and varied in its expression: ranging from grim to cheerful, from fantastical to realistic, from historical to contemporary. The images are photographic, drawn, etched or, as here, typographic. In addition, text and image are brought together in a panel that is divided into two halves, one above the other, like a domino. Inspired by movie subtitling, this amounts to a format which might be described as the vertical version of a double-page spread. Where the image is typographic, two functions of typography confront each other, the subtitle describing and the musical score evoking the reality being referred to. The slight shift of perspective indicates the difference between the two functions.

It is surprising in a country that professes separation of church and State to find a road sign in church Latin. This is even more surprising given that the sign was commissioned by the regional authority and a private-sector toll road operator. The presence of a religious symbol in public space could be explained by the impact of the national heritage in French culture and cultural policy. This patrimony includes equally medieval liturgical music as well as images and accounts of the wartime Resistance, another theme seen along this autoroute. Over the years this patrimony has come to play an important role in Bernard's vision of the social role of graphic design.

The visualization of the theme is based partly on research on the spot and conversations with the inhabitants. The monk who alerted the designer to this piece of plainsong in his gradual: 'The wind bloweth where it will, and thou hearest the voice thereof, but knowest not whence it cometh, and whither it goeth', may have been thinking not only of the celebration of the Eucharist in his abbey but also about mass tourism.

Abbaye
de Tamié
17e S.

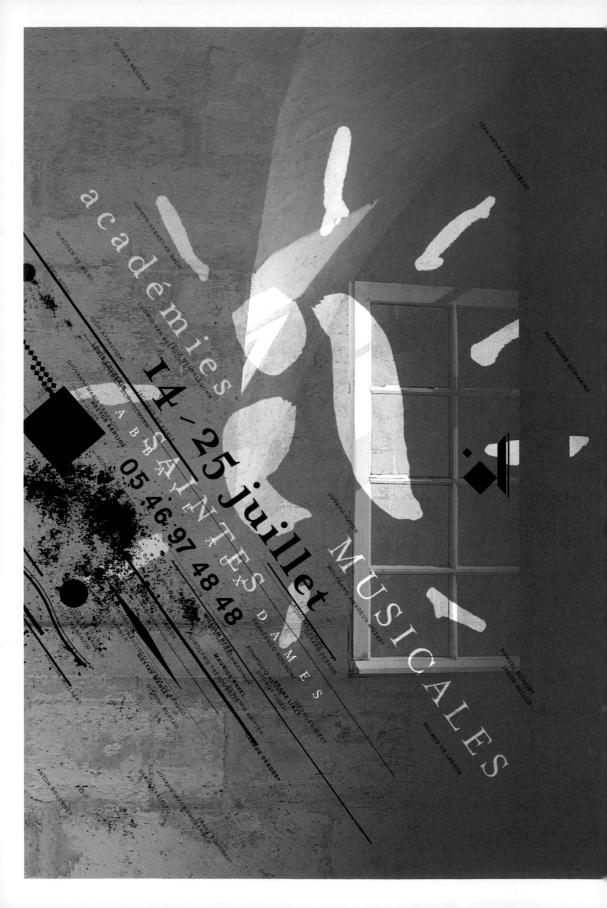

Musical Academies

This poster was commissioned by the board of a musical festival, *Académies Musicales*. The festival is held annually in July in a former abbey in Saintes, a small town in south-western France. Its fame springs from its long-standing association with Philippe Herreweghe and Paul van Nevel. Incidentally, musical academies are not institutions of musical education, but local associations of musicians in the eighteenth century that met for the pleasure of making music together.

The starting point for this poster is the emblem that Bernard had already designed for the festival, a lower case 'a' radiating rays of light. What is the meaning of this vastly enlarged minuscule? Is it the first letter of the word academies, which is also set in lower case? Or does the 'a' stand for a note in the musical scale? The answer is both. More important than its meaning, however, is its form. From the thousands of typefaces that he could have chosen, Bernard selected a Monotype variant of the typeface designed in 1767 by Bodoni. It is easily recognized by the bulb-shaped terminal on the lower-case 'a' and 'f' and its strong black/white and thick/thin contrasts. This typeface differs from handwriting in its uncompromising verticality, underlined by the horizontality of its extremely fine serifs. Huib van Krimpen observes: 'In Bodoni every trace of the calligraphic tradition has disappeared: his letterforms rely exclusively on fantastic punch-cutting technique.' [Van Krimpen 1986] It is precisely this anti-calligraphic typeface that Bernard, armed with a broad brush, attacks in a calligraphic exercise. All fine lines disappear from the 'a', leaving just one round and two curvilinear forms. If you squint, you can still make out the typical Bodoni 'a', but the brush-stroked halo that surrounds the deconstructed character causes its meaning to shift. On a pale background the radiant black 'a' takes on the character of a source of sound. Shining against a dark background, it becomes a source of light.

This character is now deployed on a poster in which typography, photography and calligraphy are ingeniously combined. The emblem moves from a typographic into an architectural space; the result is that the two-dimensional sign can be read as a three-dimensional figure. Does what looks like a humped back and bent head indicate an introverted human figure?

Against an open window in the background, the floating sign is open to another interpretation. I came across it in a recent book by Skolos and Wedell, *Type Image Message*: 'In this poster for a festival of sacred music ... Bernard used spiritual symbols. The glowing hand-painted angel appears as if he is flying out of the open windows.' [Skolos/Wedell 2006] The authors, perhaps misled by the word *Saintes*, see the emblem as an angel being sucked backwards into the black hole of the night. If it is an angel, he heralds a music festival that is certainly not restricted to sacred music.

The character 'a' floats in indefined space and assumes multiple meanings. I see a *wohltemperiert* sign of sound and light hovering on the boundary of interior and exterior space. It leaves or enters the room in the same way that music wafts through an open window on a summer evening.

Rotterdam Cultural Capital of Europe 2001

Project for a poster, part of house style presentation, not produced
1999

In collaboration with
Johannes Bergerhausen

In 1985 Melina Mercouri, then Minister of Culture in Greece, took the initiative to designate a different European city every year to be the Cultural Capital of Europe; Athens was the first. In 1998 it was decided that Rotterdam would hold the title in 2001, sharing the honour with the Portuguese city of Oporto.

Three objectives are united in the phenomenon of the cultural capital of Europe: the promotion of dialogue between the cultures of Europe; the promotion of cultural tourism; and the city festival as publicly sponsored entertainment. These objectives fit in with the genuine festival culture that arose in the eighties as a political instrument of local authorities.

In this case, Rotterdam 2001, the festival director emphasized the confluence of the various cultures in the city under the motto: 'Rotterdam is many cities'. The city organized a limited competition for which not only three Dutch agencies but also Qwer in Cologne and Atelier de Création Graphique in Paris were invited to tender. Instead of the usual monolithic logo, they were asked to develop a multifaceted logo for the festival that would do justice to the multicultural character of the great seaport.

The logo that the Atelier designed is a constellation of three circles of different sizes. One city is a dot, two cities two dots, three dots many cities. The position of the two smaller circles relative to the large one can be varied, so that by means of rotation a flexible logo system is created, to which is added the full name *Rotterdam 2001*. This construction evokes associations with an orrery or a colour circle, but one in which the colours are not defined. *All colours are beautiful.*

The flexibility of this logo system is further enhanced by the fact that the circles can be filled in in any way desired. In use, they are enriched with images taken from the historical or contemporary visual culture of Rotterdam. In this way the logo, an empty symbol, becomes the vehicle for an icon (or fragment of an icon) from either high or low culture – Mondrian or Mickey Mouse, a cartoon or a poster, typography or photography. The supersign of the circles acts as a container that is open to all languages, symbols and images without losing its own identity. It symbolizes the dynamism and integrating ability both of the organization and of the city that is harbouring it. But this planetary sign system can also function as emptiness: a blank area in an existing image. Executed as three outline circles – it can be used in publicity material for institutions participating in the festival.

Reproduced here is the proposal for the poster announcing the festival. It shows one of the most famous paintings in Rotterdam's museum of fine arts, the Boijmans Van Beuningen, Brueghel's *The Tower of Babel*. (Though the biblical story to which it refers offers a less than optimistic vision of the multilingual city.) Against the background of the tower, an edifice rising in a spiral towards Heaven, we see another circular structure: the diminishing circles of the logo. The result is a visual dialogue.

Bernard, designer of a number of powerful symbols that hold their own in the urban jungle of logos and images, approaches the assignment in reverse. He takes an age-old symbol, the tower of Babel, and punches holes in it. In so doing he creates a new image, not by addition but by abduction. Like the cloud, the new symbol floats in front of the old, and the meaning of both becomes uncertain.

Rotterdam 2001
Culturele Hoofdstad
van Europa

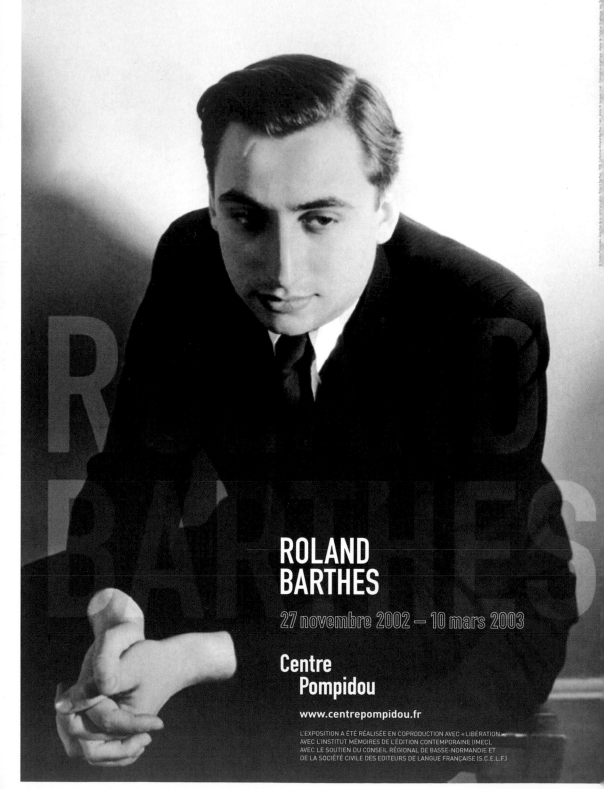

ROLAND
BARTHES

27 novembre 2002 — 10 mars 2003

Centre
Pompidou

www.centrepompidou.fr

L'EXPOSITION A ÉTÉ RÉALISÉE EN COPRODUCTION AVEC «LIBÉRATION»,
AVEC L'INSTITUT MÉMOIRES DE L'ÉDITION CONTEMPORAINE (IMEC),
AVEC LE SOUTIEN DU CONSEIL RÉGIONAL DE BASSE-NORMANDIE ET
DE LA SOCIÉTÉ CIVILE DES EDITEURS DE LANGUE FRANÇAISE (S.C.E.L.F.)

ster for an exhibition in
Pompidou Centre
× 120 / 2002

oto © Jacques Livet,
8

Roland Barthes

In 2001 the Atelier de Création Graphique developed a graphic communication programme for the Pompidou Centre. Key to the programme's overall image was a series of posters designed for important exhibitions at the Centre – a high-quality form of institutional communication. The posters share a number of elements: format, kind of information, wordmark and the use of condensed DIN capitals. For each poster in the series these recurring elements are linked to a strong image: the portrait of the artist or a work characteristic of his *oeuvre*. The changing combination of image and typography offers Bernard a latitude that he consistently explores.

The first thing that strikes one in this poster is the sitter's passivity and pensive gaze. Barthes sits bent slightly forward, his hands folded in a pose somewhere between tension and relaxation. There is also something indeterminate about his look: it is at once dreamy and concentrated. The photograph dates from 1938, when Barthes was twenty-three, studying classical languages and French at the Sorbonne, but spending more time on his Groupe de Théatre Antique de la Sorbonne, which staged classical tragedies and comedies. The photo shows him in his dual role as actor and intellectual.

The photograph is in the style of the Harcourt studio in Paris, in vogue in the thirties. Twenty years later Barthes would write: 'In France you are not an actor if you have not been photographed by the Harcourt studios.' Bathed in the soft light of the studio lamps the actor is 'reduced to a face, purified of all movement'. [Barthes 1971] In the Harcourt studios the camera, ally of the moment, produces eternity: people of flesh and blood are removed from time and space and transformed into stars. The young Barthes, allowing himself to be incorporated into this mythical universe of icons, has clearly not yet cast a 'political gaze on the sign'. [Calvet 1973]

How do the typography and the image relate in this poster? How could the image of the fragile, somewhat languid Barthes survive the confrontation with the bold German capitals? The letters are made transparent so that the subject's clothing shines through them. Indeed, their sfumato is barely distinct from the shadow on the wall. The outline of Barthes appears to pass through the capitals, so far attenuated that they merge into the image. This creates an interaction between name and man: the name floats through the man, the body becomes the message, the letters become physical. And both are modelled by the light.

The typography is as discreet as a butler. Man and letter meet at the periphery; only the head and hands are outside the text field. Both take on colour from the shifting blue and red. That, above all, is the trump card that Bernard plays in this poster: through the subtle mixing of the photographic black and white with the colours of France, Barthes is posthumously incorporated into the national heritage.

319

This book marks the award of the Erasmus Prize 2006 to
Pierre Bernard. It is published with the support of the
Praemium Erasmianum Foundation, the Erasmus Festival
's-Hertogenbosch, Fortis, ING and Theodoor Gilissen
Private Bankers.

Text
Hugues Boekraad

Picture editing
Hugues Boekraad
Reynoud Homan

Research
Frederike Huygen
Dorien Pessers

Photography
Dennis Hogers, Stedelijk Museum Amsterdam
Atelier de Création Graphique, Paris
Reynoud Homan

Design
Reynoud Homan

Acknowledgements
Carolien Glazenburg, curator graphic design, Stedelijk
Museum Amsterdam
Depot Grapus La Ville d'Aubervilliers
Atelier de Création Graphique, Paris
Max Sparreboom, Yvonne Goester, Adra Haste, Amsterdam

Printed by
Die Keure

Erasmus *festival*
's-Hertogenbosch

FORTIS

ING

Theodoor **GILISSEN**
Private Bankers

ISBN 978-3-03778-087-9
© 2008 Lars Müller Publishers

Lars Müller Publishers
5400 Baden/Switzerland
www.lars-muller-publishers.com

Cover
Héloise and Marsha looking at a rainbow in Burgundy
Photomontage by Pierre Bernard
25 × 45 / 1990